AMERICAN WOMEN

Who They Are & How They Live

AMERICAN WOMEN

Who They Are & How They Live

BY THE EDITORS OF NEW STRATEGIST PUBLICATIONS

1st EDITION

New Strategist Publications, Inc.
Ithaca, New York

New Strategist Publications, Inc.
P.O. Box 242, Ithaca, NY 14851
607/273-0913

ISBN 1-885070-08-X

Printed in the United States of America

Table of Contents

Chapter 3. Health

Chapter 4. Income

Chapter 5. Labor Force

Chapter 6. Living Arrangements

Chapter 7. Population

List of Tables

Chapter 1. Attitudes

Chapter 2. Education

Chapter 3. Health

Chapter 4. Income

Chapter 5. Labor Force

Chapter 6. Living Arrangements

Chapter 7. Population

Introduction

The lifestyles and attitudes of women have been transformed by the coming of age of the generations of women born after World War II. The changes in women have affected almost every institution of our society, from the family to the workplace, from politics to the consumer marketplace.

Women under the age of 50 have rejected the *Leave It to Beaver* lifestyle in favor of *Roseanne*, *Murphy Brown*, and *Seinfeld*. Working wives and mothers now far outnumber housewives. The "Mrs. degree" has become a quaint relic as women postpone marriage and earn a majority of bachelor's degrees. Once expected to be helpmates of their husbands, most women now believe their own careers are equally important. The average woman is not only better educated and better off than her mother or grandmother ever was, she is also far more individualistic and ambitious.

The changing attitudes and lifestyles of women are reshaping the American marketplace. Long the primary buyers of most consumer products and services, women are still the ones making most household purchasing decisions. But the female customer is not who she used to be. Compared to her mother, she is far more sophisticated, demanding, and pressed for time. The many businesses struggling to boost their bottom line in today's competitive economy must abandon their traditional notions about women and appeal to this powerful new consumer.

American Women: Who They Are & How They Live describes these new consumers. It examines the lifestyles of American women in rich detail, from the proportion who work full-time to the number sharing their homes with grown children, from the earnings of women with professional degrees to what women think about men. It also looks into the future, with projections of key data such as the female population by age, and women's labor force participation rates.

As we publish *American Women,* dramatic technological change is reshaping the demographic reference industry. The government's detailed demographic data, once widely available to all in printed reports, are now accessible only to Internet users or in unpublished tables obtained by calling the appropriate agency with a specific request. The government's web sites, which house enormous spreadsheets of data, are of great value to researchers with the time and skills to first download and then extract the important nuggets of information. The shift from printed reports to web sites—while convenient for number-crunchers—has made demographic analysis a bigger chore. For many researchers, it is more time-consuming than ever to get no-nonsense answers to their questions about the demographic characteristics of Americans.

American Women has the answers. It has the numbers and the stories behind them. Thumbing through its pages, you can gain more insight into the women's market than you could by spending all afternoon surfing databases on the Internet. By having it on your bookshelf, you can get the answers to your questions even faster than you could with the fastest modem.

How to Use This Book

American Women is designed for easy use. It is divided into nine chapters, organized alphabetically: Attitudes, Education, Health, Income, Labor Force, Living Arrangements, Population, Spending, and Wealth.

Most of the tables in the book are based on data collected and published by the federal government, in particular the Census Bureau, the Bureau of Labor Statistics, the National Center for Education Statistics, and the National Center for Health Statistics. The federal government continues to be the best source of up-to-date, reliable information on the changing characteristics of Americans. When government data are not available about an important topic, we have included data from other surveys and studies.

While the data in this book are produced by the government, we are not simply reprinting the government's spreadsheets—as do many reference books. Each table is individually compiled and created by New Strategist, with calculations performed by our statisticians to reveal the trends. A page of text accompanies most of the tables, analyzing the data and highlighting future trends.

If you want more information than the tables and text provide, you can locate the original source of the data, listed at the bottom of each table. The book contains a lengthy table list to help you locate the information you need. For a more detailed search, use the index in the back of the book. Also in the back of the book is the glossary, which defines many of the terms commonly used in the tables and text.

American Women will help you understand women's wants and needs. Explore, reflect, imagine.

CHAPTER

1

Attitudes

❖ **Most young women believe their children will be better off than they are.**
Fifty-five percent of women under age 30 believe their children will have a better standard of living than they do.

❖ **Most working women would not stop working even if they were rich.**
Seventy-five percent of working women aged 18 to 29 would continue to work even if they had enough money to live comfortably for the rest of their lives.

❖ **Younger women are more confident about single parenting.**
Among women under age 30, fully 61 percent agree that one parent can raise a child as well as two.

❖ **Few women now believe traditional sex roles are best.**
Only 32 percent of all women favor traditional roles—ranging from 18 percent of women under age 30 to 75 percent of women aged 80 or older.

❖ **Most women think they can improve their standard of living.**
Fifty-nine percent of women believe they and their families have a good chance of improving their standard of living.

❖ **Regardless of age, most women are proud to be American.**
Fully 84 percent of women say they are very or extremely proud to be an American. But the proportion drops to 77 percent among those under age 30.

❖ **Most women believe in God without any doubts.**
Two-thirds of women say they know God really exists, and they have no doubts about it. Only 14 percent say they are believers, but they have some doubts.

❖ **Most women believe there's some truth to astrology.**
Fifty-two percent of women believe astrology definitely or probably has some scientific truth to it.

Most Women Think They Are Better Off

But many younger women think their parents had a higher standard of living.

Most women believe they have a better standard of living than their parents did at the same age. But there are differences of opinion by age.

A bare majority of women in their 20s and 30s believe their standard of living exceeds the standard of living enjoyed by their parents at the same age. Twenty-one percent feel they are actually worse off. Women aged 40 to 59 are more likely than younger women to say they are better off, but substantial numbers in this age group believe they are worse off.

Women aged 60 to 79 are most likely to say they are better off. Those aged 80 or older are less likely to believe they have a better standard of living, but few feel they are worse off than their parents were in their old age.

❖ While some difference of opinion by age is related to lifestage, much of it is due to changes in the economic well-being of women over the past five decades. Today's elderly have enjoyed Social Security and other benefits extended to older Americans, while young women are struggling to get by on entry-level wages that have not kept pace with inflation.

Standard of Living Compared to Parents, 1994

"Compared to your parents when they were the age you are now, do you think your own standard of living is better, about the same, or worse than theirs was?"

(percent of women responding by age, 1994)

	better	*same*	*worse*
Total	60.8%	22.3%	14.4%
Aged 18 to 29	53.6	22.1	21.4
Aged 30 to 39	50.8	27.1	21.1
Aged 40 to 49	61.1	25.1	13.1
Aged 50 to 59	68.4	12.8	17.1
Aged 60 to 69	74.5	17.6	3.9
Aged 70 to 79	75.7	14.3	1.4
Aged 80 or older	50.0	40.0	2.5

Note: Numbers may not add to 100 because "don't know" and no answer are not included.
Source: 1994 General Social Survey, National Opinion Research Center, University of Chicago

Women Are Optimistic About Their Children's Future

Most believe their children will be better off.

Among women of all ages, half believe their children will have a better standard of living than they do. Women under age 30 and those aged 50 to 59 are most likely to believe this (55 percent). Among women in their 40s and those aged 60 or older, fewer than half feel their children will have a better standard of living, although the proportion who do is larger than the proportion who don't.

Women aged 80 or older are the most pessimistic about the future old age of their children. Only 38 percent believe that when their children are in their 80s they will have a better standard of living. Thirty-four percent believe it will be worse.

❖ While the largest percentage of women believe their children's standard of living will be an improvement over theirs, many worry about it getting worse. Women's concern about their children's future strongly influences their decisions on pocketbook and political issues.

Future Standard of Living for Children, 1994

"When your children are at the age you are now, do you think their standard of living will be better, about the same, or worse than yours is now?"

(percent of women responding by age, 1994)

	better	same	worse
Total	50.3%	23.2%	22.1%
Aged 18 to 29	55.4	17.2	23.9
Aged 30 to 39	50.3	24.6	20.3
Aged 40 to 49	44.7	26.7	23.3
Aged 50 to 59	54.5	20.9	20.9
Aged 60 to 69	46.0	26.0	18.0
Aged 70 to 79	49.2	24.6	20.0
Aged 80 or older	37.5	14.3	34.4

Note: Responses include only those with children. Numbers may not add to 100 because "don't know" and no answer are not included.
Source: 1994 General Social Survey, National Opinion Research Center, University of Chicago

Women's Incomes Are Important

Working women contribute half or more of household income.

Women's incomes make up about half or more of household income in 55 percent of all households with employed women. In 18 percent of households, employed women are the sole earner.

In 53 percent of married couples, the wife's earnings account for less than half of total household income. But in a substantial 47 percent of couples, the wife's income accounts for half or more of household income.

Women are the sole earner in 64 percent of single-parent households, compared with only 3 percent of two-parent households.

Women's incomes account for half or more of total household income in 67 percent of black households and 54 percent of white or Hispanic households.

❖ Women's earnings no longer pay for family extras, but are essential to their households' standard of living. Consequently, women are increasingly committed to their jobs and serious about getting ahead.

Importance of Women's Incomes, 1995

(percent of household income contributed by employed women, 1995)

	all income	more than half	about half	less than half
Total employed women	18%	11%	26%	44%
Marital status				
Never-married	43	7	13	35
Married	4	11	33	53
Separated/divorced/widowed	64	18	9	9
Family status				
Two-parent household	3	10	32	55
Single-parent household	64	18	8	10
Race and Hispanic origin				
White	17	11	27	46
Black	32	9	26	33
Hispanic	15	17	20	46

Source: Women: The New Providers, *Whirlpool Foundation Study Part One, Families and Work Institute, 1995*

Women Want to Work

Most would not stop working even if they were rich.

Do women work because they have to or because they want to? A majority of working women say they would continue to work even if they didn't need the money.

Women in the early years of their careers (aged 18 to 29) are most likely to say they would continue to work (75 percent). The proportion drops to 65 percent among those in their 30s and to 62 percent among those in their 40s.

The lowest percentage is found among women aged 50 to 59, with 53 percent saying they would continue to work and 44 percent saying they would quit if they could. Many women in this age group are eagerly anticipating retirement.

❖ Women work for many reasons, and money is undoubtedly a big one. But it is wrong to assume that most working women would prefer to stay at home if given the choice.

Would You Work If You Were Rich? 1994

"If you were to get enough money to live as comfortably as you would like for the rest of your life, would you continue to work or would you stop working?"

(percent of women responding by age, 1994)

	continue to work	stop working
Total	64.2%	34.0%
Aged 18 to 29	75.0	24.3
Aged 30 to 39	64.5	34.1
Aged 40 to 49	61.8	37.1
Aged 50 to 59	53.1	44.2
Aged 60 to 69	69.4	30.6
Aged 70 to 79	62.5	12.5
Aged 80 or older	60.0	20.0

Note: Asked only of those currently working. Numbers may not add to 100 because "don't know" and no answer are not included.
Source: 1994 General Social Survey, National Opinion Research Center, University of Chicago

Generations Divide on Divorce

Most older women want to make it harder to divorce.

Among women aged 60 or older, a majority say it should be more difficult to obtain a divorce than it is now. But younger women are ambivalent. Pluralities say it should be more difficult, but substantial minorities want to make it even easier to divorce.

Among women under age 60, about half or more would leave divorce laws untouched or make it even easier to divorce. Between 41 and 46 percent want to make it more difficult.

Solid majorities of women aged 70 or older would like divorce to be more difficult to obtain. Only 6 to 7 percent want to make it easier.

❖ Regardless of age, substantial numbers of women believe divorce should be more difficult to obtain. But most women do not want to return to the days when unhappy couples were forced to stay together.

Should It Be Easier to Divorce? 1994

"Should divorce in this country be easier or more difficult to obtain than it is now?"

(percent of women responding by age, 1994)

	easier	stay as is	more difficult
Total	25.3%	20.9%	47.8%
Aged 18 to 29	30.7	22.1	40.7
Aged 30 to 39	33.8	21.7	41.5
Aged 40 to 49	25.8	23.3	46.2
Aged 50 to 59	27.4	23.8	42.1
Aged 60 to 69	20.0	17.5	57.5
Aged 70 to 79	6.4	11.0	70.6
Aged 80 or older	6.7	20.0	61.7

Note: Numbers may not add to 100 because "don't know" and no answer are not included.
Source: 1994 General Social Survey, National Opinion Research Center, University of Chicago

Marriage and Children Do Not Always Go Together

Young women are less likely than older women to link the two.

Generational differences are apparent in the percentages of women who say people who want children should get married. Fewer than 10 percent of women aged 50 or older disagree with that statement. Among women under age 30, between 26 and 33 percent disagree.

Women aged 18 to 29 are least likely to feel marriage is a necessary prerequisite for children. Fewer than half agree that marriage should come first.

❖ With women's incomes rising and men's falling, women have less to gain by marrying before having children. Women's growing independence from men is reshaping the consumer marketplace.

Should People Marry Before Having Children? 1994

"People who want children ought to get married—do you agree or disagree?"

(percent of women responding by age, 1994)

	agree	neither	disagree
Total	70.7%	9.6%	17.1%
Aged 18 to 29	48.6	16.0	32.6
Aged 30 to 39	60.2	11.4	26.1
Aged 40 to 49	70.2	11.8	14.9
Aged 50 to 59	83.9	5.1	8.4
Aged 60 to 69	85.3	8.4	3.2
Aged 70 to 79	91.7	1.2	4.8
Aged 80 or older	89.5	2.6	5.3

Note: Numbers may not add to 100 because "can't choose" and no answer are not included.
Source: 1994 General Social Survey, National Opinion Research Center, University of Chicago

One Parent Is Good Enough

Younger women are more confident about single parenting.

A majority of women aged 18 to 39 agree with the statement that one parent can raise a child as well as two. Among women under age 30, fully 61 percent agree.

Among women in their 40s, only 37 percent believe one parent can do as good a job as two, while 45 percent feel it takes both parents. Women in this age group may be speaking from their own difficult experiences, since many are now raising teenagers.

Women aged 50 to 59 are divided on the question of whether one parent is as good as two, with equal percentages agreeing and disagreeing. But a solid majority of women aged 60 or older say they don't believe one parent is as good as two.

❖ If two parents are no better than one, then there is little reason for unhappy couples to stay together for the sake of the children. With so many young women believing one parent can be as good as two, divorce levels are likely to remain high.

Is One Parent as Good as Two? 1994

"One parent can bring up a child as well as two parents together—do you agree or disagree?"

(percent of women responding by age, 1994)

	agree	*neither*	*disagree*
Total	42.6%	13.6%	41.6%
Aged 18 to 29	61.1	13.9	23.7
Aged 30 to 39	54.0	12.8	32.2
Aged 40 to 49	37.3	14.9	45.3
Aged 50 to 59	44.9	9.3	45.7
Aged 60 to 69	29.5	14.7	51.6
Aged 70 to 79	19.1	16.7	60.7
Aged 80 or older	10.6	15.8	65.8

Note: Numbers may not add to 100 because "don't know" and no answer are not included.
Source: 1994 General Social Survey, National Opinion Research Center, University of Chicago

Marriage Is Not the Key to Happiness

Younger women do not link marriage and happiness.

Only 41 percent of all women agree that "married people are generally happier than unmarried people." But there are sharp differences of opinion among women by age, with older women far more likely to agree than younger women.

The proportion of women saying married people are happier than the unmarried rises with each successive age group, from only 24 percent among women under age 30 to more than two-thirds of women aged 70 or older. Among women under age 50, between 25 and 29 percent disagree that the married are happier than the unmarried. This drops to 19 percent among women in their 50s and to only 5 percent among those in their 70s.

Younger women are also more likely than older women to say they neither agree nor disagree that married people are happier.

❖ Young women are postponing marriage and discovering they can be happy without being married. Their growing independence shapes their consumer behavior, making it important to target women as individuals.

Are Married People Happier? 1994

"Married people are generally happier than unmarried people—do you agree or disagree?"

(percent of women responding by age, 1994)

	agree	*neither*	*disagree*
Total	41.3%	32.2%	22.3%
Aged 18 to 29	23.7	43.1	29.2
Aged 30 to 39	35.1	34.1	28.9
Aged 40 to 49	36.6	32.3	24.8
Aged 50 to 59	46.6	30.5	19.4
Aged 60 to 69	50.6	27.4	16.9
Aged 70 to 79	66.7	22.6	4.8
Aged 80 or older	68.4	18.4	10.5

Note: Numbers may not add to 100 because "can't choose" and no answer are not included.
Source: 1994 General Social Survey, National Opinion Research Center, University of Chicago

Working Women Do Not Harm Family Life

Most women believe they can work without causing the family to suffer.

Only about one-third of women believe family life suffers when a woman has a full-time job. The proportions are even lower among women under age 50.

The majority of women aged 18 to 59 say family life doesn't suffer when women have full-time jobs. Two-thirds of women under age 30 feel this way. But among women aged 70 or older, a majority believe family life suffers when women work full-time. Those most likely to say this are women aged 80 or older (63 percent).

• As women's roles have changed, so have women's attitudes. Because most women born after World War II have had to work, they have a better opinion about combining jobs and family life than do older women—most of whom did not have to work.

Do Families Suffer If Mother Works? 1994

"All in all, family life suffers when the woman has a full-time job—do you agree or disagree?"

(percent of women responding by age, 1994)

	agree	*neither*	*disagree*
Total	33.5%	11.8%	53.8%
Aged 18 to 29	21.5	10.4	66.7
Aged 30 to 39	25.6	15.2	58.7
Aged 40 to 49	30.5	8.7	60.2
Aged 50 to 59	35.6	12.7	51.7
Aged 60 to 69	43.2	9.5	45.2
Aged 70 to 79	52.4	15.5	31.0
Aged 80 or older	63.1	5.3	29.0

Note: Numbers may not add to 100 because "can't choose" and no answer are not included.
Source: 1994 General Social Survey, National Opinion Research Center, University of Chicago

Working Mothers Are OK

Most women think mothers don't need to stay home.

Fully 62 percent of women do not agree that preschoolers suffer if their mothers work. But older and younger women have different opinions on this issue.

The older the woman, the more likely she is to believe that working mothers are bad for young children. Among women in their 70s, 59 percent agree that preschoolers suffer if their mothers work, as do 70 percent of those aged 80 or older.

Among women under age 60, however, at least two-thirds say they disagree. Among women aged 18 to 29—the group most likely to have had working mothers as children—fully 74 percent say they don't believe preschoolers suffer.

❖ Young women believe they can juggle family and career successfully. Contrary to the stereotype, they don't feel guilty about working while their children are young.

Do Preschoolers Suffer If Mother Works? 1994

"A preschool child is likely to suffer if his or her mother works—do you agree or disagree?"

(percent of women responding by age, 1994)

	agree	*disagree*
Total	36.2%	62.2%
Aged 18 to 29	24.1	74.4
Aged 30 to 39	29.4	69.8
Aged 40 to 49	32.2	67.3
Aged 50 to 59	32.3	66.4
Aged 60 to 69	47.5	50.9
Aged 70 to 79	58.7	34.9
Aged 80 or older	70.0	28.3

Note: Numbers may not add to 100 because "don't know" and no answer are not shown.
Source: 1994 General Social Survey, National Opinion Research Center, University of Chicago

Traditional Sex Roles Are Out

The old division of labor is of no interest to young women.

Few women now believe traditional sex roles—man as breadwinner and woman as homemaker—are best. Only 32 percent of all women favor traditional roles.

Support for traditional roles is strongest among women aged 70 or older, a solid majority of whom favor this arrangement. But support declines among younger women. The majority of women under age 60 say they do not agree that traditional roles are best. Among women under age 30, only 18 percent believe the traditional division of labor between men and women is best.

❖ Generational replacement is an important part of social change. As older generations die, certain beliefs and attitudes die with them. Support for traditional sex roles is disappearing as older women are replaced by younger, working women.

Should the Man Be the Achiever Outside the Home? 1994

"It is much better for everyone involved if the man is the achiever outside the home and the woman takes care of the home and family—do you agree or disagree?"

(percent of women responding by age, 1994)

	agree	disagree
Total	31.9%	65.8%
Aged 18 to 29	17.6	82.4
Aged 30 to 39	21.6	76.4
Aged 40 to 49	23.4	74.1
Aged 50 to 59	33.0	63.4
Aged 60 to 69	45.0	53.4
Aged 70 to 79	61.5	32.1
Aged 80 or older	75.0	21.7

Note: Numbers may not add to 100 because "don't know" and no answer are not included.
Source: 1994 General Social Survey, National Opinion Research Center, University of Chicago

Women Take Work Seriously

Most consider a woman's career as important as her husband's.

Few women believe a husband's career should take precedence over a wife's. Only 21 percent of women say it is more important for a wife to help her husband's career than to have her own career.

A majority of women aged 70 or older believe it is more important for a woman to help her husband than to have a career herself, but this proportion falls to 33 percent among women in their 60s. Among younger women, only 9 to 15 percent agree.

Least likely to agree are women in their 30s. No longer in entry-level jobs, women in this age group are moving up the career ladder. Few believe women should play a supporting role.

❖ Younger women are far more career-oriented than their elders, making them a different kind of consumer than older women. Businesses must adapt to the changing attitudes of women or lose them as customers.

Is a Husband's Career More Important? 1994

"It is more important for a wife to help her husband's career than to have one herself—do you agree or disagree?"

(percent of women responding by age, 1994)

	agree	disagree
Total	20.5%	76.3%
Aged 18 to 29	12.5	87.0
Aged 30 to 39	8.8	88.2
Aged 40 to 49	15.2	81.8
Aged 50 to 59	14.6	81.7
Aged 60 to 69	33.3	64.1
Aged 70 to 79	52.3	38.6
Aged 80 or older	51.6	43.4

Note: Numbers may not add to 100 because "don't know" and no answer are not included.
Source: 1994 General Social Survey, National Opinion Research Center, University of Chicago

Women Control the Purse Strings

But as they grow older, they enjoy shopping less.

Most women, regardless of age, say they handle the checkbook and pay the bills. But on many other issues there are important differences by age.

The women of Generation X (under age 32) are still struggling with their image of themselves as homemakers. They are more likely than boomer women (aged 32 to 50) or older women to say they are uncomfortable when their house is not completely clean—72 percent compared with 58 to 60 percent of boomers and older women. Forty-one percent of Gen Xers, but only one-third of older women, feel guilty for relying on convenience foods.

Boomer women are least likely to say dressing well is important to them (60 percent compared with 66 percent of Gen Xers and 72 percent of older women). And while 38 percent say they no longer enjoy shopping, this is less than the 49 percent of older women who feel this way. Generation Xers are most likely to enjoy shopping—only 30 percent say it's no fun anymore.

❖ Over half of Generation Xers, and nearly as many older women, say they wish they knew how to relax. Businesses offering women ways to relax will tap into a powerful need.

Women's Attitudes Toward Family and Self, 1996

(percent of women agreeing with selected statements by age, 1996)

	under age 32	aged 32 to 50	aged 50 or older
Family			
In our family, I take care of the checkbook and pay the bills.	82%	83%	87%
When making important family decisions, consideration of the children should come first.	85	75	60
It seems as though everyone in our family is always on the run.	72	72	64
Meal preparation should take as little time as possible.	64	66	63
I am uncomfortable when the house is not completely clean.	72	58	60
I feel guilty when I serve convenience foods to my family.	41	34	33
Self			
I am a homebody.	61	69	71
I have more self-confidence than most of my friends.	72	66	71
Everything is changing too fast today.	60	64	70
Dressing well is an important part of my life.	66	60	72
I wish I knew how to relax.	55	46	47
Changes in routine disturb me.	37	40	44
Television is my primary form of entertainment.	55	46	49
Shopping is no fun anymore.	30	38	49

Source: The Changing American: Life Style Trends 1975-1996, *DDB Needham Worldwide, Inc., Chicago, Illinois*

Women Do Most Shopping and Cooking

Men do most small repairs around the house.

Stereotypical roles are still common in American homes. In married-couple households, wives usually or always do the laundry, shop for groceries, plan dinner, and care for sick family members. Husbands usually make small repairs around the house.

Change may be on the horizon, however. The younger the woman, the more likely she is to say her husband or partner shares chores equally with her. Among women under age 30, over half say small repairs, grocery shopping, planning dinner, and caring for the sick are shared equally with her husband or partner.

Laundry remains a woman's domain, for some reason. But among women aged 18 to 24, who are most likely to have egalitarian households, only one-third say they always or usually do the wash.

❖ Although housekeeping is becoming more egalitarian, women still do most of the chores. Because they shoulder a disproportionate share of housework, stress and time pressures are bigger problems for women than for men.

Who Shops for Groceries? 1994

"In your household, who shops for groceries?"

(percent of women responding by age, 1994)

	always the woman	usually the woman	equal/both	usually the man	always the man
Total	22.4%	29.3%	43.1%	4.4%	0.7%
Aged 18 to 24	11.1	22.2	66.7	0.0	0.0
Aged 25 to 34	21.1	28.1	46.5	3.5	0.9
Aged 35 to 44	22.4	31.9	39.7	6.0	0.0
Aged 45 to 54	29.1	22.8	46.8	1.3	0.0
Aged 55 to 64	18.6	27.1	44.1	8.5	1.7
Aged 65 or older	23.4	39.1	31.3	4.7	1.6

Note: Percentages are based on respondents who were married or living as married.
Source: 1994 General Social Survey, National Opinion Research Center, University of Chicago

Who Plans Dinner? 1994

"In your household, who decides what to have for dinner?"

(percent of women responding by age, 1994)

	always the woman	*usually the woman*	*equal/both*	*usually the man*	*always the man*
Total	24.7%	36.0%	35.6%	3.3%	0.4%
Aged 18 to 24	11.1	22.2	61.1	5.6	0.0
Aged 25 to 34	22.8	28.9	44.7	2.6	0.9
Aged 35 to 44	20.7	39.7	35.3	4.3	0.0
Aged 45 to 54	34.2	35.4	27.8	2.5	0.0
Aged 55 to 64	20.7	37.9	36.2	5.2	0.0
Aged 65 or older	30.8	44.6	21.5	1.5	1.5

Note: Percentages are based on respondents who were married or living as married.
Source: 1994 General Social Survey, National Opinion Research Center, University of Chicago

Who Does the Laundry? 1994

"In your household, who does the laundry?"

(percent of women responding by age, 1994)

	always the woman	usually the woman	equal/both	usually the man	always the man
Total	39.2%	32.2%	25.5%	2.3%	0.9%
Aged 18 to 24	22.2	33.3	44.4	0.0	0.0
Aged 25 to 34	25.2	38.7	33.3	0.9	1.8
Aged 35 to 44	38.3	31.3	27.8	2.6	0.0
Aged 45 to 54	39.0	29.9	26.0	3.9	1.3
Aged 55 to 64	45.8	30.5	18.6	3.4	1.7
Aged 65 or older	64.1	26.6	7.8	1.6	0.0

Note: Percentages are based on respondents who were married or living as married.
Source: 1994 General Social Survey, National Opinion Research Center, University of Chicago

Who Cares for the Sick? 1994

"In your household, who cares for sick family members?"

(percent of women responding by age, 1994)

	always the woman	usually the woman	equal/both	usually the man	always the man
Total	22.1%	32.4%	44.5%	0.7%	0.2%
Aged 18 to 24	11.8	17.6	70.6	0.0	0.0
Aged 25 to 34	21.4	30.4	48.2	0.0	0.0
Aged 35 to 44	19.5	37.2	43.4	0.0	0.0
Aged 45 to 54	20.0	38.7	41.3	0.0	0.0
Aged 55 to 64	27.1	18.6	50.8	3.4	0.0
Aged 65 or older	29.0	37.1	30.6	1.6	1.6

Note: Percentages are based on respondents who were married or living as married.
Source: 1994 General Social Survey, National Opinion Research Center, University of Chicago

Who Makes Small Repairs? 1994

"In your household, who makes the small repairs around the house?"

(percent of women responding by age, 1994)

	always the woman	usually the woman	equal/both	usually the man	always the man
Total	3.7%	5.1%	26.6%	49.9%	14.8%
Aged 18 to 24	0.0	0.0	55.6	44.4	0.0
Aged 25 to 34	2.8	4.7	26.2	51.4	15.0
Aged 35 to 44	4.4	7.9	28.1	45.6	14.0
Aged 45 to 54	3.9	3.9	25.0	55.3	11.8
Aged 55 to 64	3.6	3.6	28.6	46.4	17.9
Aged 65 or older	4.8	4.8	16.1	53.2	21.0

Note: Percentages are based on respondents who were married or living as married.
Source: 1994 General Social Survey, National Opinion Research Center, University of Chicago

Mothers Outlive Fathers

Until their 50s, most women can still call on their mothers.

As one would expect, the older the woman the less likely that her parents are still living. Since men have shorter life expectancies than women, women are more likely to have a living mother than a living father.

Among women under age 40, the majority have both parents still living. Among women in their 40s, only 47 percent have fathers who are still alive, but 70 percent have living mothers. By the time women are in their 50s, fewer than half (46 percent) say their mothers are still alive, while only 21 percent have living fathers.

❖ Beginning in their 40s, women face one of life's most profound experiences—the death of parents. The baby-boom generation is reaching this milestone now, resulting in growing interest in family history, spirituality, and staying healthy.

Women with Living Mothers, 1994

"Is your mother alive?"

(percent of women responding by age, 1994)

	yes	*no*
Total	58.9%	39.8%
Aged 18 to 29	95.3	4.7
Aged 30 to 39	86.2	12.9
Aged 40 to 49	70.0	28.8
Aged 50 to 59	45.9	51.6
Aged 60 to 69	18.6	80.4
Aged 70 to 79	1.1	96.8
Aged 80 or older	0.0	95.0

Note: Numbers may not add to 100 because "don't know" and no answer are not included.
Source: 1994 General Social Survey, National Opinion Research Center, University of Chicago

Women with Living Fathers, 1994

"Is your father still living?"

(percent of women responding by age, 1994)

	yes	no
Total	43.5%	53.4%
Aged 18 to 29	87.2	9.4
Aged 30 to 39	67.3	30.0
Aged 40 to 49	46.5	50.0
Aged 50 to 59	21.3	73.8
Aged 60 to 69	5.2	93.8
Aged 70 to 79	0.0	97.8
Aged 80 or older	0.0	95.0

Note: Numbers may not add to 100 because "don't know" and no answer are not included.
Source: 1994 General Social Survey, National Opinion Research Center, University of Chicago

Most Women Think Men Are Self-Centered

Women and men often disagree about men's changing roles.

On some issues, women and men agree. Women are only slightly more likely than men to say it's no longer fair for men to make all the household decisions (86 percent of women compared with 82 percent of men.) Three-quarters of both men and women believe fathers are more involved with their children than they were 20 years ago. Most men and women also believe men are confused about what women want from them.

Disagreements remain, however. Sixty-two percent of men, but only 54 percent of women, believe men are re-examining the "macho" role. While a 57 percent majority of women think most men are basically self-centered, only 43 percent of men agree. Fully 70 percent of men, but only 57 percent of women, believe women are too quick to call men sexist. Only 61 percent of women, compared to 72 percent of men, believe men have become more understanding of women's needs.

❖ Many men and women have negative opinions of one another because sex roles are changing. People in their 40s and 50s are most likely to be struggling with changing roles because they were raised to be traditional and have had to adapt to new norms.

What Women Think about Men, 1995

(percent of persons agreeing with selected statements about men, by sex, 1995)

	women	men
It's no longer fair for men to be the sole decision maker in the household.	86%	82%
Men are just as competitive as ever.	84	85
People admire men who show a more sensitive side.	81	80
Men still find it difficult to think of women completely as equals.	79	70
Men are much more involved in their children's lives than they were 20 years ago.	74	73
Most men are confused about what women expect of them nowadays.	68	69
Men have become more able to express their feelings.	68	76
When it comes to housework and childrearing, women still want to be in charge.	65	67
Men have become more understanding of women's needs.	61	72
Most men are basically self-centered.	57	43
Many women are too quick to call men sexist.	57	70
Men are much more comfortable than they used to be about expressing their feelings to their male friends.	56	62
More and more men are questioning the "macho" role.	54	62
Employers unfairly penalize men who rearrange their work schedules to take care of things for their family.	46	49
All this talk about a new "men's movement" is just media hype.	46	50
Men who occasionally rearrange their work schedules in order to take care of family things—such as taking kids to the doctor and attending school functions—are often not as serious about their careers as other men.	28	32

Source: The 1995 Virginia Slims Opinion Poll, Roper Starch Worldwide, New York

Most Believe in the Good Life

Most women think they can improve their standard of living.

Fifty-nine percent of women agree with the statement, "The way things are in America, people like me and my family have a good chance of improving our standard of living." Among younger women, the proportion is even higher. Sixty-four percent of women under age 30 believe a better standard of living is attainable.

As women get older, however, fewer believe they will improve their lot in life. Among women in their 40s, 59 percent say they have a chance for a better standard of living. This proportion falls to 54 percent among women in their 60s.

A substantial minority of women (27 percent) do not believe they can attain a better standard of living. Elderly women are most likely to feel this way. Fully 35 percent of women aged 80 or older don't believe things will improve for them.

❖ Most women are optimistic about the future, believing their standard of living will improve. This belief motivates them to get an education and find a good-paying job.

Can You Achieve the Good Life? 1994

"The way things are in America, people like me and my family have a good chance of improving our standard of living. Do you agree or disagree?"

(percent of women responding by age, 1994)

	agree	*neither*	*disagree*
Total	59.1%	12.1%	26.7%
Aged 18 to 29	63.5	6.4	27.9
Aged 30 to 39	61.8	11.6	25.6
Aged 40 to 49	58.8	15.4	23.4
Aged 50 to 59	56.4	12.8	29.9
Aged 60 to 69	53.9	14.7	29.4
Aged 70 to 79	64.2	10.0	21.4
Aged 80 or older	42.5	15.0	35.0

Note: Numbers may not add to 100 because "can't choose" and no answer are not included.
Source: 1994 General Social Survey, National Opinion Research Center, University of Chicago

Women Are Proud to Be Americans

But younger women are not as proud as older women.

Fully 84 percent of women say they are very or extremely proud to be an American. But among younger women, the proportion is lower.

Virtually all women from the generations that lived through World War II are very proud to be American. Between 89 and 93 percent of women aged 50 or older say they are very or extremely proud. The proportion saying this stands at 85 percent among women in their 40s. It drops to 79 percent among those in their 30s and to 77 percent among those under age 30.

❖ Younger women came of age during difficult times for the United States, including the Vietnam War and Watergate. Those experiences contributed to their diminished pride in being American.

Proud to Be an American? 1994

"How proud are you to be an American?"

(percent of women responding by age, 1994)

	extremely or very proud	somewhat proud	not very proud
Total	84.1%	13.1%	1.2%
Aged 18 to 29	76.8	17.6	3.5
Aged 30 to 39	78.8	18.7	1.6
Aged 40 to 49	84.5	13.8	0.6
Aged 50 to 59	89.3	8.9	0.0
Aged 60 to 69	93.1	5.7	0.0
Aged 70 to 79	88.8	9.5	1.6
Aged 80 or older	93.0	2.3	0.0

Note: Numbers may not add to 100 because "don't know" and no answer are not included.
Source: 1994 General Social Survey, National Opinion Research Center, University of Chicago

Most Women Are Pretty Happy

Age has little relationship to happiness.

Among all women, 59 percent say they are "pretty" happy, while 28 percent say they are "very" happy. Only 13 percent say they are "not too" happy.

The percentage saying they are very happy, pretty happy, or not too happy varies little with age. Those least likely to say they are very happy are women aged 18 to 24 (23 percent), while those most likely to be very happy are aged 45 to 54 (31 percent). Women aged 55 to 64 are most likely to say they are not too happy (14 percent).

❖ Happiness varies by lifestage. It declines during times of transition, such as when young women leave their parents' home (ages 18 to 24) or when husbands and wives retire (ages 55 to 64).

Are You Happy? 1994

"Taken all together, how would you say things are these days? Would you say that you are very happy, pretty happy, or not too happy?"

(percent of women responding by age, 1994)

	very happy	*pretty happy*	*not too happy*
Total	27.8%	58.9%	12.9%
Aged 18 to 24	23.2	64.3	12.5
Aged 25 to 34	25.8	60.5	13.2
Aged 35 to 44	26.5	60.3	12.7
Aged 45 to 54	30.5	57.9	11.6
Aged 55 to 64	29.6	56.6	13.8
Aged 65 or older	30.1	55.6	13.4

Source: 1994 General Social Survey, National Opinion Research Center, University of Chicago

Young Women Find Life Exciting

Excitement wanes among older women.

A majority of women aged 18 to 24 say they find life exciting (54 percent). Only 40 percent say their lives are "pretty routine." But 6 percent say life is dull—a higher proportion than is found in all but the oldest age group. Eight percent of women aged 65 or older say life is dull.

As women get older, fewer find life exciting. Women aged 25 to 54 are split almost evenly between those who find life exciting and those for whom life is pretty routine. Among women aged 55 to 64, a majority (51 percent) say life is routine, as do 54 percent of those aged 65 or older.

❖ The differences in the excitement level of older and younger women may be due to differences in educational attainment between the two groups. Younger, better-educated women are more in touch with the world, adding to their excitement. Older, less-educated women are more isolated, which contributes to their boredom.

Is Life Exciting?, 1994

"In general, do you find life exciting, pretty routine, or dull?"

(percent of women responding by age, 1994)

	exciting	pretty routine	dull
Total	45.2%	49.6%	4.5%
Aged 18 to 24	53.8	40.0	6.3
Aged 25 to 34	46.9	50.2	2.9
Aged 35 to 44	48.1	48.5	3.3
Aged 45 to 54	47.4	48.4	4.2
Aged 55 to 64	44.6	51.2	3.3
Aged 65 or older	34.3	54.3	8.1

Source: 1994 General Social Survey, National Opinion Research Center, University of Chigago

Fear Is a Fact of Life for Women

For most women, walking alone at night is scary.

Sixty percent of women are afraid to walk alone at night in an area near their home. Among men, only 30 percent express such a fear.

The older the woman, the more likely she is to be afraid—with one exception. Young women under age 30 are almost as likely as elderly women to say they are sometimes afraid to walk alone.

Nearly seven out of ten women aged 70 or older say there are places nearby where they are afraid to walk alone, as do two-thirds of women in their 60s, and 64 percent of women under age 30. Women in their 30s and 50s are less fearful: 58 percent say there are areas nearby where they would be afraid to walk alone. Those least likely to be afraid (51 percent) are women in their 40s.

❖ Women have always been safety-conscious. Rising crime rates have added to their concerns. As the female population ages, the demand for security will grow at home, in the workplace, when traveling, and during leisure pursuits.

Are You Afraid to Walk Alone at Night? 1994

"Is there any area right around here—that is, within a mile—where you would be afraid to walk alone at night?"

(percent of women responding by age, 1994)

	yes	*no*
Total	59.8%	39.1%
Aged 18 to 29	64.1	35.4
Aged 30 to 39	58.0	41.6
Aged 40 to 49	51.1	47.6
Aged 50 to 59	58.2	41.2
Aged 60 to 69	66.1	33.0
Aged 70 to 79	67.6	29.5
Aged 80 or older	68.8	27.1

Note: Numbers may not add to 100 because "don't know" and no answer are not included.
Source: 1994 General Social Survey, National Opinion Research Center, University of Chicago

Belief in God Is Strong

Most women believe in God without any doubts.

Two-thirds of women say they know God really exists, and they have no doubts about it. Only 14 percent say they are believers, but they have some doubts.

Younger women are slightly less likely to believe in God than are older women. Only 59 percent of women aged 18 to 29 believe in God without a doubt. Seventeen percent are believers with some doubts. Four percent are nonbelievers.

Boomer women in their 40s are most likely to view God as a "higher power" rather than a "personal God." Eleven percent of women in this age group see God as a higher power, as do 8 percent of women in their 30s.

Women aged 50 or older are most likely to have no doubts about the existence of God. Between 71 and 77 percent of this age group believe with no doubts.

❖ Religion is important in the lives of most women. Many are searching for meaning, which explains why books, television programs, and organizations devoted to spirituality are finding such an enormous audience.

Belief in God, 1994

"Which statement comes closest to expressing what you believe about God?
- **I know God really exists and I have no doubts about it.**
- **While I have doubts, I feel that I do believe in God.**
- **I find myself believing in God some of the time, but not at others.**
- **I don't believe in a personal God, but I do believe in a Higher Power of some kind.**
- **I don't know whether there is a God and I don't believe there is any way to find out.**
- **I don't believe in God."**

(percent of women responding by age, 1994)

	no doubts	believe, but have doubts	believe sometimes	higher power	don't know, no way to find out	don't believe
Total	67.6%	13.7%	3.0%	6.9%	2.2%	2.0%
Aged 18 to 29	58.5	16.9	4.6	4.6	6.2	3.8
Aged 30 to 39	66.3	17.4	2.2	7.6	2.2	0.5
Aged 40 to 49	63.7	15.5	3.6	10.7	1.8	2.4
Aged 50 to 59	75.5	10.4	2.8	6.6	0.9	0.9
Aged 60 to 69	76.7	8.1	2.3	5.8	0.0	1.2
Aged 70 to 79	71.2	6.8	3.4	3.4	1.7	3.4
Aged 80 or older	75.0	8.3	0.0	2.8	0.0	2.8

Note: Numbers may not add to 100 because "don't know" and no answer are not included.
Source: 1994 General Social Survey, National Opinion Research Center, University of Chicago

Religious Diversity Is Increasing

There are fewer Protestants and more Catholics among the young.

Three-quarters of women aged 70 or older are Protestant, but within each successively younger age group the Protestant proportion declines. Between 60 and 62 percent of women aged 30 to 49 are Protestant. Among women under age 30, only 50 percent say they are Protestant.

About one-quarter of all women and 27 percent of women under age 30 are Catholic. But among women under age 50, increasing proportions say their religious preference is something other than Protestant, Catholic, or Jewish. Seven percent of women under age 30 say they have some other religion.

The percentage of women saying they have no religious preference is also higher among the young. Seven percent of women in their 40s, 10 percent of those in their 30s, and 14 percent of those under age 30 say they have no religious preference.

❖ The young are more diverse than their elders in many ways, including religion. Businesses must consider a variety of cultures and beliefs when marketing to women under the age of 50.

Religious Preference, 1994

"What is your religious preference?"

(percent of women responding by age, 1994)

	Protestant	Catholic	Jewish	other	none
Total	62.8%	24.4%	1.8%	3.6%	7.0%
Aged 18 to 29	50.5	27.1	1.7	6.5	13.7
Aged 30 to 39	60.0	23.4	2.2	4.6	9.5
Aged 40 to 49	61.9	25.9	1.7	3.5	7.0
Aged 50 to 59	67.9	25.6	1.7	2.1	2.6
Aged 60 to 69	66.8	25.5	1.6	2.7	2.7
Aged 70 to 79	76.3	19.2	1.9	0.6	1.3
Aged 80 or older	74.7	18.1	1.2	0.0	3.6

Note: Numbers may not add to 100 because "don't know" and "no answer" are not included.
Source: 1994 General Social Survey, National Opinion Research Center University of Chicago

Religion Is More Important for Older Women

Weekly attendance at religious services is more common among older women.

A majority of women attend religious services at least once a month. But fewer than half attend every week.

Weekly attendance is most common among women aged 60 to 79, with 44 to 45 percent attending weekly. Only 37 percent of women aged 80 or older attend religious services weekly, probably because health problems limit the ability of many in this age group to get around.

About three out of ten women aged 40 to 59 attend religious services every week. The proportion is even lower among younger women. Only 23 percent of women in their 30s and 19 percent of those under age 30 attend religious services weekly. Twenty-one percent of women under age 30 and 23 percent of those aged 30 to 39 say they attend religious services less than once a year or never.

❖ In their struggle to attract young adults, religious institutions face two obstacles: the time pressure felt by working parents, and the difficulty of appealing to generations accustomed to being entertained.

Religious Attendance, 1994

"How often do you attend religious services?"

(percent of women responding by age, 1994)

	at least weekly	at least monthly but less than once a week	several times a year	less than once a year or never
Total	30.3%	22.7%	25.3%	19.9%
Aged 18 to 29	19.2	24.0	35.1	21.3
Aged 30 to 39	23.2	24.2	28.0	23.4
Aged 40 to 49	31.4	24.7	27.3	15.1
Aged 50 to 59	32.1	25.7	22.7	16.2
Aged 60 to 69	45.1	15.8	17.9	19.6
Aged 70 to 79	43.5	17.9	15.4	20.5
Aged 80 or older	37.3	18.0	13.2	27.7

Note: Numbers may not add to 100 because "don't know" and "no answer" are not included.
Source: 1994 General Social Survey, National Opinion Research Center University of Chicago

Many Women Believe in Astrology

Most think there's some truth to it.

Newspapers have a reason for publishing daily astrology columns. Over half of all women believe that there is definitely or probably some scientific basis for astrology.

Surprisingly, women aged 70 or older are least likely to believe in astrology. Only 47 to 48 percent say they believe it has scientific validity. Among younger women, from 50 to 55 percent think there's some truth to it.

Not all women are believers, however. Women aged 40 to 49 are least likely to grant astrology any scientific basis. Forty-six percent say there is probably or definitely no scientific basis to it. But that leaves a 50 percent majority of this age group who say there is science behind it.

❖ Few women plan their day based on an astrologer's predictions. But most are open to the idea of a spiritual force that shapes events.

Belief in Astrology, 1994

"Astrology—the study of star signs—has some scientific truth."

(percent of women responding by age, 1994)

	definitely or probably true	*definitely or probably not true*	*can't choose*
Total	52.3%	37.9%	7.8%
Aged 18 to 29	53.1	39.3	7.7
Aged 30 to 39	54.9	38.6	4.9
Aged 40 to 49	50.0	45.8	3.0
Aged 50 to 59	54.6	37.7	5.7
Aged 60 to 69	51.0	30.2	18.7
Aged 70 to 79	47.5	28.9	20.3
Aged 80 or older	47.2	27.8	16.7

Note: Numbers may not add to 100 because no answer is not included.
Source: 1994 General Social Survey, National Opinion Research Center, University of Chicago

Young Women Distrust Others

Most believe people are only looking out for themselves.

Cynicism and distrust are much greater among younger Americans than older generations. Only 35 percent of women under age 30 believe other people are trying to be helpful most of the time. Fully 58 percent think others are just looking out for themselves. Half of women in their 30s also feel this way.

Women aged 50 to 79 are most likely to have faith in others. Between 57 and 60 percent of people in this age group say most people want to be helpful.

The percentage of women aged 80 or older who believe most people are helpful is lower than among women aged 40 to 79. This may reflect their increased sense of vulnerability because of their old age.

❖ The distrust felt by younger women makes them difficult to reach with marketing messages. Building rapport with this age group is important.

Helpfulness of Others, 1994

"Would you say that most of the time people try to be helpful, or that they are mostly just looking out for themselves?"

(percent of women responding by age, 1994)

	trying to be helpful	*looking out for themselves*	*depends*
Total	49.6%	43.6%	6.0%
Aged 18 to 29	35.1	58.0	6.4
Aged 30 to 39	43.4	50.0	6.6
Aged 40 to 49	52.9	40.3	5.9
Aged 50 to 59	57.0	38.4	4.0
Aged 60 to 69	60.3	32.4	5.9
Aged 70 to 79	59.2	34.7	6.1
Aged 80 or older	51.7	34.5	8.6

Note: Numbers may not add to 100 because "don't know" and no answer are not included.
Source: 1994 General Social Survey, National Opinion Research Center, University of Chicago

CHAPTER

2

Education

❖ **Women are more likely to have a college degree.**

In 1995, 20 percent of women had completed college, compared with just 4 percent in 1940.

❖ **Sharp generational differences are apparent in educational attainment.**

The best-educated women are those in their 40s and early 50s—10 percent of women aged 40 to 44 have a graduate-level degree.

❖ **Young women are equal to young men in educational attainment.**

Among 60-to-64-year-olds, 24 percent of men, but only 12 percent of women have completed college. Among 25-to-29-year-olds, the gap virtually disappears.

❖ **Most college students are women.**

In 1950, there were two men for every woman enrolled in college. Today, women account for 55 percent of all college students.

❖ **College women are older than they once were.**

In 1994, 60 percent of women in college were aged 22 or older. More than 20 percent were aged 35 or older.

❖ **Most older women are part-time students.**

About 60 percent of all women college students are enrolled full-time, but among those aged 25 or older, part-time is the norm.

❖ **Most college degrees are earned by women.**

Women earned 55 percent of bachelor's degrees in 1993-94.

One in Five Women Is a College Graduate

Women are more likely than ever to have a college degree.

The educational attainment of Americans has soared as the well-educated baby-boom generation grew up, graduated from high school, and went to college. In 1940, few women or men were even high school graduates—only 26 percent of women and 23 percent of men had a high school diploma. By 1970, a majority of both women and men were high school graduates. Today, 82 percent of both men and women have a high school degree.

Men have always been more likely than women to have a college degree. In 1940, just 4 percent of women and 6 percent of men were college graduates. These figures have grown substantially as baby boomers went to college. By 1995, 20 percent of women and 26 percent of men had completed college.

❖ Among young adults aged 25 to 29, men and women are equally likely to be college graduates because women are pursuing higher education with the same seriousness as men.

Educational Attainment by Sex, 1940 to 1995

(percent of persons aged 25 or older who are high school or college graduates by sex, selected years 1940-95)

	high school		college	
	women	men	women	men
1995	81.6%	81.7%	20.2%	26.0%
1990	77.5	77.7	18.4	24.4
1985	73.5	74.4	16.0	23.1
1980	68.1	69.2	13.6	20.9
1975	62.1	63.1	10.6	17.6
1970	55.4	55.0	8.2	14.1
1965	49.9	48.0	7.1	12.0
1959	45.2	42.2	6.0	10.3
1950	36.0	32.6	5.2	7.3
1940	26.3	22.7	3.8	5.5

Source: Bureau of the Census, Educational Attainment in the United States: March 1995, *PPL-48, 1996*

Younger Women Are Better Educated

Sharp generational differences are apparent in educational attainment.

Among women aged 65 or older, only 64 percent are high school graduates. But among women under age 50, nearly 90 percent have completed high school. Only 10 percent of women aged 65 or older have a college diploma versus one-quarter of women under age 50.

Most older women were raised to be homemakers, dependent on breadwinner husbands. Getting a high school or college degree was not considered a necessity. Today's young women have been brought up to be economically independent. For them, diplomas are vital to earning a living.

Many women continue their education past the bachelor's degree level, pursuing higher degrees as they juggle work and family. The best educated women are those in their 40s and early 50s. Ten percent of women aged 40 to 44 have a graduate-level degree.

❖ Differences in educational attainment are a major reason for the generation gap in attitudes between older and younger women. Younger women are more career oriented and independent than older women, making them different consumers than their mothers.

Educational Attainment by Age, 1995

(number and percent distribution of women aged 25 or older by age and educational attainment, 1995; numbers in thousands)

			high school graduate or more								
							bachelor's degree or more				
	total women	not a high school graduate	total	high school graduate only	some college	associate's degree	total	bachelor's degree only	master's degree	professional degree	doctoral degree
Total number	105,028	24,003	81,026	34,786	20,141	7,353	18,746	13,282	4,267	719	478
Aged 25 to 29	9,712	1,225	8,486	3,065	2,123	880	2,418	2,017	308	79	14
Aged 30 to 34	11,088	1,234	9,855	3,820	2,148	1,135	2,752	2,108	471	122	51
Aged 35 to 39	11,200	1,247	9,953	3,776	2,290	1,144	2,743	1,956	566	144	77
Aged 40 to 44	10,163	1,088	9,075	3,454	1,975	991	2,655	1,648	793	132	82
Aged 45 to 49	8,813	1,025	7,789	3,064	1,688	792	2,245	1,401	683	74	87
Aged 50 to 54	6,858	1,109	5,749	2,553	1,279	464	1,453	864	484	48	57
Aged 55 to 59	5,680	1,150	4,531	2,385	948	325	873	526	269	37	41
Aged 60 to 64	5,198	1,349	3,850	2,179	748	283	640	405	198	23	14
Aged 65 or older	18,264	6,565	11,699	6,776	2,363	743	1,817	1,255	454	58	50
Aged 65 to 69	5,263	1,563	3,701	2,119	746	238	598	401	151	23	23
Aged 70 to 74	4,854	1,508	3,347	1,997	681	234	435	305	101	15	14
Aged 75 or older	8,147	3,494	4,652	2,660	936	271	785	549	202	20	14

(continued)

(continued from previous page)

	total women	not a high school graduate	high school graduate or more								
							bachelor's degree or more				
			total	high school graduate only	some college	associate's degree	total	bachelor's degree only	master's degree	professional degree	doctoral degree
Total percent	100.0%	22.9%	77.1%	33.1%	19.2%	7.0%	17.8%	12.6%	4.1%	0.7%	0.5%
Aged 25 to 29	100.0	12.6	87.4	31.6	21.9	9.1	24.9	20.8	3.2	0.8	0.1
Aged 30 to 34	100.0	11.1	88.9	34.5	19.4	10.2	24.8	19.0	4.2	1.1	0.5
Aged 35 to 39	100.0	11.1	88.9	33.7	20.4	10.2	24.5	17.5	5.1	1.3	0.7
Aged 40 to 44	100.0	10.7	89.3	34.0	19.4	9.8	26.1	16.2	7.8	1.3	0.8
Aged 45 to 49	100.0	11.6	88.4	34.8	19.2	9.0	25.5	15.9	7.7	0.8	1.0
Aged 50 to 54	100.0	16.2	83.8	37.2	18.6	6.8	21.2	12.6	7.1	0.7	0.8
Aged 55 to 59	100.0	20.2	79.8	42.0	16.7	5.7	15.4	9.3	4.7	0.7	0.7
Aged 60 to 64	100.0	26.0	74.1	41.9	14.4	5.4	12.3	7.8	3.8	0.4	0.3
Aged 65 or older	100.0	35.9	64.1	37.1	12.9	4.1	9.9	6.9	2.5	0.3	0.3
Aged 65 to 69	100.0	29.7	70.3	40.3	14.2	4.5	11.4	7.6	2.9	0.4	0.4
Aged 70 to 74	100.0	31.1	69.0	41.1	14.0	4.8	9.0	6.3	2.1	0.3	0.3
Aged 75 or older	100.0	42.9	57.1	32.7	11.5	3.3	9.6	6.7	2.5	0.2	0.2

Source: Bureau of the Census, Educational Attainment in the United States: March 1995*, PPL-48, 1996; calculations by New Strategist*

Women Equal Men in Educational Attainment

Young women have closed the gap.

At all ages, women are as likely as men to have graduated from high school. Overall, 82 percent of both men and women have a high school degree. Men are more likely to be college graduates, however. Among people aged 25 or older, 26 percent of men and 20 percent of women have a college degree.

The gap in college graduation rates between men and women varies sharply by age. It is greatest among people in their early 60s: 24 percent of men aged 60 to 64, but only 12 percent of women in that age group, have completed college.

The gap narrows in each successively younger age group, however. Among people in their late 40s, 35 percent of men and 26 percent of women have a college degree. Among 40-to-44-year-olds, the gap is just 4 percentage points. Among young adults aged 25 to 29, the gap virtually disappears.

❖ Women are pursuing higher education in record numbers. As their college graduation rates match—and possibly overtake—those of men, women will narrow the earnings gap with men.

High School and College Graduates by Age and Sex, 1995

(percent of persons aged 25 or older who are high school or college graduates by age and sex, 1995)

	high school graduates		college graduates	
	women	men	women	men
Total	81.6%	81.7%	20.2%	26.0%
Aged 25 to 29	87.4	86.3	24.9	24.5
Aged 30 to 34	88.9	85.9	24.8	25.7
Aged 35 to 39	88.9	87.8	24.5	26.6
Aged 40 to 44	89.3	87.4	26.1	29.6
Aged 45 to 49	88.4	87.7	25.5	35.0
Aged 50 to 54	83.8	84.0	21.2	29.6
Aged 55 to 59	79.8	79.9	15.4	25.4
Aged 60 to 64	74.1	74.7	12.3	23.8
Aged 65 or older	64.1	63.5	10.0	17.2
Aged 65 to 69	70.3	69.1	11.3	19.9
Aged 70 to 74	69.0	66.7	9.0	18.4
Aged 75 or older	57.1	56.2	9.6	13.9

Source: Bureau of the Census, Educational Attainment in the United States: March 1995, *PPL-48, 1996*

White Women Are Better Educated Than Minority Women

The difference is greatest at the college level.

While 79 percent of white women aged 25 or older are high school graduates, the proportions are lower among blacks and Hispanics. In 1995, only 69 percent of black women and 51 percent of Hispanic women were high school graduates. The gap in educational attainment is even greater at the college level. Nineteen percent of white women aged 25 or older have a college diploma, versus 11 percent of black and 7 percent of Hispanic women.

At the high school level, young black women are closing the educational gap with white women. Among women aged 25 to 29, 88 percent of whites and 85 percent of blacks have high school diplomas. Hispanics still lag far behind at 59 percent.

Even among young adults, there is an enormous gap in the proportion of women who have a college diploma by race and ethnicity. Twenty-seven percent of white women aged 25 to 29 have a college degree, versus only 14 percent of black and 10 percent of Hispanic women.

❖ The cost of a college education keeps black and Hispanic women—who typically have lower incomes than white women—from earning degrees. Until minorities can better afford a college education, they will continue to trail whites in educational attainment.

High School and College Graduates by Age, Race, and Hispanic Origin, 1995

(percent of women aged 25 or older who are high school or college graduates by age, race, and Hispanic origin, 1995)

	high school graduates			college graduates		
	white	black	Hispanic	white	black	Hispanic
Total	78.7%	69.2%	50.9%	18.7%	10.9%	6.9%
Aged 25 to 29	88.2	85.1	58.7	26.6	13.6	10.1
Aged 30 to 34	90.0	84.4	64.2	26.5	13.3	9.9
Aged 35 to 39	89.8	87.6	61.1	25.7	15.6	9.8
Aged 40 to 44	90.8	83.3	62.5	27.0	16.6	10.0
Aged 45 to 49	90.1	78.3	53.4	26.9	14.7	7.7
Aged 50 to 54	85.5	75.0	50.6	21.5	15.7	8.6
Aged 55 to 59	81.9	67.7	43.1	16.2	8.9	4.0
Aged 60 to 64	76.3	57.0	35.5	12.4	9.6	5.9
Aged 65 or older	67.0	38.2	27.5	10.3	6.6	4.0
Aged 65 to 69	73.2	47.0	32.1	11.5	9.4	6.0
Aged 70 to 74	72.5	40.5	22.9	9.4	4.5	4.0
Aged 75 or older	59.7	30.3	26.3	10.1	5.7	1.9

Source: Bureau of the Census, Educational Attainment in the United States: March 1995*, detailed tables for Current Population Reports P20-489, PPL-48, 1996*

Equal Numbers of Males and Females in School

Women are more likely to continue their education into adulthood, however.

The value Americans place on education is apparent in school enrollment statistics. Virtually all children aged 5 to 17 are enrolled in school. And although it was once rare for children to be in preschool, today nearly half of 3- and 4-year-olds are in school.

Women aged 18 and 19 are as likely as men that age to be in school (60 percent). But among people aged 20 or older, women are more likely than men to be enrolled in school—with one exception. Among 22 to 24 year olds, men and women are about equally likely to be in school.

Women in their 30s and 40s are continuing their education in significant numbers. There are 2.7 million women aged 30 or older enrolled in school. Some are completing a college education that had been interrupted by work or family demands, while others are pursuing specialized degrees. Among students aged 30 or older, women outnumber men by nearly 1 million.

❖ Increasingly, education is viewed as a lifelong pursuit rather than something reserved for the young. Highly-educated women will continue to be interested in learning opportunities not only for career advancement, but also for self-fulfillment.

School Enrollment by Age and Sex, 1994

(number and percent of persons aged 3 or older enrolled in school by age and sex, 1994; numbers in thousands)

	females		males	
	number	*percent*	*number*	*percent*
Total, aged 3 or older	34,654	27.2%	34,618	28.7%
Aged 3 and 4	1,893	46.9	2,024	47.6
Aged 5 and 6	3,787	96.4	3,965	97.0
Aged 7 to 9	5,609	99.5	5,878	99.2
Aged 10 to 13	7,459	99.4	7,823	99.4
Aged 14 and 15	3,694	98.7	3,825	98.8
Aged 16 and 17	3,362	94.4	3,533	94.3
Aged 18 and 19	2,076	60.0	2,104	60.4
Aged 20 and 21	1,665	47.0	1,467	42.7
Aged 22 to 24	1,360	23.9	1,364	24.2
Aged 25 to 29	1,079	11.1	992	10.5
Aged 30 to 34	832	7.5	636	5.9
Aged 35 to 44	1,213	5.7	715	3.5
Aged 45 to 54	522	3.4	221	1.5
Aged 55 or older	103	0.4	72	0.3

Source: Bureau of the Census, School Enrollment: Social and Economic Characteristics of Students: October 1994, *Current Population Reports, P20-487, 1996*

Women's College Enrollment Rate Has Soared

Women are now as likely as men to go to college.

In 1960, only 38 percent of women entered college within 12 months of graduating from high school. Today, 61 percent of women go from high school into college. The college enrollment rate of men has also increased, rising from 54 percent in 1960 to 63 percent in 1995.

The gap in the college enrollment rates of men and women was a full 16 percentage points in 1960. This gap narrowed in the 1960s and 1970s as the women of the baby-boom generation went to college. By 1988, women's college enrollment rates surpassed those of men and continued to do so until 1995. In that year, men's enrollment rate surged to a record high, while the rate for women fell slightly. Women's enrollment rate is off substantially from the 67 percent record high of the early 1990s—when it surpassed men's college enrollment rate by nearly 10 percentage points.

❖ Because both women and men need educational credentials to establish themselves in a financially rewarding career, the gap between their college enrollment rates is likely to disappear in the years ahead.

College Enrollment Rates by Sex, 1960 to 1995

(percent of persons aged 16 to 24 who graduated from high school in the previous 12 months and were enrolled in college as of October of each year, by sex; percentage point difference in enrollment rates of women and men; selected years, 1960-95)

	women	men	percentage point difference
1995	61.4%	62.6%	-1.2
1994	63.2	60.6	2.6
1993	65.4	59.7	5.7
1992	63.8	59.6	4.2
1991	67.1	57.6	9.5
1990	62.0	57.8	4.2
1989	61.6	57.6	4.0
1988	60.8	57.0	3.8
1987	55.3	58.4	-3.1
1986	51.9	55.9	-4.0
1985	56.9	58.6	-1.7
1980	51.8	46.7	5.1
1975	49.0	52.6	-3.6
1970	48.5	55.2	-6.7
1965	45.3	57.3	-12.0
1960	37.9	54.0	-16.1

Source: National Center for Education Statistics, Digest of Education Statistics 1996, NCES 96-133; calculations by New Strategist

Most College Students Are Women

Before 1980, men accounted for the majority of college students.

In 1950, there were two men for every woman enrolled in college. Today, women account for a 55 percent majority of students. Of the 15 million people enrolled in college in 1994, 8.3 million were women.

Women's rising share of the college population reflects the changing roles of women in society. No longer content to be housewives, women are earning the educational credentials that will further their career opportunities. Among young adults, women are the educational equals of men. As they embark on careers, their earnings should reflect their high levels of education.

❖ Because women are now responsible for their own economic well-being, they are a prime market for higher and continuing education—no matter what their age.

College Enrollment, 1950 to 1994

(total number of college students aged 15 or older, and number and percent women; selected years 1950-94; numbers in thousands)

	total students	women	
		number	percent
1994	15,022	8,258	55.0%
1993	14,394	7,795	54.2
1992	14,035	7,844	55.9
1991	14,057	7,618	54.2
1990	13,621	7,429	54.5
1985	12,524	6,618	52.8
1980	11,387	5,957	52.3
1975	10,880	4,969	45.7
1970	7,413	3,013	40.6
1965	5,675	2,172	38.3
1960	3,570	1,231	34.5
1955	2,379	800	33.6
1950	2,175	701	32.2

Source: Bureau of the Census, School Enrollment—Social and Economic Characteristics of Students: October 1994, *Current Population Reports, P20-487, 1996; calculations by New Strategist*

College Women Are Older Than They Once Were

Only 39 percent of students are aged 18 to 21.

The 18-to-21 age group once dominated the college crowd, accounting for well over half of all female college students until 1980.

Today, the picture has changed dramatically as women stay in school longer or return to school well beyond traditional college age. The average length of time it takes students to obtain a bachelor's degree has increased to about six years as more students pursue their education part-time, or interrupt schooling altogether to work or raise a family.

In 1994, 60 percent of women in college were aged 22 or older. More than one in five were aged 35 or older, a proportion that has nearly doubled since 1975.

❖ The college market, once dominated by teens and young adults, has aged considerably. Many older students have families and jobs, making their needs different from those of younger students.

Women in College by Age, 1950 to 1994

(number and percent distribution of women college students aged 15 or older by age; selected years 1950-94; numbers in thousands)

	total	14 to 17	18 and 19	20 and 21	22 to 24	25 to 29	30 to 34	35+
Number								
1994	8,258	85	1,635	1,613	1,328	1,054	776	1,766
1993	7,795	75	1,663	1,487	1,243	1,022	692	1,613
1992	7,844	107	1,566	1,594	1,269	984	748	1,575
1991	7,618	83	1,603	1,549	1,066	965	715	1,636
1990	7,429	91	1,576	1,403	1,063	1,017	732	1,546
1985	6,618	129	1,559	1,303	926	941	658	1,100
1980	5,957	153	1,565	1,178	882	788	590	802
1975	4,969	164	1,517	1,058	668	590	357	614
1970	3,013	130	1,248	774	452	255	154	-
1965	2,172	151	997	522	241	156	105	-
1960	1,231	123	565	287	98	92	66	-
1955	800	90	313	285*		69	43	-
1950	701	106	338	247*		10	-	-
Percent distribution								
1994	100.0%	1.0%	19.8%	19.5%	16.1%	12.8%	9.4%	21.4%
1993	100.0	1.0	21.3	19.1	15.9	13.1	8.9	20.7
1992	100.0	1.4	20.0	20.3	16.2	12.5	9.5	20.1
1991	100.0	1.1	21.0	20.3	14.0	12.7	9.4	21.5
1990	100.0	1.2	21.2	18.9	14.3	13.7	9.9	20.8
1985	100.0	1.9	23.6	19.7	14.0	14.2	9.9	16.6
1980	100.0	2.6	26.3	19.8	14.8	13.2	9.9	13.5
1975	100.0	3.3	30.5	21.3	13.4	11.9	7.2	12.4
1970	100.0	4.3	41.4	25.7	15.0	8.5	5.1	-
1965	100.0	7.0	45.9	24.0	11.1	7.2	4.8	-
1960	100.0	10.0	45.9	23.3	8.0	7.5	5.4	-
1955	100.0	11.3	39.1	35.6*		8.6	5.4	-
1950	100.0	15.1	48.2	35.2*		1.4	-	-

** Data are for 20-to-24 age group.*
Note: (-) means data not available.
Source: Bureau of the Census, School Enrollment—Social and Economic Characteristics of Students: October 1994, *Current Population Reports, P20-487, 1996; calculations by New Strategist*

Female Students Are Racially Diverse

One in five female college students is a minority.

The racial composition of college students has grown more diverse over the past few decades. In 1955, 91 percent of women enrolled in college were white. By 1994, the proportion had fallen to 81 percent as more black and Hispanic women went to college.

While college enrollment among black and Hispanic women has increased, these minorities are still underrepresented in higher education. Thirteen percent of female college students are black, versus 15 percent of all women aged 18 to 24. Only 8 percent of female college students are Hispanic, versus 13 percent of women in the 18-to-24 age group.

❖ Behind the lagging college enrollment of blacks and Hispanics is their lower incomes. The relentless rise in the cost of college makes it difficult for minority women to afford higher education.

Women in College by Race and Hispanic Origin, 1955 to 1994

(number and percent distribution of women college students aged 15 or older by race and Hispanic origin; selected years 1955-94; numbers in thousands)

	total	*white*	*black*	*Hispanic*
Number				
1994	8,258	6,698	1,054	659
1993	7,795	6,331	947	630
1992	7,844	6,499	897	530
1991	7,618	6,382	848	483
1990	7,429	6,253	807	384
1985	6,618	5,679	712	299
1980	5,957	5,121	686	221
1975	4,969	4,284	577	193
1970	3,013	2,693	269	-
1965	2,172	1,991	148	-
1960	1,231	1,128	102	-
1955	800	729	71	-
Percent distribution				
1994	100.0%	81.1%	12.8%	8.0%
1993	100.0	81.2	12.1	8.1
1992	100.0	82.9	11.4	6.8
1991	100.0	83.8	11.1	6.3
1990	100.0	84.2	10.9	5.2
1985	100.0	85.8	10.8	4.5
1980	100.0	86.0	11.5	3.7
1975	100.0	86.2	11.6	3.9
1970	100.0	89.4	8.9	-
1965	100.0	91.7	6.8	-
1960	100.0	91.6	8.3	-
1955	100.0	91.1	8.9	-

Note: (-) means data not available. Numbers will not add to total because Hispanics may be of any race and not all races are shown.

Source: Bureau of the Census, School Enrollment—Social and Economic Characteristics of Students: October 1994, *Current Population Reports, P20-487, 1996; calculations by New Strategist*

Most Older Women Are Part-Time Students

Only younger women have the luxury of pursuing an education full-time.

About 60 percent of women enrolled in college are full-time students, but among those aged 25 or older, part-time is the norm.

Most female students under age 25 are enrolled full-time at four-year institutions. Older students are more evenly split between two- and four-year institutions and graduate programs.

For many women, the dream of attaining a college diploma never disappears. Fully 600,000 women aged 45 or older are college students.

❖ The women most likely to pursue educational opportunities as adults are those who are already well-educated. Today's highly-educated young women will be eager for learning opportunities throughout their lives.

Women in College by Age and Attendance Status, 1994

(number and percent distribution of women college students aged 15 or older by age and attendance status, 1994; numbers in thousands)

		undergraduate						graduate		
		two year college			four-year college					
	total	total	full-time	part-time	total	full-time	part-time	total	full-time	part-time
Total	8,258	2,504	1,234	1,270	4,379	3,246	1,134	1,375	505	870
Aged 15 to 17	85	16	12	4	69	67	3	-	-	-
Aged 18 and 19	1635	528	415	113	1104	1032	72	3	3	-
Aged 20 and 21	1613	352	228	124	1255	1127	128	6	4	2
Aged 22 to 24	1328	332	171	161	713	521	192	283	166	117
Aged 25 to 29	1054	337	121	217	351	165	186	366	182	183
Aged 30 to 34	776	315	100	214	265	117	148	196	65	131
Aged 35 to 39	681	265	93	172	244	88	156	172	44	128
Aged 40 to 44	486	142	54	88	186	69	117	158	16	142
Aged 45 to 49	352	109	17	92	135	47	88	108	14	94
Aged 50 to 54	154	69	23	46	36	7	30	49	5	44
Aged 55 to 59	55	16	-	16	14	7	8	24	5	19
Aged 60 to 64	21	12	-	12	4	-	4	5	-	5
Aged 65 or older	18	11	1	10	2	-	2	5	-	5

(continued)

(continued from previous page)

Percent distribution by age	total	undergraduate: two year college total	two year college full-time	two year college part-time	four-year college total	four-year college full-time	four-year college part-time	graduate total	graduate full-time	graduate part-time
Total	100.0%	100.0%	100.0%	100.0%	100.0%	100.0%	100.0%	100.0%	100.0%	100.0%
Aged 15 to 17	1.0	0.6	1.0	0.3	1.6	2.1	0.3	-	-	-
Aged 18 and 19	19.8	21.1	33.6	8.9	25.2	31.8	6.3	0.2	0.6	-
Aged 20 and 21	19.5	14.1	18.5	9.8	28.7	34.7	11.3	0.4	0.8	0.2
Aged 22 to 24	16.1	13.3	13.9	12.7	16.3	16.1	16.9	20.6	32.9	13.4
Aged 25 to 29	12.8	13.5	9.8	17.1	8.0	5.1	16.4	26.6	36.0	21.0
Aged 30 to 34	9.4	12.6	8.1	16.9	6.1	3.6	13.1	14.3	12.9	15.1
Aged 35 to 39	8.2	10.6	7.5	13.5	5.6	2.7	13.8	12.5	8.7	14.7
Aged 40 to 44	5.9	5.7	4.4	6.9	4.2	2.1	10.3	11.5	3.2	16.3
Aged 45 to 49	4.3	4.4	1.4	7.2	3.1	1.4	7.8	7.9	2.8	10.8
Aged 50 to 54	1.9	2.8	1.9	3.6	0.8	0.2	2.6	3.6	1.0	5.1
Aged 55 to 59	0.7	0.6	-	1.3	0.3	0.2	0.7	1.7	1.0	2.2
Aged 60 to 64	0.3	0.5	-	0.9	0.1	-	0.4	0.4	-	0.6
Aged 65 or older	0.2	0.4	0.1	0.8	0.0	-	0.2	0.4	-	0.6

(continued)

(continued from previous page)

		undergraduate						graduate		
		two year college			four-year college					
Percent distribution by attendance status	total	total	full-time	part-time	total	full-time	part-time	total	full-time	part-time
Total	100.0%	30.3%	14.9%	15.4%	53.0%	39.3%	13.7%	16.7%	6.1%	10.5%
Aged 15 to 17	100.0	18.8	14.1	4.7	81.2	78.8	3.5	-	-	-
Aged 18 and 19	100.0	32.3	25.4	6.9	67.5	63.1	4.4	0.2	0.2	-
Aged 20 and 21	100.0	21.8	14.1	7.7	77.8	69.9	7.9	0.4	0.2	0.1
Aged 22 to 24	100.0	25.0	12.9	12.1	53.7	39.2	14.5	21.3	12.5	8.8
Aged 25 to 29	100.0	32.0	11.5	20.6	33.3	15.7	17.6	34.7	17.3	17.4
Aged 30 to 34	100.0	40.6	12.9	27.6	34.1	15.1	19.1	25.3	8.4	16.9
Aged 35 to 39	100.0	38.9	13.7	25.3	35.8	12.9	22.9	25.3	6.5	18.8
Aged 40 to 44	100.0	29.2	11.1	18.1	38.3	14.2	24.1	32.5	3.3	29.2
Aged 45 to 49	100.0	31.0	4.8	26.1	38.4	13.4	25.0	30.7	4.0	26.7
Aged 50 to 54	100.0	44.8	14.9	29.9	23.4	4.5	19.5	31.8	3.2	28.6
Aged 55 to 59	100.0	29.1	-	29.1	25.5	12.7	14.5	43.6	9.1	34.5
Aged 60 to 64	100.0	57.1	-	57.1	19.0	-	19.0	23.8	-	23.8
Aged 65 or older	100.0	61.1	5.6	55.6	11.1	-	11.1	27.8	-	27.8

Note: (-) means sample is too small to make a reliable estimate.
Source: Bureau of the Census, School Enrollment—Social and Economic Characteristics of Students: October 1994, *Current Population Reports, P20-487, 1996; calculations by New Strategist*

Racial Makeup of Female Students Varies by Type of Institution

Two-year colleges are most diverse.

Fifteen percent of female students attending two-year colleges are black, while 11 percent are Hispanic. The black and Hispanic proportions are slightly smaller at four-year institutions, at 13 and 7 percent, respectively. At the graduate level, only 8 percent of female students are black, while just 5 percent are Hispanic.

Over half of black and white female college students attend four-year institutions, while the share among Hispanics is 48 percent. Forty-two percent of Hispanic women in college attend two-year institutions, versus a 35 percent share among blacks and 30 percent among whites.

❖ Because black and Hispanic students typically have lower incomes than white students, they are more likely to go to less expensive, two-year schools such as community colleges.

Women in College by Race, Hispanic Origin, and Attendance Status, 1994

(number and percent distribution of women college students aged 15 or older by race, Hispanic origin, and attendance status, 1994; numbers in thousands)

		undergraduate							graduate		
		two year college			four-year college						
	total	total	full-time	part-time	total	full-time	part-time		total	full-time	part-time
Total	8,258	2,504	1,234	1,270	4,379	3,246	1,134		1,375	505	870
White	6,698	1,993	964	1,029	3,540	2,631	909		1,166	410	756
Black	1,054	368	200	169	573	419	154		113	42	71
Hispanic	659	277	126	151	314	204	110		68	29	39
Percent distribution by race and Hispanic origin											
Total	100.0%	100.0%	100.0%	100.0%	100.0%	100.0%	100.0%		100.0%	100.0%	100.0%
White	81.1	79.6	78.1	81.0	80.8	81.1	80.2		84.8	81.2	86.9
Black	12.8	14.7	16.2	13.3	13.1	12.9	13.6		8.2	8.3	8.2
Hispanic	8.0	11.1	10.2	11.9	7.2	6.3	9.7		4.9	5.7	4.5
Percent distribution by attendance status											
Total	100.0%	30.3%	14.9%	15.4%	53.0%	39.3%	13.7%		16.7%	6.1%	10.5%
White	100.0	29.8	14.4	15.4	52.9	39.3	13.6		17.4	6.1	11.3
Black	100.0	34.9	19.0	16.0	54.4	39.8	14.6		10.7	4.0	6.7
Hispanic	100.0	42.0	19.1	22.9	47.6	31.0	16.7		10.3	4.4	5.9

Note: numbers will not add to total because Hispanics may of of any race and not all races are shown.
Source: Bureau of the Census, School Enrollment—Social and Economic Characteristics of Students: October 1994, *Current Population Reports, P20-487, 1996; calculations by New Strategist*

College Women Value Money More

Most college freshman seek financial security.

The priorities of women entering college have changed enormously in the past three decades. In 1967, few women freshmen cited financial objectives as being "essential" or "very important" to them. Fully 88 percent said they were in college to "develop a meaningful philosophy of life." Three-quarters wanted to "help others in difficulty." Only 30 percent said they wanted to be "very well off financially."

Times have changed. In 1995, 73 percent of female college freshmen said it was "essential" or "very important" to be very well off financially. Although a majority still want to help others, the percentage is lower than in 1967. Developing a meaningful life philosophy must seem silly to a generation raised on economic insecurity. The proportion citing this objective as important fell to only 42 percent.

A shift from the arts to the sciences is also apparent. The proportion of women saying they want to make a "theoretical contribution to science" more than doubled, from 6 to 15 percent between 1967 and 1995. The percentage wanting to "create artistic work" or "become accomplished in a performing art" fell substantially.

❖ Today's young women want financial security. While they haven't abandoned more altruistic objectives entirely, their goals have become far more self-centered.

Important Objectives of Women College Freshmen, 1967 and 1995

(percent of women college freshmen citing objective as "essential" or "very important," 1967 and 1995; percentage point change, 1967-95; ranked by percentage in 1995)

	1995	1967	percentage point change, 1967-95
Be very well off financially	72.5%	30.0%	42.5%
Help others in difficulty	69.3	73.6	-4.3
Become an authority in my field	63.4	63.7	-0.3
Obtain recognition from colleagues	53.3	34.9	18.4
Develop a meaningful philosophy of life	42.4	87.6	-45.2
Be successful in my own business	36.0	32.8	3.2
Be a community leader	29.1	18.9	10.2
Keep up to date with political affairs	25.7	49.1	-23.4
Write original works	12.9	16.7	-3.8
Create artistic work	12.5	22.1	-9.6
Become accomplished in a performing art	11.4	14.6	-3.2
Theoretical contribution to science	14.8	6.1	8.7

Source: Dey, E.L., Astin, A.W., & Korn, W.S. (1991). The American Freshman: Twenty-Five Year Trends. *Los Angeles: Higher Education Research Institute, UCLA. Astin, A.W., Korn, W.S., Sax, L.J., & Mahoney, K.M. (1995).* The American Freshman: National Norms for Fall 1995. *Los Angeles: Higher Education Research Institute, UCLA.*

College Women Are Highly Confident

Today's young women are more confident than those of 30 years ago.

Like the children of Lake Woebegon, the majority of women entering college believe they are "above average" in many ways. By definition, a majority can't be above average, but one thing is clear: the young women of 1995 are even more confident in their abilities than were those of 1966.

Most freshmen women say they are above average in their understanding of others, in their drive to achieve, and in their academic ability, according to a survey by UCLA's Higher Education Research Institute. Young college women today are more likely than their counterparts of 30 years ago to say they are above average in their leadership ability; intellectual and social self-confidence; mathematical, writing and public-speaking ability; stubbornness; and popularity. Academic ability is the only characteristic on which today's college freshmen rate themselves lower than did the college freshmen of 30 years ago.

❖ Self-confidence is a prerequisite for success. Today's young women are more determined to succeed and have greater confidence in their abilities than did baby-boom women in 1966. Look out world, here they come.

Self-Confidence of Women College Freshmen, 1966 and 1995

(percent of women college freshmen rating themselves above average or in the top 10 percent in selected characteristics, 1966 and 1995; percentage point change, 1966-95; ranked by percentage in 1995)

	1995	*1966*	*percentage point change, 1966-95*
Understanding of others	73.7%	66.0%	7.7%
Drive to achieve	64.7	57.9	6.8
Academic ability	52.8	58.5	-5.7
Leadership ability	49.7	46.1	3.6
Self-confidence (intellectual)	44.5	30.7	13.8
Stubborness	44.2	37.5	6.7
Writing ability	41.8	28.9	12.9
Self-confidence (social)	41.3	26.0	15.3
Mathematical ability	32.3	26.0	6.3
Popularity	30.0	28.5	1.5
Public speaking ability	27.8	20.7	7.1

Source: Dey, E.L., Astin, A.W., & Korn, W.S. (1991). The American Freshman: Twenty-Five Year Trends. *Los Angeles: Higher Education Research Institute, UCLA. Astin, A.W., Korn, W.S., Sax, L.J., & Mahoney, K.M. (1995).* The American Freshman: National Norms for Fall 1995. *Los Angeles: Higher Education Research Institute, UCLA.*

Most College Degrees Are Earned by Women

But some types of degrees are more likely to go to men.

In 1996, more women than men received college degrees, with 55 percent of diplomas awarded to women. The proportions vary sharply by type of degree, however.

The share of degrees earned by women drops with increasing educational level. Women earned 61 percent of all associate's degrees conferred in 1996. Of the 1.2 million bachelor's degrees awarded in that year, 56 percent were earned by women, as were 51 percent of master's degrees. But only 39 percent of doctoral degrees and 41 percent of first-professional degrees were earned by women.

The share of associate's, master's, and doctoral degrees earned by women should rise between 1996 and 2006, according to projections by the National Center for Education Statistics. In 1996, nearly 17,000 women received doctoral degrees. By 2006, women are expected to earn half of all doctoral degrees.

❖ The gender gap in educational attainment has been narrowing for decades. As it does, the income gap is also narrowing—making women more important consumers than ever.

Degrees Conferred by Level of Degree and Sex, 1996 to 2006

(number and percent distribution of degrees conferred by level of degree and sex of degree-holder, 1996 and 2006; percent change in number, 1996-2006)

	1996		2006		percent change
	number	percent	number	percent	1996-2006
Associate's degree	534,000	100.0%	584,000	100.0%	9.4%
Women	323,000	60.5	360,000	61.6	11.5
Men	212,000	39.7	224,000	38.4	5.7
Bachelor's degree	1,195,000	100.0	1,316,000	100.0	10.1
Women	663,000	55.5	725,000	55.1	9.4
Men	533,000	44.6	591,000	44.9	10.9
Master's degree	409,000	100.0	462,000	100.0	13.0
Women	210,000	51.3	250,000	54.1	19.0
Men	199,000	48.7	212,000	45.9	6.5
Doctoral degree	43,300	100.0	43,200	100.0	-0.2
Women	16,800	38.8	21,400	49.5	27.4
Men	26,500	61.2	21,800	50.5	-17.7
First-professional degree	78,000	100.0	91,700	100.0	17.6
Women	32,100	41.2	36,500	39.8	13.7
Men	45,900	58.8	55,200	60.2	20.3

Source: National Center for Education Statistics, Projections of Education Statistics to 2006, *Internet web site,* http://www.ed.gov/NCES; *calculations by New Strategist*

Women's Share of Degrees Varies by Field of Study

Female professions are still dominated by women.

Women still dominate many fields that have traditionally been their province. They earned most of the bachelor's, master's, and doctoral degrees in education, health professions, home economics, and library sciences in 1993-94.

Women are still a minority in many fields traditionally dominated by men. Women received only one-third of bachelor's degrees in physical sciences, 28 percent of those in computer and information sciences, and 15 percent of those in engineering. The share of master's or doctoral degrees awarded to women in these fields was even lower. But women earned 46 percent of bachelor's degrees in mathematics and 48 percent of bachelor's degrees in business in 1993-94.

❖ Professions traditionally dominated by women typically pay less than those dominated by men. Until women break into the hard sciences—such as engineering—they will have difficulty narrowing the pay gap with men.

Bachelor's Degrees Conferred by Field of Study, 1993-94

(total number of bachelor's degrees conferred by field of study, and number and percent awarded to women, 1993-1994)

		women	
	total	*number*	*percent*
All fields	1,169,275	636,853	54.5%
Agriculture and natural recources	18,070	6,322	35.0
Architecture and related programs	8,975	3,211	35.8
Area, ethnic, and cultural studies	5,573	3,615	64.9
Biological sciences/life sciences	51383	26,333	51.2
Business and management	246,654	117493	47.6
Communications and communications technologies	51,827	30,468	58.8
Computer and information sciences	24,200	6,883	28.4
Education	107,600	83,150	77.3
Engineering and engineering-related technologies	78,225	11,628	14.9
English language and literature	53,924	35,499	65.8
Foreign languages	14,378	10,074	70.1
Health professions and related sciences	74,421	61,359	82.4
Home economics and vocational home economics	15,522	13,589	87.5
Law and legal studies	2,171	1,523	70.2
Liberal/general studies	33,397	20,280	60.7
Library sciences	62	57	91.9
Mathematics	14,396	6,661	46.3
Multi-disciplinary studies	25,167	16,109	64.0
Parks and recreation	11,470	5,647	49.2
Philosophy and religion	7,546	2,702	35.8
Physical sciences and science technologies	18,400	6,177	33.6
Protective services	23,009	8,840	38.4
Psychology	69,259	50,617	73.1
Public administration and services	17,815	13,896	78.0
Social sciences and history	133,680	61,674	46.1
Theological studies	5,434	1,309	24.1
Visual and performing arts	49,053	29,515	60.2

Source: National Center for Education Statistics, Digest of Education Statistics 1996, *NCES 96-133; calculations by New Strategist*

Master's Degrees Conferred by Field of Study, 1993-94

(total number of master's degrees conferred by field of study, and number and percent awarded to women, 1993-1994)

		women	
	total	number	percent
All fields	387,050	210,985	54.5%
Agriculture and natural recources	4,119	1,604	38.9
Architecture and related programs	3,943	1,515	38.4
Area, ethnic, and cultural studies	1,633	865	53.0
Biological sciences/life sciences	5,196	2,731	52.6
Business and management	93,437	34,102	36.5
Communications and communications technologies	5,419	3,321	61.3
Computer and information sciences	10,416	2,692	25.8
Education	98,938	75,930	76.7
Engineering and engineering-related technologies	29,754	4,600	15.5
English language and literature	7,885	5,173	65.6
Foreign languages	3,288	2,201	66.9
Health professions and related sciences	28,025	22,211	79.3
Home economics and vocational home economics	2,421	2,016	83.3
Law and legal studies	2,432	824	33.9
Liberal/general studies	2,496	1,583	63.4
Library sciences	5,116	4,076	79.7
Mathematics	4,100	1,564	38.1
Multi-disciplinary studies	2,464	1,270	51.5
Parks and recreation	1,625	780	48.0
Philosophy and religion	1,350	513	38.0
Physical sciences and science technologies	5,679	1,661	29.2
Protective services	1,437	535	37.2
Psychology	12,181	8,780	72.1
Public administration and services	21833	15427	70.7
Social sciences and history	14561	6409	44.0
Theological studies	4956	1922	38.8
Visual and performing arts	9925	5696	57.4

Source: National Center for Education Statistics, Digest of Education Statistics 1996, *NCES 96-133; calculations by New Strategist*

Doctoral Degrees Conferred by Field of Study, 1993-94

(total number of doctoral degrees conferred by field of study, and number and percent awarded to women, 1993-1994)

		women	
	total	number	percent
All fields	43,185	16,633	38.5%
Agriculture and natural recources	1,278	296	23.2
Architecture and related programs	161	50	31.1
Area, ethnic, and cultural studies	155	80	51.6
Biological sciences/life sciences	4,534	1,844	40.7
Business and management	1,364	384	28.2
Communications and communications technologies	345	171	49.6
Computer and information sciences	810	125	15.4
Education	6,908	4,202	60.8
Engineering and engineering-related technologies	5,979	664	11.1
English language and literature	1,344	776	57.7
Foreign languages	886	531	59.9
Health professions and related sciences	1,902	1,113	58.5
Home economics and vocational home economics	365	272	74.5
Law and legal studies	79	16	20.3
Liberal/general studies	80	34	42.5
Library sciences	45	31	68.9
Mathematics	1,157	253	21.9
Multi-disciplinary studies	227	76	33.5
Parks and recreation	116	46	39.7
Philosophy and religion	528	145	27.5
Physical sciences and science technologies	4,650	1,008	21.7
Protective services	25	11	44.0
Psychology	3,563	2,217	62.2
Public administration and services	519	281	54.1
Social sciences and history	3627	1310	36.1
Theological studies	1448	213	14.7
Visual and performing arts	1054	469	44.5

Source: National Center for Education Statistics, Digest of Education Statistics 1996, *NCES 96-133; calculations by New Strategist*

Women Are a Growing Share of Lawyers and Physicians

Women earn most degrees awarded in pharmacy and veterinary medicine.

Not long ago, it was unusual to find women physicians, lawyers, dentists, or pharmacists. Now, women make up a substantial share of those earning degrees in these and other professions.

As of 1993-94, women earned a majority of degrees in pharmacy (67 percent) and veterinary medicine (62 percent). They earned nearly half of degrees in optometry (49 percent) and law (43 percent). Women accounted for more than one-third of those earning degrees in medicine and dentistry (38 percent each) and osteopathy (35 percent). Women's representation at the professional level is lowest in theology, at 25 percent of graduates in 1993-94.

❖ As recent graduates from professional programs replace older professionals who are overwhelmingly men, women's presence in these high-paying fields will become commonplace.

First-Professional Degrees Conferred by Field of Study, 1993-94

(total number of first-professional degrees conferred by field of study, and number and percent awarded to women, 1993-1994)

		women	
	total	*number*	*percent*
Total	75,418	30,711	40.7%
Dentistry (D.D.S. or D.M.D.)	3,787	1,457	38.5
Medicine (M.D.)	15,368	5,824	37.9
Optometry (O.D.)	1,103	549	49.8
Osteopathic medicine (D.O.)	1,798	633	35.2
Pharmacy (Pharm.D.)	1,936	1,293	66.8
Podiatry (Pod.D., D.P. or D.P.M.)	465	135	29.0
Veterinary medicine (D.V.M.)	2,089	1,291	61.8
Chiropractic (D.C. or D.C.M.)	2,806	796	28.4
Law (LL.B. or J.D.)	40,044	17,218	43.0
Theology (M. Div., M.H.L., B.D., or Ord.)	5,967	1,481	24.8

Source: National Center for Education Statistics, Digest of Education Statistics 1996, *NCES 96-133; calculations by New Strategist*

Women Marry Educational Equals

Most husbands and wives have the same level of education.

People tend to seek mates who have similar backgrounds and interests It is no surprise, then, that for most couples both husband and wife have the same level of educational attainment. Fifty-four percent of husbands and wives are educationally matched, with both having, for example, bachelor's degrees.

The greater educational attainment of younger generations is apparent in the larger number of couples with diplomas. In 19 percent of married couples with a husband aged 35 to 44, both spouses have a bachelor's degree. This is also true for 20 percent of couples with a husband aged 45 to 54. The proportion of couples in the 35-to-54 age group in which both husband and wife have a bachelor's degree is greater than the proportion in which both spouses are only high school graduates. Among older couples, the opposite is true. In only 8 percent of couples with a husband aged 65 or older do both spouses have a bachelor's degree. In 19 percent of these couples, both spouses went no further than high school. For an even larger 20 percent, neither spouse completed high school.

❖ As well-educated baby-boom couples replace older, less-educated couples, the older market will be transformed. Businesses should prepare for much more sophisticated older consumers.

Educational Attainment of Husbands and Wives by Age of Husband, 1995

(percent distribution of married couples by educational attainment of husbands and wives, by age of husband, 1995)

	education of wife				
	total wives	less than high school	high school graduate only	some college or associate's degree	bachelor's degree or more
Education and age of husband					
Total husbands	100.0%	14.6%	37.1%	26.7%	21.6%
Less than high school	16.9	9.2	5.7	1.6	0.3
High school graduate only	31.6	3.8	18.7	6.8	2.3
Some college or associate's degree	24.3	1.3	8.1	11.2	3.8
Bachelor's degree or more	27.2	0.3	4.6	7.1	15.2
Husbands aged 18 to 24	100.0	22.0	38.1	32.7	7.1
Less than high school	22.3	13.4	7.0	1.9	-
High school graduate only	42.1	7.6	22.6	10.6	1.3
Some college or associate's degree	28.9	1.0	7.8	17.7	2.4
Bachelor's degree or more	6.7	0.1	0.8	2.4	3.4
Husbands aged 25 to 34	100.0	11.7	32.8	31.9	23.6
Less than high school	12.6	6.7	4.3	1.4	0.2
High school graduate only	34.7	3.7	18.7	9.3	3.0
Some college or associate's degree	27.3	1.1	6.9	15.2	4.1
Bachelor's degree or more	25.4	0.2	2.8	6.0	16.4
Husbands aged 35 to 44	100.0	8.8	34.4	29.1	30.0
Less than high school	9.8	5.1	3.4	1.0	0.6
High school graduate only	30.7	2.6	17.8	7.5	4.9
Some college or associate's degree	28.0	1.0	8.8	12.8	5.4
Bachelor's degree or more	31.4	0.2	4.4	7.8	19.0
Husbands aged 45 to 54	100.0	10.6	35.9	27.4	26.1
Less than high school	12.2	6.2	4.3	1.5	0.2
High school graduate only	28.8	3.0	17.6	6.0	2.1
Some college or associate's degree	24.1	1.1	8.3	10.8	3.9
Bachelor's degree or more	34.9	0.3	5.7	9.1	19.8

continued

(continued from previous page)

		education of wife			
	total wives	less than high school	high school graduate only	some college or associate's degree	bachelor's degree or more
Husbands aged 55 to 64	100.0%	17.1%	43.3%	23.5%	16.1%
Less than high school	20.3	10.4	7.6	1.8	0.4
High school graduate only	32.7	4.7	20.8	5.8	1.4
Some college or associate's degree	21.3	1.6	9.0	8.1	2.5
Bachelor's degree or more	25.8	0.4	5.9	7.8	11.7
Husbands aged 65 or older	100.0	27.4	42.1	18.7	11.9
Less than high school	33.4	19.7	10.5	2.6	0.6
High school graduate only	30.3	5.3	19.1	4.4	1.5
Some college or associate's degree	17.8	1.9	7.3	6.4	2.2
Bachelor's degree or more	18.5	0.5	5.1	5.3	7.8

Source: Bureau of the Census, Educational Attainment in the United States: March 1995, *PPL-48, 1996; calculations by New Strategist*

CHAPTER

3

Health

❖ **Even most older women feel good to excellent.**

Most women say their health is good or excellent, with the largest percentage (48 percent) saying it is good.

❖ **A majority of women aged 20 to 44 use some form of contraception.**

Birth control pills and condoms are more popular among young women, while 48 percent of contracepting women aged 35 to 44 have been sterilized.

❖ **Over half of women giving birth in 1995 were aged 20 to 29.**

Births to teenagers and older women receive a lot of media attention, but they are not the norm.

❖ **More than one-third of births are to blacks, Hispanics, or Asians.**

Although blacks are still the largest minority, births to Hispanics outnumber births to blacks by a considerable margin.

❖ **The average hospital stay for women is getting shorter.**

The average hospital stay for women fell by nearly one full day between 1991 and 1994, while men's average hospital stays remained the same.

❖ **Acute health conditions are more common among the young.**

The rate of acute infections is highest among children under age 5 and lowest among older people.

❖ **Women are more likely to die of heart disease than from any other cause.**

The second most common cause of death is cancer, followed by cerebrovascular disease. AIDS is not in the top-ten list.

Women Say They Are in Good Health

Even most older women feel good to excellent.

Most women say their health is good or excellent, with the largest percentage (48 percent) saying it is good. Another 30 percent say they are in excellent health. Seventeen percent say their health is fair, while only 4 percent say it is poor.

There are some predictable differences by age, however. Among women aged 18 to 24, fully 41 percent say they are in excellent health. This drops with increasing age to only 22 percent among women aged 65 or older.

The proportion saying their health is only fair or poor stands at less than 15 percent among women under age 35, hovers between 20 and 25 percent among women aged 35 to 64, and rises to 37 percent among women aged 65 or older. But a 62 percent majority of elderly women say their health is good or excellent.

❖ The percentage of older women who say their health is good to excellent is rising as Americans take better care of themselves. With older women feeling better, they are becoming more important consumers.

Health Status by Age, 1994

"Would you say your own health, in general, is excellent, good, fair, or poor?"

(percent of women responding by age, 1994)

	excellent	*good*	*fair*	*poor*
Total	30.1%	48.0%	17.4%	4.4%
Aged 18 to 24	41.3	46.3	12.5	0.0
Aged 25 to 34	37.6	50.6	11.0	0.8
Aged 35 to 44	28.1	50.0	20.0	1.9
Aged 45 to 54	31.8	47.4	16.7	4.2
Aged 55 to 64	24.0	54.5	13.2	8.3
Aged 65 or older	21.9	40.0	26.2	11.4

Source: 1994 General Social Survey, National Opinion Research Center, University of Chicago

Women Are Heavier Than Ever

Low-fat may be in, but women aren't getting any thinner.

Women are more conscious of their health than ever before. They are more likely to exercise and eat a low-fat diet than they were in decades past. Unfortunately, they are also more likely to be overweight.

The youngest women are least likely to be heavy. Twenty-five percent of women aged 25 to 34 are overweight, but this is up by more than 11 percentage points from 13 percent in 1960-62. Women aged 55 to 64 are most likely to be overweight, with 49 percent having a body mass index that signifies too much weight. This is up from 43 percent of this age group who were overweight in 1960-62. Women aged 65 to 74 are slightly less likely to be overweight now than they were 30 years ago, but the change is small.

❖ With so many women being overweight, the struggling women's apparel market could benefit from offering more clothes designed to flatter fuller figures.

Overweight Women by Age, 1960-62 to 1988-91

(percent of women aged 20 or older who are overweight by age, 1960-62 and 1988-91; percentage point change, 1960-62 to 1988-91)

	1988-91	1960-62	percentage point change 1960-62 to 1988-91
Aged 20 to 34	24.5%	13.2%	11.3
Aged 35 to 44	35.1	24.1	11.0
Aged 45 to 54	39.8	30.7	9.1
Aged 55 to 64	48.7	43.2	5.5
Aged 65 to 74	39.7	42.9	-3.2
Aged 75 or older	31.5	-	-

Note: Overweight for women is defined as a body mass index greater than or equal to 27.3 kilograms/meter. (-) means data not available. Excludes pregnant women.
Source: National Center for Health Statistics, Health United States 1995, *(PHS)96-1232, 1996; calculations by New Strategist*

Fewer Women Smoke

The anti-smoking campaigns are working.

Public health campaigns against cigarette smoking have had an effect on women. In 1965, 34 percent of women smoked. By 1993, the proportion had fallen to 23 percent.

Women aged 25 to 44 are most likely to smoke. In this age group, 27 percent of women are smokers. But in 1965, fully 44 percent of women in this age group smoked.

The oldest age group is the only one to show any increase in the percentage who smoke. But this is also the age group in which women are least likely to smoke. In 1965, 10 percent of women aged 65 or older smoked. In 1993, 11 percent did.

❖ Anti-smoking campaigns and pharmaceutical aids aimed at mothers- and fathers-to-be may achieve greater success than those aimed at the population at large.

Cigarette Smoking by Age, 1965 and 1993

(percent of women aged 18 or older who smoke cigarettes by age, 1965 and 1993; and percentage point change, 1965-93)

	1993	*1965*	*percentage point change 1965-93*
Total	22.5%	33.9%	-11.4
Aged 18 to 24	22.9	38.1	-15.2
Aged 25 to 34	27.3	43.7	-16.4
Aged 35 to 44	27.4	43.7	-16.3
Aged 45 to 64	23.0	32.0	-9.0
Aged 65 or older	10.5	9.6	0.9

Source: National Center for Health Statistics, Health United States 1995, *(PHS)96-1232, 1996; calculations by New Strategist*

Most Women Drink Sometimes

But one-third are teetotalers.

Young women are most likely to drink. Fully 83 percent say they drink alcoholic beverages at least occasionally. Among women in their 30s, three-quarters say they sometimes drink. A majority of women aged 50 to 69 also enjoy beer, wine, or liquor at least occasionally.

Women in their 40s are more likely than any other age group, except those aged 70 or older, to abstain from drinking. Nearly half say they never drink. The real teetotalers, however, are older women. Among women aged 70 or older, 61 to 64 percent say they never drink.

❖ One reason for the lower drinking levels among older women is the sex role stereotypes in effect when they were young. Younger women, who were not raised to follow the stereotypes, may be more likely to drink when they are older.

Drinking by Age, 1994

"Do you ever have occasion to use any alcoholic beverages such as liquor, wine, or beer, or are you a total abstainer?"

(percent of women responding by age, 1994)

	use alcohol	*abstain*
Total	64.3%	35.7%
Aged 18 to 29	83.3	16.7
Aged 30 to 39	76.0	24.0
Aged 40 to 49	52.2	47.8
Aged 50 to 59	70.6	29.4
Aged 60 to 69	58.8	41.2
Aged 70 to 79	35.7	64.3
Aged 80 or older	38.9	61.1

Source: 1994 General Social Survey, National Opinion Research Center, University of Chicago

Women Enjoy Walking

Fitness walking is the most popular activity among females.

Out of 18 popular fitness activities, the only one that attracts a substantial percentage of females aged 6 or older is fitness walking. About 9 percent of females take a fitness walk at least 100 days a year. A smaller 5 percent use a stationary bike that often. Other fitness and sports activities attract only between 1 and 3 percent of females.

Overall, 62 percent of frequent fitness walkers are females. Aerobics is the most female-dominated activity: 82 to 89 percent of frequent participants in aerobics are female. Females also account for more than half of frequent participants on the treadmill, stationary bike, and stair-climbing machine.

❖ Walking has become the most popular fitness activity among women for good reasons. It requires no special equipment, location, or time—important benefits to busy workers, mothers, and homemakers.

Fitness and Sports Participation, 1995

(number and percent of females aged 6 or older who are frequent participants in selected sports and fitness activities and percent of frequent participants who are female, 1995; numbers in thousands)

	number of females who participate frequently	percent of females who participate frequently	females as a percent of frequent participants
Aerobic dancing (regular)	1,287	1.1%	82.3%
Aerobic dancing (low-impact)	2,106	1.7	89.0
Aerobic dancing (step)	1,916	1.6	88.0
Bicycling (touring/fitness/training)	1,795	1.5	39.0
Bowling	3,823	3.2	40.7
Fitness walking	10,599	8.7	61.6
Golf	1,237	1.0	16.4
Free weights	3,623	3.0	31.9
Resistance machine	2,367	2.0	38.0
Stationary bike	6,072	5.0	64.7
Treadmill	4,124	3.4	58.9
Stair-climbing machine	2,568	2.1	67.7
In-line skating	3,537	2.9	37.5
Running/jogging	3,732	3.1	39.4
Softball (slow pitch)	4,076	3.4	50.2
Swimming (laps/fitness only)	2,738	2.3	55.8
Tennis	2,437	2.0	49.2
Volleyball (hard surface/grass)	3,888	3.2	62.9

Note: The definition of frequent participation is 100 or more days per year, except for the following: 25 or more days per year—bowling, golf, in-line skating, softball, tennis, and volleyball; 52 days per year—swimming.
Source: Sports Participation Index, 1995, *prepared for the Sporting Goods Manufacturers Association, North Palm Beach, Florida, by American Sports Data, Inc., Hartsdale, New York, 1996*

Contraceptive Preferences Vary by Age

Younger women favor the pill.

A majority of women aged 20 to 44 use some form of contraception, but the preferred method differs by age. Younger women are more likely than their elders to use reversible methods of birth control. Birth control pills and condoms are most popular with women under age 25. Among women in this age group who practice contraception, over half rely on the pill. Condom use is highest among contracepting 15-to-19-year-olds, at 44 percent. This share drops to 25 percent among women aged 20 to 24.

Birth control pills are still the most popular method of contraception among women aged 25 to 34, used by 35 percent. Twenty-six percent of contracepting women in this age group have been sterilized.

Sterilization is the most popular method of contraception for women aged 35 to 44. Fully 48 percent of women in this age group who practice contraception have been sterilized. Another 23 percent rely on male sterilization to prevent pregnancy. Only 7 percent are on the pill and just 10 percent use condoms.

❖ The many women aged 35 to 44 who have opted for sterilization have taken control of their futures. Once their children are grown, they will focus their attention on career and leisure pursuits.

Contraception by Age, 1990

(percent of women aged 15 to 44 using contraception by age, and percent distribution of women by age and type of contraceptive, 1990)

	percent using contraception	contra-cepting women	female sterili-zation	male sterili-zation	birth control pill	intra-uterine device	diaphragm	condom
Total	59.3%	100.0%	29.5%	12.6%	28.5%	1.4%	2.8%	17.7%
Aged 15 to 19	31.5	100.0	-	-	52.0	-	-	44.0
Aged 20 to 24	55.3	100.0	8.0	1.8	55.4	0.8	0.6	25.3
Aged 25 to 34	63.2	100.0	25.6	9.3	34.7	0.7	3.6	17.3
Aged 35 to 44	68.9	100.0	47.8	22.9	6.8	2.6	3.5	9.8

Note: (-) means sample is too small to make a reliable estimate. Numbers will not add to 100 because not all methods are shown.
Source: National Center for Health Statistics, Health United States 1995, *(PHS)96-1232, 1996*

More Childless Women

Some waited too long, while others have chosen to remain childless.

In 1976, only a little more than one-third of women aged 18 to 44 had never had children. By 1994, fully 42 percent of women in this age group were childless.

Women are delaying childbearing to a later age and this is reflected in the numbers. In 1976, only 31 percent of women aged 25 to 29 were childless, but by 1994, 44 percent of women in this age group had no children.

The longer a woman waits to have children, the more likely she is to confront fertility problems. This fact is behind the rising percentage of older women who are childless. Among women in their late 30s, 20 percent were childless in 1994, up from 11 percent in 1976. Among those in their early 40s, 18 percent had no children in 1994, compared with 10 percent in 1976.

❖ The soaring demand for fertility services in recent years is due to the fertility problems of baby-boom women, many of whom delayed having children until their late 30s or early 40s.

Childless Women by Age, 1976 and 1994

(percent of women aged 18 to 44 who are childless by age, 1976 and 1994, and percentage point change, 1976-94)

	1994	*1976*	*percentage point change, 1976-94*
Total	42.0%	35.1%	6.9
Aged 18 to 24	77.9	69.0	8.9
Aged 25 to 29	43.6	30.8	12.8
Aged 30 to 34	26.3	15.6	10.7
Aged 35 to 39	19.6	10.5	9.1
Aged 40 to 44	17.5	10.2	7.3

Source: Bureau of the Census, Internet web site, http://www.census.gov*; calculations by New Strategist*

Most New Mothers Are Twentysomething

Over half of women giving birth in 1995 were aged 20 to 29.

Births to teenagers and older women receive a lot of media attention, but they are not the norm. Three-quarters of all births in 1995 were to women aged 20 to 34. Over half were to women in their 20s.

Only 12 percent of the women giving birth in 1995 were aged 35 or older, and just 13 percent were teens aged 15 to 19.

Although many women wait until they are in their 30s to begin a family, most of those aged 30 to 39 who gave birth in 1995 already had children. Among women in their 40s who gave birth in 1995, most were having baby number three, four, or more.

❖ Businesses marketing to new parents should target women aged 20 to 34, since younger and older women account for a fraction of total births.

Births by Age of Mother and Birth Order, 1995

(number and percent distribution of births by age of mother and birth order, 1995)

	total births	*first birth*	*second birth*	*third birth*	*fourth birth or more*
Total number	3,900,089	1,609,925	1,245,390	617,664	398,615
Under age 15	12,318	11,901	291	6	2
Aged 15 to 19	500,744	390,237	88,322	15,616	2,626
Aged 20 to 24	967,591	460,880	321,435	125,916	52,904
Aged 25 to 29	1,064,984	401,370	369,989	182,145	104,042
Aged 30 to 34	904,143	248,587	326,422	191,640	130,742
Aged 35 to 39	381,455	82,709	120,910	88,632	86,067
Aged 40 to 44	66,195	13,688	17,459	13,317	21,104
Aged 45 to 49	2,660	553	562	393	1,127
Percent distribution by birth order					
Total	100.0%	41.3%	31.9%	15.8%	10.2%
Under age 15	100.0	96.6	2.4	0.0	0.0
Aged 15 to 19	100.0	77.9	17.6	3.1	0.5
Aged 20 to 24	100.0	47.6	33.2	13.0	5.5
Aged 25 to 29	100.0	37.7	34.7	17.1	9.8
Aged 30 to 34	100.0	27.5	36.1	21.2	14.5
Aged 35 to 39	100.0	21.7	31.7	23.2	22.6
Aged 40 to 44	100.0	20.7	26.4	20.1	31.9
Aged 45 to 49	100.0	20.8	21.1	14.8	42.4
Percent distribution by age					
Total	100.0%	100.0%	100.0%	100.0%	100.0%
Under age 15	0.3	0.7	0.0	0.0	0.0
Aged 15 to 19	12.8	24.2	7.1	2.5	0.7
Aged 20 to 24	24.8	28.6	25.8	20.4	13.3
Aged 25 to 29	27.3	24.9	29.7	29.5	26.1
Aged 30 to 34	23.2	15.4	26.2	31.0	32.8
Aged 35 to 39	9.8	5.1	9.7	14.3	21.6
Aged 40 to 44	1.7	0.9	1.4	2.2	5.3
Aged 45 to 49	0.1	0.0	0.0	0.1	0.3

Note: Births by birth order will not add to total because "not stated" is not included.
Source: National Center for Health Statistics, Births and Deaths: United States, 1995, *Monthly Vital Statistics Report, Vol. 45, No. 3, Supplement 2, 1996; calculations by New Strategist*

More Than One in Three Births Is to a Black, Hispanic, or Asian

The share is even larger among young women.

Among the 3.9 million babies born in 1995, 17 percent were born to Hispanics, 15 percent to blacks, 4 percent to Asians, and 1 percent to Native Americans. Overall, 80 percent of births were to white women. But because Hispanics may be of any race and most are white, many of those white births are to Hispanics.

Only 70 percent of births to 15-to-19-year-olds were to whites (including Hispanics). Fully 27 percent were to blacks and 24 percent to Hispanics. In contrast, among births to women aged 30 to 34 in 1994, 84 percent were to whites (including Hispanics), 13 percent to Hispanics, and 11 percent to blacks.

Although blacks are still the largest minority in the United States, births to Hispanics outnumber births to blacks by a considerable margin—671,849 Hispanic and 598,558 black babies were born in 1995.

❖ Businesses targeting new parents must take into account the racial and ethnic diversity of this market.

Births by Age, Race, and Hispanic Origin of Mother, 1995

(number and percent distribution of births by age, race, and Hispanic origin of mother, 1995)

	total births	white	black	Asian	Native American	Hispanic
Total number	3,900,089	3,105,315	598,558	158,447	37,769	671,849
Under age 15	12,318	5,911	5,910	289	209	3,209
Aged 15 to 19	500,744	350,999	132,846	9,069	7,830	117,907
Aged 20 to 24	967,591	745,822	182,644	27,023	12,102	206,430
Aged 25 to 29	1,064,984	876,074	132,389	47,806	8,714	175,962
Aged 30 to 34	904,143	755,955	95,059	47,210	5,920	113,085
Aged 35 to 39	381,455	314,962	41,941	22,066	2,486	45,887
Aged 40 to 44	66,195	53,447	7,530	4,724	494	9,004
Aged 45 to 49	2,660	2,147	240	260	14	365
Percent distribution by race and Hispanic origin						
Total	100.0%	79.6%	15.3%	4.1%	1.0%	17.2%
Under age 15	100.0	48.0	48.0	2.3	1.7	26.1
Aged 15 to 19	100.0	70.1	26.5	1.8	1.6	23.5
Aged 20 to 24	100.0	77.1	18.9	2.8	1.3	21.3
Aged 25 to 29	100.0	82.3	12.4	4.5	0.8	16.5
Aged 30 to 34	100.0	83.6	10.5	5.2	0.7	12.5
Aged 35 to 39	100.0	82.6	11.0	5.8	0.7	12.0
Aged 40 to 44	100.0	80.7	11.4	7.1	0.7	13.6
Aged 45 to 49	100.0	80.7	9.0	9.8	0.5	13.7
Percent distribution by age						
Total	100.0%	100.0%	100.0%	100.0%	100.0%	100.0%
Under age 15	0.3	0.2	1.0	0.2	0.6	0.5
Aged 15 to 19	12.8	11.3	22.2	5.7	20.7	17.5
Aged 20 to 24	24.8	24.0	30.5	17.1	32.0	30.7
Aged 25 to 29	27.3	28.2	22.1	30.2	23.1	26.2
Aged 30 to 34	23.2	24.3	15.9	29.8	15.7	16.8
Aged 35 to 39	9.8	10.1	7.0	13.9	6.6	6.8
Aged 40 to 44	1.7	1.7	1.3	3.0	1.3	1.3
Aged 45 to 49	0.1	0.1	0.0	0.2	0.0	0.1

Note: Births by race and Hispanic origin will not add to total because Hispanics may be of any race and "not stated" is not included.
Source: National Center for Health Statistics, Births and Deaths: United States, 1995, *Monthly Vital Statistics Report, Vol. 45, No. 3, Supplement 2, 1996; calculations by New Strategist*

Most Mothers Are Married

But one-third of women giving birth in 1994 were not married.

The younger the mother, the more likely she is to be unmarried when she gives birth. Over 90 percent of girls under age 15 who gave birth in 1994 were unmarried, as were 76 percent of 15-to-19-year-old mothers. Among new mothers in their early 20s, a near majority of 45 percent were unmarried. Even among new mothers aged 30 or older, a substantial 15 percent are unmarried.

Black women are more likely to have children out of wedlock than either white or Hispanic women. Overall, 70 percent of births to black women are out-of-wedlock, compared with 25 percent of births to white women and 43 percent of those to Hispanic women. While most white and Hispanic women in their 20s who gave birth in 1994 were married, most black women in this age group who gave birth were single.

❖ The proportion of babies born out-of-wedlock has soared in recent years because women who become pregnant outside of marriage are no longer forced into "shotgun" weddings.

Births by Marital Status of Mother, 1994

(total number of births and number and percent to unmarried women, by age, race, and Hispanic origin of mother, 1994)

	total births	births to unmarried women	
		number	percent
Total	3,952,767	1,289,592	32.6%
Under age 15	12,901	12,186	94.5
Aged 15 to 19	505,488	381,499	75.5
Aged 20 to 24	1,001,418	449,246	44.9
Aged 25 to 29	1,088,845	237,636	21.8
Aged 30 to 34	906,498	136,991	15.1
Aged 35 to 39	371,608	59,701	16.1
Aged 40 or older	66,009	12,333	18.7
White	3,121,004	794,261	25.4
Under age 15	5,978	5,407	90.4
Aged 15 to 19	348,081	235,263	67.6
Aged 20 to 24	764,085	277,364	36.3
Aged 25 to 29	889,581	146,527	16.5
Aged 30 to 34	754,871	83,870	11.1
Aged 35 to 39	305,291	37,594	12.3
Aged 40 or older	53,117	8,236	15.5
Black	636,391	448,315	70.4
Under age 15	6,465	6,404	99.1
Aged 15 to 19	140,968	134,371	95.3
Aged 20 to 24	197,841	156,304	79.0
Aged 25 to 29	142,355	81,599	57.3
Aged 30 to 34	99,155	47,044	47.4
Aged 35 to 39	42,029	19,242	45.8
Aged 40 or older	7,578	3,351	44.2
Hispanic	665,026	286,469	43.1
Under age 15	3,147	2,805	89.1
Aged 15 to 19	115,232	80,319	69.7
Aged 20 to 24	205,732	96,594	47.0
Aged 25 to 29	176,031	58,474	33.2
Aged 30 to 34	111,461	31,899	28.6
Aged 35 to 39	44,370	13,437	30.3
Aged 40 or older	9,053	2,941	32.5

Source: National Center for Health Statistics, Advance Report of Final Natality Statistics, 1994, *Vol. 44, No. 11 Supplement, 1996; calculations by New Strategist*

Hospitals Are Still the Most Popular Place for Giving Birth

But 40,000 women gave birth elsewhere in 1994.

The great majority of babies are born in hospitals. Only 17 percent of newborns in 1994 arrived in a different setting. Most of those born outside of a hospital were attended by someone other than a physician—usually a midwife.

Among women who did not give birth in a hospital, most gave birth at home. Forty-five percent of home births were attended by midwives. Nearly 12,000 births in 1994 took place in a freestanding birthing center, with 83 percent of those births attended by midwives. Only 5 percent of hospital births were attended by midwives.

❖ Recognizing trends is a key to success in any business. By developing birthing centers with a home-like decor, many hospitals have successfully headed off competition from freestanding birthing centers.

Births by Place of Delivery and Attendant, 1994

(number and percent distribution of births by place of delivery and attendant, 1994)

		attendant		
	total births	physician	midwife	other
Total number	3,952,767	3,707,606	218,466	24,173
In hospital	3,912,195	3,700,399	196,977	13,283
Not in hospital	40,119	6,979	21,476	10,856
Freestanding birthing center	11,787	1,813	9,765	201
Clinic or doctor's office	923	376	316	208
Residence	24,694	3,924	11,033	9,073
Other	2,715	866	362	1,374
Total percent	100.0%	93.8%	5.5%	0.6%
In hospital	100.0	94.6	5.0	0.3
Not in hospital	100.0	17.4	53.5	27.1
Freestanding birthing center	100.0	15.4	82.8	1.7
Clinic or doctor's office	100.0	40.7	34.2	22.5
Residence	100.0	15.9	44.7	36.7
Other	100.0	31.9	13.3	50.6

Note: Numbers will not add to total because unspecified is not shown.
Source: National Center for Health Statistics, Advance Report of Final Natality Statistics, 1994, *Vol. 44, No. 11 Supplement, 1996; calculations by New Strategist*

Cesarean Rates Rise with Age

One out of five women giving birth in 1994 had a cesarean delivery.

As mothers-to-be grow older, it becomes increasingly likely that they will have a cesarean delivery. Among babies born to women under age 20, only 15 percent were delivered by cesarean section. This share rises to 31 percent for babies born to women aged 40 to 44.

Most women have vaginal deliveries, but among women who have already had a cesarean, vaginal deliveries are not common. Out of all births in 1994, only 3 percent were women delivering vaginally after having a previous cesarean.

❖ Older women giving birth are more likely to encounter complications than are younger women, which accounts for their greater likelihood of having a cesarean delivery.

Births by Delivery Method, 1994

(number and percent distribution of births by age of mother and method of delivery, 1994)

		vaginal		cesarean		
	total births	total	after previous cesarean	total	first	repeat
Total number	3,952,767	3,087,576	110,341	830,517	520,647	309,870
Under age 20	518,389	437,183	4,134	77,194	68,070	9,124
Aged 20 to 24	1,001,418	811,377	22,419	181,680	125,077	56,603
Aged 25 to 29	1,088,845	847,290	32,994	231,809	141,917	89,892
Aged 30 to 34	906,498	680,678	34,379	217,469	118,532	98,937
Aged 35 to 39	371,608	266,276	14,304	101,796	54,812	46,984
Aged 40 to 44	66,009	44,772	2,111	20,569	12,239	8,330
Total percent	100.0%	78.1%	2.8%	21.0%	13.2%	7.8%
Under age 20	100.0	84.3	0.8	14.9	13.1	1.8
Aged 20 to 24	100.0	81.0	2.2	18.1	12.5	5.7
Aged 25 to 29	100.0	77.8	3.0	21.3	13.0	8.3
Aged 30 to 34	100.0	75.1	3.8	24.0	13.1	10.9
Aged 35 to 39	100.0	71.7	3.8	27.4	14.7	12.6
Aged 40 to 44	100.0	67.8	3.2	31.2	18.5	12.6

Source: National Center for Health Statistics, Advance Report of Final Natality Statistics, 1994, *Vol. 44, No. 11 Supplement, 1996; calculations by New Strategist*

Three out of Four Women Have Had Children

Two children is most common.

Among all women aged 18 or older, a plurality of 27 percent have had two children. This is followed by the 26 percent of women who have had no children—most of whom eventually will. Sixteen percent of women have had one child, while 31 percent have had three or more.

Women aged 45 to 64 in 1992 have had the most children, with 51 percent having had three or more children. Many of these women are the mothers of the baby-boom generation, born between 1946 and 1964. Among boomers themselves, families are much smaller. Nearly one in five (19 percent) women aged 35 to 39 was childless in 1992, while only 28 percent had three or more children.

The number of only children is increasing, according to these statistics. Among women in their early 40s, 17 percent have had only one child and for most there will be no others. Among women aged 45 to 64, 11 percent have had just one child.

❖ Smaller families means greater spending on each child. Today's parents are willing to indulge their children's wants and needs like no other generation of parents.

Children Ever Born by Age of Mother, 1992

(number and percent distribution of women by age and number of children ever born, 1992; numbers in thousands)

	total women	number of children ever born							
		total	none	one	two	three	four	five to six	seven or more
Total	97,362	100.0%	26.0%	16.3%	26.5%	15.5%	8.2%	5.3%	2.3%
18 to 19	3,429	100.0	84.9	12.6	1.9	0.5	0.1	-	-
20 to 24	9,592	100.0	65.6	20.7	10.2	2.4	0.9	0.2	-
25 to 29	10,262	100.0	42.4	23.1	22.0	9.1	2.5	0.8	0.1
30 to 34	11,282	100.0	24.1	21.1	32.8	14.8	4.8	1.9	0.4
35 to 39	10,697	100.0	18.9	17.0	36.1	17.6	7.1	2.5	0.7
40 to 44	9,580	100.0	16.4	17.3	37.3	18.6	6.9	2.7	0.7
45 to 64	24,824	100.0	10.8	10.9	27.4	22.2	13.9	10.3	4.6
65 or older	17,696	100.0	15.5	14.3	25.5	17.5	12.4	9.7	5.1

Source: Bureau of the Census, Fertility of American Men, *Population Division Working Paper No. 14, 1996*

Young Women Need Health Insurance

Those aged 18 to 24 are most likely to be without coverage.

Most women have health insurance coverage, but a substantial portion of those aged 18 to 34 do not. Among women aged 18 to 24, fully one-quarter do not have health insurance. Among women aged 25 to 34, 19 percent are without health insurance coverage.

Most working-age women with health insurance are covered by a private plan, usually through an employer. Many young women do not work for an employer who provides health insurance or they do not work enough hours to be eligible. Seventeen percent of women aged 18 to 24 are covered by Medicaid, a smaller proportion than is without coverage entirely.

❖ Many young women would find catastrophic health care coverage appealing if they understood the benefits of such a plan—and it was affordable.

Health Insurance Coverage by Age, 1995

(number and percent distribution of females by age and type of health insurance coverage, 1995; numbers in thousands)

		covered by private or government health insurance								
			private health insurance		government health insurance					
	total	total	total	group health	total	Medicaid	Medicare	military	not covered
Number									
Total	135,171	116,237	94,606	80,709	39,110	18,452	19,769	4,338	18,934
Under 18	34,746	29,933	22,854	21,240	9,236	8,142	175	1,157	4,813
18 to 24	12,441	9,270	7,305	6,058	2,627	2,130	77	505	3,171
25 to 34	20,528	16,680	14,217	13,283	3,084	2,519	160	543	3,849
35 to 44	21,805	18,626	16,816	15,605	2,486	1,837	295	577	3,179
45 to 54	16,260	14,128	13,026	11,943	1,784	1,018	384	557	2,132
55 to 64	10,992	9,397	8,177	6,954	2,018	882	832	602	1,595
65 or older	18,398	18,202	12,211	5,626	17,876	1,922	17,846	396	196
Percent distribution by type of coverage									
Total	100.0%	86.0%	70.0%	59.7%	28.9%	13.7%	14.6%	3.2%	14.0%
Under 18	100.0	86.1	65.8	61.1	26.6	23.4	0.5	3.3	13.9
18 to 24	100.0	74.5	58.7	48.7	21.1	17.1	0.6	4.1	25.5
25 to 34	100.0	81.3	69.3	64.7	15.0	12.3	0.8	2.6	18.8
35 to 44	100.0	85.4	77.1	71.6	11.4	8.4	1.4	2.6	14.6
45 to 54	100.0	86.9	80.1	73.5	11.0	6.3	2.4	3.4	13.1
55 to 64	100.0	85.5	74.4	63.3	18.4	8.0	7.6	5.5	14.5
65 or older	100.0	98.9	66.4	30.6	97.2	10.4	97.0	2.2	1.1
Percent distribution by age									
Total	100.0%	100.0%	100.0%	100.0%	100.0%	100.0%	100.0%	100.0%	100.0%
Under 18	25.7	25.8	24.2	26.3	23.6	44.1	0.9	26.7	25.4
18 to 24	9.2	8.0	7.7	7.5	6.7	11.5	0.4	11.6	16.7
25 to 34	15.2	14.3	15.0	16.5	7.9	13.7	0.8	12.5	20.3
35 to 44	16.1	16.0	17.8	19.3	6.4	10.0	1.5	13.3	16.8
45 to 54	12.0	12.2	13.8	14.8	4.6	5.5	1.9	12.8	11.3
55 to 64	8.1	8.1	8.6	8.6	5.2	4.8	4.2	13.9	8.4
65 or older	13.6	15.7	12.9	7.0	45.7	10.4	90.3	9.1	1.0

Note: Numbers will not add to total because people may have more than one type of health insurance coverage.
Source: Bureau of the Census, unpublished tables from the 1996 Current Population Survey; calculations by New Strategist

Physician Contacts Increase with Age

Older women are more likely to seek a doctor's advice.

Women of all ages average seven physician "contacts" (by telephone, at the physician's office, in a hospital, or other setting) a year. But the number of visits varies by age.

As women get older, they are more likely to have conditions requiring a doctor's advice. Girls under age 18 averaged slightly more than 4 physician contacts in 1994, but contacts increase with age to an average of 12 a year for women aged 65 or older.

Women are more likely than men to contact a physician. Of all physician contacts made by people aged 18 to 44, for example, women accounted for fully 64 percent—in large part because of pregnancy and childbirth. Of the contacts made by people aged 65 or older, women accounted for 61 percent.

❖ Women already dominate the health care market. As the large baby-boom generation ages, the importance of women to the health care industry will increase.

Physician Contacts by Age, 1994

(number of physician contacts by females, contacts per female, and female share of total contacts, by age and place of contact, 1994)

	total	telephone	office	hospital	other
Total contacts (in 000s)	929,619	124,716	521,487	108,267	168,355
Under age 18	150,364	22,176	88,187	19,535	19,032
Aged 18 to 44	350,187	51,036	201,842	44,790	50,743
Aged 45 to 64	216,114	32,555	119,794	25,631	35,826
Aged 65 or older	212,952	18,949	111,665	18,311	62,754
Contacts per female					
Total	7.0	0.9	3.9	0.8	1.3
Under age 18	4.4	0.6	2.6	0.6	0.6
Aged 18 to 44	6.4	0.9	3.7	0.8	0.9
Aged 45 to 64	8.3	1.2	4.6	1.0	1.4
Aged 65 or older	11.8	1.0	6.2	1.0	3.5
Female share of total					
Total	58.8%	63.1%	59.4%	52.0%	58.7%
Under age 18	48.4	51.7	48.3	45.5	48.0
Aged 18 to 44	63.6	70.4	65.8	59.8	55.0
Aged 45 to 64	58.3	62.6	59.2	46.5	61.9
Aged 65 or older	60.7	62.9	60.0	52.1	64.6

Source: National Center for Health Statistics, Current Estimates From the National Health Interview Survey, 1994, *Series 10, No. 193, 1995; calculations by New Strategist*

Women Account for Most Health Care Visits

A majority of those visiting health care facilities are women.

Women accounted for 59 percent of all those visiting physicians' offices, hospital emergency rooms, and outpatient departments in 1993. Although a majority of children under age 15 visiting the three types of health care facilities are boys, at older ages women's share ranges from 53 to 70 percent.

Women averaged four health care visits in 1993, 3.3 of them to physicians' offices. The annual number of visits per person rises with age, from 2.8 for girls under age 15 to 7.0 for women aged 75 or older.

❖ With most women in the work force, finding time to visit a health care facility has become difficult. This difficulty is driving the demand for after-hours medical services and convenient care centers.

Health Care Visits by Age, 1993

(number of health care visits by females, visits per female, and female share of total visits; by age and place of visit; 1993)

	total	physician offices	hospital emergency rooms	hospital outpatient departments
Total visits (in 000s)	516,204	430,170	47,099	38,935
Under age 15	77,342	60,664	10,258	6,420
Aged 15 to 44	211,649	170,262	22,608	18,779
Aged 45 to 64	110,131	96,011	6,732	7,388
Aged 65 to 74	61,725	55,215	3,070	3,440
Aged 75 or older	55,356	48,017	4,431	2,908
Visits per female				
Total	4.0	3.3	0.4	0.3
Under age 15	2.8	2.2	0.4	0.2
Aged 15 to 44	3.6	2.9	0.4	0.3
Aged 45 to 64	4.3	3.7	0.3	0.3
Aged 65 to 74	6.0	5.4	0.3	0.3
Aged 75 or older	7.0	6.1	0.6	0.4
Female share of total				
All ages	59.3%	60.0%	52.2%	62.3%
Under age 15	46.9	46.9	45.2	49.7
Aged 15 to 44	65.0	66.4	53.3	70.0
Aged 45 to 64	59.5	60.0	54.1	59.7
Aged 65 to 74	58.7	58.8	56.9	58.7
Aged 75 or older	61.8	61.9	60.6	63.7

Source: National Center for Health Statistics, Health United States 1995, *(PHS)96-1232, 1996; calculations by New Strategist*

Women's Hospital Stays Are Shorter

The average hospital stay for women was 5.1 days in 1994, down from 6.0 days in 1991.

As insurance companies try to cut costs, hospital stays have shortened—but only for women. The average hospital stay for women fell by nearly one full day between 1991 and 1994, while men's hospital stays averaged 7.0 days in both years.

Drive-through deliveries account for only a fraction of the drop in women's average hospital stay, since the decline was greatest in older age groups. The average hospital stay for women of childbearing age fell by less than one day between 1991 and 1994, while the average stay for women aged 45 to 64 fell by 1.1 days. Among women aged 65 or older, the average stay fell from 8.8 to 7.3 days—a decline of 1.5 days. Among men aged 45 to 64, there was a decline of 0.2 days, while there was no change in the length of hospital stays for men aged 65 or older.

❖ As hospital stays shorten, the public is beginning to resist. The average length of a hospital stay may stabilize in the next few years as the government steps in to regulate the insurers.

Hospital Stays by Age, 1994

(number of inpatients discharged from short-stay, non-Federal hospitals and average length of stay, by age and sex, 1994)

	total	*women*	*men*
Discharges, total (in 000s)	27,400	13,641	11,059
Under age 18	3,068	1,534	1,535
Aged 18 to 44	9,848	7,064	2,785
Aged 45 to 64	6,142	3,156	2,986
Aged 65 or older	8,341	4,587	3,754
Length of stay, total (days)	5.9	5.1	7.0
Under age 18	5.8	5.0	6.4
Aged 18 to 44	4.1	3.6	6.4
Aged 45 to 64	5.8	5.4	6.3
Aged 65 or older	7.8	7.3	8.3

Source: National Center for Health Statistics, Current Estimates from the National Health Interview Survey, 1994, *Series 10, No. 193, 1995*

Children Are Most Likely to Catch Colds

Acute health conditions are more common among the young.

Young people have the greatest incidence of acute health conditions, such as colds, flu, and ear infections. In general, the rate of acute infections is highest among girls under age 5 and lowest among women aged 45 or older.

There are a few conditions that don't follow this pattern, however. Although acute bronchitis is most common among girls under age 5 (a rate of 12.6 per 100 girls in that age group), older females had similar rates: 4.5 for girls aged 5 to 17, 5.6 for women aged 18 to 44, and 4.9 for women aged 45 or older.

Sprains and strains are most common among women aged 18 to 44 (a rate of 7.9, compared with 0.7 to 3.9 among females of other ages). Acute musculoskeletal conditions are most common among women aged 45 or older.

❖ Mothers are one of the most important markets for non-prescription drugs as they care for their children's colds and other acute illnesses.

Acute Health Conditions by Age, 1994

(number of acute conditions and rate per 100 females by type of acute condition and age, 1994; numbers in thousands)

	total		under age 5		aged 5-17		aged 18-44		aged 45 or older	
	number	rate	number	rate	number	rate	number	rate	number	rate
Total acute conditions	249,251	187.2	34,591	345.6	56,062	231.8	99,991	182.5	58,606	132.7
Infective and parasitic diseases	30,370	22.8	5,451	54.5	10,576	43.7	10,554	19.3	3,789	8.6
Common childhood diseases	1,731	1.3	892	8.9	493	2.0	346	0.6		
Intestinal virus	5,861	4.4	788	7.9	2,243	9.3	2,308	4.2	522	1.2
Viral infections	9,976	7.5	2,148	21.5	3,175	13.1	2,993	5.5	1,660	3.8
Other	12,802	9.6	1,624	16.2	4,665	19.3	4,907	9.0	1,607	3.6
Respiratory conditions	113,712	85.4	14,685	146.7	25,930	107.2	47,522	86.7	25,575	57.9
Common cold	35,669	26.8	6,627	66.2	7,533	31.1	14,254	26.0	7,255	16.4
Other acute upper respiratory infections	17,497	13.1	2,181	21.8	5,767	23.8	6,111	11.2	3,438	7.8
Influenza	47,296	35.5	3,404	34.0	11,196	46.3	21,690	39.6	11,006	24.9
Acute bronchitis	7,585	5.7	1,266	12.6	1,083	4.5	3,053	5.6	2,184	4.9
Pneumonia	2,576	1.9	739	7.4	162	0.7	945	1.7	729	1.7
Other respiratory conditions	3,088	2.3	468	4.7	189	0.8	1,469	2.7	962	2.2
Digestive system conditions	8,963	6.7	841	8.4	2,283	9.4	3,515	6.4	2,324	5.3
Dental conditions	1,316	1.0	157	1.6	165	0.7	664	1.2	330	0.7
Indigestion, nausea, and vomiting	4,813	3.6	453	4.5	1,639	6.8	1,882	3.4	839	1.9
Other digestive conditions	2,835	2.1	231	2.3	479	2.0	969	1.8	1,156	2.6

(contnued)

(continued from previous page)

	total		under age 5		aged 5-17		aged 18-44		aged 45 or older	
	number	rate	number	rate	number	rate	number	rate	number	rate
Injuries	29,247	22.0	1,986	19.8	5,834	24.1	12,393	22.6	9,034	20.5
Fractures and dislocations	3,387	2.5	239	2.4	992	4.1	797	1.5	1,359	3.1
Sprains and strains	7,040	5.3	68	0.7	929	3.8	4,309	7.9	1,733	3.9
Open wounds and lacerations	3,640	2.7	276	2.8	982	4.1	1,544	2.8	838	1.9
Contusions & superficial injuries	6,342	4.8	617	6.2	1,381	5.7	1,663	3.0	2,681	6.1
Other current injuries	8,838	6.6	786	7.9	1,550	6.4	4,079	7.4	2,423	5.5
Selected other acute conditions	46,766	35.1	9,127	91.2	8,526	35.3	18,222	33.3	10,891	24.7
Eye conditions	2,158	1.6	353	3.5	209	0.9	562	1.0	1,034	2.3
Acute ear infections	12,489	9.4	5,879	58.7	3,569	14.8	1,814	3.3	1,228	2.8
Other ear conditions	2,175	1.6	359	3.6	562	2.3	689	1.3	565	1.3
Acute urinary conditions	7,327	5.5	520	5.2	544	2.2	3,802	6.9	2,461	5.6
Disorders of menstruation	1,146	0.9	-	-	480	2.0	621	1.1	45	0.1
Other disorders of female genital tract	2,652	2.0	-	-	117	0.5	2,063	3.8	473	1.1
Delivery and other conditions of pregnancy	3,707	2.8	-	-	91	0.4	3,616	6.6	-	-
Skin conditions	3,583	2.7	746	7.5	742	3.1	1,001	1.8	1,095	2.5
Acute musculoskeletal conditions	5,951	4.5	113	1.1	480	2.0	2,398	4.4	2,960	6.7
Headache, excluding migraine	2,646	2.0	669	2.8	1,271	2.3	705	1.6		
Fever, unspecified	2,933	2.2	1,158	11.6	1,063	4.4	386	0.7	326	0.7
All other acute conditions	20,193	15.2	2,502	25.0	2,914	12.0	7,785	14.2	6,993	15.8

Note: The acute conditions shown here are those that caused people to restrict their activity for at least half a day, or that caused people to contact a physician about the illness or injury. (-) means not applicable or sample is too small to make a reliable estimate.
Source: National Center for Health Statistics, Current Estimates From the National Health Interview Survey, 1994, *Series 10, No. 193, 1995*

Chronic Conditions Will Get More Attention

As the elderly population grows, chronic conditions will become more common.

The prevalence of chronic conditions increases as women get older. Arthritis, for example, afflicts only 38 out of 1,000 women under age 45, but the rate rises steadily with age to 554 per 1,000 among women aged 65 or older—or more than half. Likewise, heart disease is a condition almost entirely limited to the years after menopause.

A few chronic conditions are found most often among women aged 45 to 64, however. Migraines, for example, are most common among younger women. Of every 1,000 women under age 45, 67 suffer from migraines. This rate drops to just 28 per 1,000 among women aged 65 or older.

❖ As the women of the baby-boom generation age, the prevention and treatment of chronic conditions will become increasingly important health care issues.

Chronic Health Conditions by Age, 1994

(number of chronic conditions and rate per 1,000 females by type of chronic condition and age, 1994; numbers in thousands)

	total		under age 45		aged 45 to 64		aged 65 or older					
							total		aged 65 to 74		aged 75 or older	
	number	rate	number	rate	number	rate	number	rate	number	rate	number	rate
Selected skin & musculoskeletal conditions												
Arthritis	21,155	158.9	3,399	38.2	7,741	297.0	10,015	553.5	5,209	513.6	4,806	604.4
Gout	724	5.4	91	1.0	191	7.3	442	24.4	136	13.4	306	38.5
Intervertebral disc disorders	2,819	21.2	1,006	11.3	1,284	49.3	529	29.2	329	32.4	200	25.2
Bone spur or tendinitis	1,645	12.4	603	6.8	700	26.9	342	18.9	272	26.8	70	8.8
Disorders of bone or cartilage	1,040	7.8	230	2.6	340	13.0	470	26.0	225	22.2	245	30.8
Trouble with bunions	2,643	19.9	915	10.3	799	30.7	929	51.3	415	40.9	514	64.6
Bursitis	3,183	23.9	976	11.0	1,292	49.6	915	50.6	500	49.3	416	52.3
Sebaceous skin cyst	491	3.7	270	3.0	110	4.2	111	6.1	100	9.9	11	1.4
Trouble with acne	3,037	22.8	2,811	31.6	184	7.1	42	2.3	42	4.1	-	-
Psoriasis	1,408	10.6	777	8.7	369	14.2	262	14.5	103	10.2	159	20.0
Dermatitis	5,754	43.2	3,880	43.6	1,162	44.6	712	39.4	391	38.6	320	40.2
Trouble with dry (itching) skin	3,395	25.5	1,821	20.5	940	36.1	634	35.0	312	30.8	322	40.5
Trouble with ingrown nails	3,262	24.5	1,462	16.4	775	29.7	1,025	56.6	537	52.9	488	61.4
Trouble with corns and calluses	2,870	21.6	1,090	12.2	846	32.5	934	51.6	472	46.5	462	58.1
Impairments												
Visual impairment	3,502	26.3	1,144	12.9	991	38.0	1,367	75.5	487	48.0	880	110.7
Color blindness	530	4.0	179	2.0	206	7.9	145	8.0	96	9.5	49	6.2

(continued)

(continued from previous page)

	total		under age 45		aged 45 to 64		aged 65 or older					
							total		aged 65 to 74		aged 75 or older	
	number	rate	number	rate	number	rate	number	rate	number	rate	number	rate
Cataracts	4,276	32.1	222	2.5	572	21.9	3,482	192.4	1,420	140.0	2,061	259.2
Glaucoma	1,483	11.1	159	1.8	271	10.4	1,053	58.2	352	34.7	701	88.2
Hearing impairment	9,293	69.8	2,705	30.4	2,281	87.5	4,307	238.0	1,859	183.3	2,448	307.8
Tinnitus	3,055	22.9	869	9.8	864	33.2	1,322	73.1	687	67.7	635	79.9
Speech impairment	1,019	7.7	735	8.3	183	7.0	101	5.6	87	8.6	14	1.8
Absence of extremities	240	1.8	84	0.9	52	2.0	104	5.7	33	3.3	71	8.9
Paralysis of extremities	618	4.6	219	2.5	181	6.9	218	12.0	97	9.6	120	15.1
Deformity or orthopedic impairment	16,679	125.3	9,015	101.3	4,513	173.2	3,151	174.1	1,641	161.8	1,510	189.9
Selected digestive conditions												
Ulcer	2,400	18.0	1,183	13.3	606	23.3	611	33.8	434	42.8	177	22.3
Hernia of abdominal cavity	2,613	19.6	513	5.8	815	31.3	1,285	71.0	710	70.0	575	72.3
Gastritis or duodenitis	2,043	15.3	938	10.5	429	16.5	676	37.4	399	39.3	276	34.7
Frequent indigestion	3,478	26.1	1,686	18.9	1,017	39.0	775	42.8	416	41.0	360	45.3
Enteritis or colitis	1,480	11.1	596	6.7	515	19.8	369	20.4	192	18.9	177	22.3
Spastic colon	1,689	12.7	754	8.5	546	21.0	389	21.5	226	22.3	163	20.5
Diverticula of intestines	1,328	10.0	107	1.2	504	19.3	717	39.6	392	38.7	324	40.7
Frequent constipation	3,085	23.2	1,340	15.1	452	17.3	1,293	71.5	480	47.3	813	102.2
Selected conditions of the genitourinary, nervous, endocrine, metabolic, or blood systems												
Goiter or other disorders of the thyroid	3,819	28.7	1,297	14.6	1,316	50.5	1,206	66.7	759	74.8	447	56.2
Diabetes	4,187	31.4	792	8.9	1,641	63.0	1,754	96.9	1,024	101.0	730	91.8

(continued)

(continued from previous page)

	total		under age 45		aged 45 to 64		aged 65 or older					
							total		aged 65 to 74		aged 75 or older	
	number	rate	number	rate	number	rate	number	rate	number	rate	number	rate
Anemias	3,874	29.1	2,610	29.3	779	29.9	485	26.8	246	24.3	239	30.1
Epilepsy	645	4.8	472	5.3	100	3.8	73	4.0	63	6.2	10	1.3
Migraine	8,540	64.1	5,972	67.1	2,057	78.9	511	28.2	303	29.9	208	26.2
Neuralgia or neuritis	405	3.0	145	1.6	140	5.4	120	6.6	72	7.1	48	6.0
Kidney trouble	2,347	17.6	1,481	16.6	470	18.0	396	21.9	137	13.5	259	32.6
Bladder disorders	3,076	23.1	1,412	15.9	721	27.7	943	52.1	535	52.8	408	51.3
Diseases of female genital organs	5,052	37.9	3,480	39.1	1,332	51.1	240	13.3	166	16.4	73	9.2
Selected circulatory conditions												
Rheumatic fever	1,463	11.0	687	7.7	417	16.0	359	19.8	239	23.6	121	15.2
Heart disease	11,261	84.6	2,949	33.1	2,894	111.0	5,418	299.4	2,544	250.8	2874	361.4
Ischemic heart disease	3,193	24.0	115	1.3	847	32.5	2,231	123.3	958	94.5	1273	160.1
Heart rhythm disorders	5,424	40.7	2,300	25.8	1,384	53.1	1,740	96.2	843	83.1	897	112.8
Other selected diseases of the heart,												
excl. hypertension	2,645	19.9	534	6.0	663	25.4	1,448	80.0	743	73.3	705	88.7
High blood pressure (hypertension)	15,899	119.4	2,887	32.4	5,851	224.5	7,161	395.8	3,841	378.7	3320	417.5
Cerebrovascular disease	1,682	12.6	165	1.9	423	16.2	1,094	60.5	422	41.6	671	84.4
Hardening of the arteries	967	7.3	-	219	8.4	748	41.3	311	30.7	438	55.1	
Varicose veins of lower extremities	5,950	44.7	2,069	23.3	2,110	81.0	1,771	97.9	1,105	109.0	666	83.8
Hemorrhoids	5,212	39.1	2,579	29.0	1,455	55.8	1,178	65.1	712	70.2	466	58.6

(continued)

(continued from previous page)

	total		under age 45		aged 45 to 64		aged 65 or older					
							total		aged 65 to 74		aged 75 or older	
	number	rate	number	rate	number	rate	number	rate	number	rate	number	rate
Selected respiratory conditions												
Chronic bronchitis	8,396	63.1	5,028	56.5	2,156	82.7	1,212	67.0	801	79.0	411	51.7
Asthma	8,019	60.2	5,338	60.0	1,773	68.0	908	50.2	637	62.8	271	34.1
Hay fever	13,870	104.2	8,831	99.2	3,477	133.4	1,562	86.3	935	92.2	627	78.8
Chronic sinusitis	20,710	155.6	12,053	135.5	5,477	210.2	3,180	175.7	1,780	175.5	1400	176.1
Deviated nasal septum	1,076	8.1	606	6.8	321	12.3	149	8.2	115	11.3	34	4.3
Chronic disease of tonsils or adenoids	1,839	13.8	1,717	19.3	110	4.2	12	0.7	12	1.2	-	-
Emphysema	796	6.0	13	0.1	248	9.5	535	29.6	372	36.7	162	20.4

Note: Chronic conditions are those that last at least three months or belong to a group of conditions that are considered to be chronic regardless of when they began.
(-) means sample is too small to make a reliable estimate.
Source: National Center for Health Statistics, Current Estimates From the National Health Interview Survey, 1994, *Series 10, No. 193, 1995*

Few Women Are Physically Limited

Even among the elderly, disability rates are relatively low.

Fourteen percent of women have a chronic condition that limits their activities. Only 4 percent of women are so disabled by a chronic condition that they are unable to carry on a major activity, however.

Chronic conditions causing some degree of limitation become more prevalent after age 44. Among women aged 45 to 64, one-quarter have a limiting condition, a proportion that rises to one-third among those aged 65 to 74, and to 46 percent among women aged 75 or older. But only 9 percent of women aged 45 to 64 and 12 percent of those aged 75 or older are unable to carry on a major life activity as a result.

❖ The disability rates of older Americans have been falling as healthier generations of elderly replace frailer older people. Disability rates among the elderly are likely to continue downward because baby boomers take better care of themselves than did today's older Americans in middle-age.

Limitations Caused by Chronic Conditions by Age, 1994

(percent of females with activity limitations caused by chronic conditions by age and type of limitation, 1994)

	total with activity limitation	limited, but not in major activity	limited in amount or kind of major activity	unable to carry on major activity
Total	14.3%	4.6%	5.7%	4.0%
Under age 15	5.1	1.4	3.1	0.6
Aged 15 to 44	10.1	3.5	4.0	2.6
Aged 45 to 64	23.9	6.4	8.8	8.6
Aged 65 to 74	33.5	13.2	11.2	9.2
Aged 75 or older	46.2	17.3	17.1	11.7

Source: National Center for Health Statistics, Health United States 1995, *(PHS)96-1232, 1996*

Work Disabilities Increase with Age

Nearly one in four women aged 55 to 64 has a work disability.

Seventeen million Americans between the ages of 16 and 64 have a work disability, or 10 percent of the working-age population. Fifty-one percent of those with a work disability are women. The Census Bureau collects work disability data by asking people whether there is anyone in the household with a condition that limits the kind or amount of work they can do at a job. Those with work disabilities may be limited in the kind or amount of work they can do, or they may be unable to work at all.

Overall, 12 percent of women aged 25 to 64 have a work disability, while 8 percent have a severe work disability. Work disabilities are least common among women aged 25 to 34. Only 7 percent of this age group are disabled, compared with 24 percent of women aged 55 to 64. Among the older age group, 17 percent have a severe work disability.

❖ The Americans with Disabilities Act has enabled many women to continue working despite their disabilities. An aging work force—and the likelihood that baby boomers will have to work well into their 60s and 70s—makes it vital for employers to accommodate the disabled in the workplace.

Women with a Work Disability, 1996

(number and percent of women aged 25 to 64 by age and work disability status, 1996; numbers in thousands)

		with a work disability					
				not severe		severe	
	total	number	percent of total	number	percent of total	percent number	of total
Total	69,550	8,153	11.7%	2,878	4.1%	5,275	7.6%
25 to 34	20,510	1,408	6.9	605	2.9	803	3.9
35 to 44	21,790	2,053	9.4	796	3.7	1,257	5.8
45 to 54	16,259	2,107	13.0	727	4.5	1,380	8.5
55 to 64	10,991	2,585	23.5	750	6.8	1,835	16.7

Source: Bureau of the Census, Internet web site, http://www.census.gov

Women Are Increasingly at Risk from AIDS

Once a man's disease, more women now are victims.

Women make up only 13.5 percent of all AIDS cases diagnosed in the U.S. through June 1995. They are a larger share of cases among the young, which is one of the reasons health care professionals believe the disease is becoming more common among women. Females account for 34 percent of AIDS cases diagnosed among 13-to-19-year-olds, for example, compared with only 11 percent of cases diagnosed among people aged 40 to 49.

Women in their 30s are more likely to be diagnosed with AIDS than are those in any other age group. Of all the women with AIDS in the U.S., 46 percent were aged 30 to 39 at the time of diagnosis. One-quarter were aged 20 to 29, while 20 percent were in their 40s.

Most females who have been diagnosed with AIDS are non-Hispanic blacks—57 percent through June 1995. Non-Hispanic whites account for 25 percent of all females diagnosed with AIDS, while 16.5 percent are Hispanic females.

❖ AIDS is a disease of increasing concern to young, heterosexual women. Businesses targeting young adults can perform an important public service by encouraging safe sex.

AIDS by Age, Race, and Hispanic Origin, 1995

(total number of cumulative AIDS cases among persons aged 13 or older, number and percent distribution of cases for females, and female share of total cases; by age, race, and Hispanic origin; through June 1995)

		female		
	total	number	percent	female share of total
Total	455,101	61,653	100.0%	13.5%
Aged 13 to 19	2,090	717	1.2	34.3
Aged 20 to 29	84,022	14,506	23.5	17.3
Aged 30 to 39	209,901	28,602	46.4	13.6
Aged 40 to 49	112,350	12,181	19.8	10.8
Aged 50 to 59	33,711	3,470	5.6	10.3
Aged 60 or older	13,027	2,177	3.5	16.7
White, non-Hispanic	227,341	15,565	25.2	6.8
Black, non-Hispanic	156,253	35,332	57.3	22.6
Hispanic	66,402	10,173	16.5	15.3
American Indian	1,183	173	0.3	14.6
Asian	3,209	323	0.5	10.1

Source: National Center for Health Statistics, Health United States 1995, *(PHS)96-1232, 1996; calculations by New Strategist*

Heart Disease Is the Leading Killer of Women

Women are more likely to die of heart disease than from any other cause.

Among females of all ages who died in 1994, one-third died from heart disease. The second most common cause of death is cancer, responsible for 23 percent of the deaths of females in 1994.

The only other condition that accounts for a significant percentage of deaths among women is cerebrovascular disease, primarily strokes. Other causes, such as pneumonia, diabetes, or Alzheimer's account for fewer than 5 percent of deaths. AIDS is not one of the top ten causes of death for women.

❖ Most heart disease research has focused on men, but that's about to change. As baby boomers age and their risk of heart disease increases, expect this vocal generation to demand more research into the prevention and treatment of heart disease among women.

Causes of Death, 1994

(total number of deaths of females, and number and percent accounted for by the ten leading causes of death, 1994)

		number	percent
	All causes	1,116,247	100.0%
1	Diseases of the heart	371,133	33.2
2	Malignant neoplasms	253,845	22.7
3	Cerebrovascular diseases	93,081	8.3
4	Chronic obstructive pulmonary diseases and allied conditions	47,899	4.3
5	Pneumonia and influenza	44,134	4.0
6	Diabetes mellitus	31,934	2.9
7	Accidents and adverse effects	30,928	2.8
8	Alzheimer's disease	12,207	1.1
9	Nephritis, nephrotic syndrome, and nephrosis	12,110	1.1
10	Septicemia	11,550	1.0
	All other causes	207,426	18.6

Source: National Center for Health Statistics, Advance Report of Final Mortality Statistics, 1994, *Vol. 45, No. 3 Supplement, 1996; calculations by New Strategist*

Women Are Living Longer

The number of elderly women will grow substantially.

A girl born in 1995 can expect to live to 78.9 years. But the longer she lives, the longer she can expect to live. A 20-year-old can expect to live to age 80. A 60-year-old can expect to live to age 83, while a 85-year-old may pass 90.

Black and white women have different life expectancies, however. At birth, a black woman can expect to live to age 74, compared with nearly 80 for a white woman. The gap narrows with age, however. By the time women celebrate their 80th birthdays, they have about the same life expectancy whether they're black or white.

❖ Because women live longer than men, there are many more elderly women than elderly men. As life expectancy increases and boomers age, the population of elderly women will expand enormously.

Life Expectancy by Age and Race, 1995

(years of life remaining at selected ages for females, by race, 1995)

	total	*white*	*black*
Aged 0	78.9	79.6	74.0
Aged 1	78.5	79.0	74.0
Aged 5	74.6	75.1	70.2
Aged 10	69.7	70.2	65.3
Aged 15	64.7	65.2	60.3
Aged 20	59.9	60.3	55.5
Aged 25	55.0	55.5	50.7
Aged 30	50.2	50.6	46.1
Aged 35	45.4	45.8	41.5
Aged 40	40.7	41.0	37.0
Aged 45	36.0	36.3	32.7
Aged 50	31.4	31.7	28.5
Aged 55	27.0	27.2	24.5
Aged 60	22.8	23.0	20.7
Aged 65	18.9	19.0	17.2
Aged 70	15.3	15.3	14.0
Aged 75	11.9	12.0	11.2
Aged 80	8.9	8.9	8.5
Aged 85	6.3	6.3	6.3

Source: National Center for Health Statistics, Births and Deaths: United States, 1995, *Monthly Vital Statistics Report, Vol. 45, No. 3, Supplement 2, 1996*

CHAPTER

4

Income

❖ **Women's incomes have climbed sharply since 1970.**

The median income of all women with income was $8,254 in 1970. By 1995 it had climbed 47 percent to $12,130.

❖ **Incomes are highest among women aged 45 to 54.**

Full-time workers in this age group have a median income of $26,143.

❖ **Women now earn 71 percent as much as men.**

The earnings of women who work full-time were up 15 percent between 1970 and 1995, while men's earnings fell 5 percent.

❖ **Women with professional degrees earn the most.**

Among women working full-time, those with professional degrees earned a median of $48,111 in 1995.

❖ **Middle-aged married couples make the most money.**

Fully 19 percent of couples aged 45 to 54 had incomes of $100,000 or more in 1995. The number of affluent couples aged 45 to 54 will rise significantly as baby boomers fill this age group.

❖ **Over 7 million women earn more than their husbands.**

The proportion of wives who earn more than their husbands rose from 16 to 22 percent between 1981 and 1995.

Rising Incomes for Women

All but the youngest saw their incomes grow between 1980 and 1995.

Women's incomes have climbed sharply since 1970. The median income of all women with income (including part-time and full-time workers as well as retirees) stood at $8,254 in 1970. By 1995 it had increased by fully 47 percent to $12,130, after adjusting for inflation.

Behind this dramatic growth are the working women of the baby-boom generation. Not only are boomers and the women of Generation X more likely to work than older women, but they often command higher salaries than their older counterparts.

Among women, only those under age 25 have experienced an income decline since 1970. The median income of young women was 8 percent lower in 1995 than in 1980, after adjusting for inflation. Even this decline is not necessarily bad news because it is partly due to the growing share of young women who are in college rather than in the labor force.

❖ Young women are pursuing college and careers like never before, boosting women's incomes. But the gender gap in income is likely to persist because women are more likely than men to drop out of the labor force temporarily while their children are young.

Median Income of Women by Age, 1970 to 1995

(median income of women with income by age, 1970 to 1995; percent change for selected years; in 1995 dollars)

	total	*< 25*	*25 to 34*	*35 to 44*	*45 to 54*	*55 to 64*	*65 or older*
1995	$12,130	$5,310	$15,557	$17,397	$17,723	$12,381	$9,355
1994	11,791	5,664	15,306	16,648	17,534	11,175	9,204
1993	11,650	5,644	14,753	16,711	17,216	11,421	8,964
1992	11,638	5,616	14,807	16,747	17,21:	11,007	8,889
1991	11,722	5,815	14,506	16,924	16,475	11,079	9,164
1990	11,742	5,716	14,680	16,912	16,592	10,961	9,379
1989	11,828	5,825	15,032	16,967	16,153	11,261	9,408
1988	11,444	5,778	14,899	16,162	15,485	10,791	9,150
1987	11,128	5,914	14,729	16,091	15,109	10,117	9,251
1986	10,582	5,623	14,336	15,385	14,434	10,258	8,934
1985	10,222	5,369	13,993	14,553	13,623	10,160	8,941
1984	10,074	5,294	13,776	14,025	13,059	10,028	8,830
1983	9,668	5,290	13,011	13,557	12,555	9,378	8,567
1982	9,385	5,343	12,708	12,516	11,960	9,417	8,553
1981	9,232	3,376	12,851	12,459	11,891	9,092	7,960
1980	9,111	5,784	12,912	11,972	11,857	9,121	7,826
1979	8,963	5,814	13,077	12,124	11,525	9,033	7,745
1978	9,185	5,830	13,183	13,104	12,806	10,099	7,631
1977	9,503	5,520	14,232	13,354	13,673	10,931	7,468
1976	9,175	5,152	13,783	13,234	13,678	10,402	7,297
1975	9,179	5,109	13,700	12,759	13,738	10,575	7,319
1974	9,050	5,203	13,255	13,070	13,857	10,638	7,162
1973	9,028	-	13,374	13,271	13,894	11,078	6,842
1972	8,921	-	13,060	13,256	13,960	11,015	6,519
1971	8,515	-	12,535	12,843	13,858	10,894	6,032
1970	8,254	-	11,901	12,731	13,642	10,871	5,617
Percent change							
1994 to 1995	2.9%	-6.3%	1.6%	4.5%	1.1%	10.8%	1.6%
1990 to 1995	3.3	-7.1	6.0	2.9	6.8	13.0	-0.3
1980 to 1995	33.1	-8.2	20.5	45.3	49.5	35.7	19.5
1970 to 1995	47.0	-	30.7	36.7	29.9	13.9	66.6

Note: (-) means data not available.
Source: Bureau of the Census, Internet web site, http://www.census.gov; *calculations by New Strategist*

Incomes Are Highest for Women Aged 45 to 54

But younger women aren't far behind.

In 1995, the median income of all women with income stood at $12,130. Among women who work full-time, median income was a much higher $23,777. About one-third of all women aged 15 or older work full-time.

Incomes are highest among women aged 45 to 54, with a median of $26,143 for full-time workers in this age group. Slightly more than half of women aged 45 to 54 work full-time, the highest share among all age groups. The median income of women aged 35 to 44 who work full-time was not far behind, at $26,121. Nearly half of women aged 35 to 44 also work full-time.

Women's incomes do not rise to as prominent a peak in the 45-to-54 age group as do men's incomes. Behind the flatter income distribution of women are generational differences: Many older working women are in low-paying clerical jobs, while many younger career-oriented women do not yet have the job experience to command higher earnings.

Women aged 65 or older, who are largely dependent on Social Security, have median incomes below $10,000. The few who work full-time, however, have higher incomes than women in any other age group.

❖ As career-oriented baby-boom women entirely fill the 45-to-54 age group, they will boost incomes for women in these peak-earning years.

Income Distribution of Women by Age, 1995

(number and percent distribution of women aged 15 or older by income and age, 1995; median income of women by work status and percent working year-round, full-time; women in thousands as of 1996)

	total	< 25	25 to 34	35 to 44	45 to 54	55 to 64	65 to 74	75 or older
Total, number	106,031	18,047	20,528	21,805	16,260	10,992	10,057	8,341
Without income	10,025	4,498	1,672	1,347	1,121	978	231	177
With income	96,007	13,550	18,856	20,458	15,139	10,014	9,826	8,163
Under $10,000	41,101	9,595	6,431	6,473	4,488	4,311	5,352	4,451
$10,000 to $19,999	24,619	2,823	5,248	4,797	3,783	2,522	2,817	2,629
$20,000 to $29,999	14,097	841	3,795	3,845	2,727	1,410	886	596
$30,000 to $39,999	7,831	197	1,929	2,458	1,833	758	396	260
$40,000 to $49,999	3,971	29	764	1,392	1,112	438	165	70
$50,000 to $64,999	2,456	40	428	821	644	313	122	89
$65,000 to $74,999	680	3	101	253	213	65	28	17
$75,000 to $84,999	433	2	67	141	109	77	20	17
$85,000 to $99,999	275	10	34	102	75	40	12	2
$100,000 or more	544	10	62	178	155	81	27	31
Total with income, percent	100.0%	100.0%	100.0%	100.0%	100.0%	100.0%	100.0%	100.0%
Under $10,000	42.8	70.8	34.1	31.6	29.6	43.0	54.5	54.5
$10,000 to $19,999	25.6	20.8	27.8	23.4	25.0	25.2	28.7	32.2
$20,000 to $29,999	14.7	6.2	20.1	18.8	18.0	14.1	9.0	7.3
$30,000 to $39,999	8.2	1.5	10.2	12.0	12.1	7.6	4.0	3.2
$40,000 to $49,999	4.1	0.2	4.1	6.8	7.3	4.4	1.7	0.9
$50,000 to $64,999	2.6	0.3	2.3	4.0	4.3	3.1	1.2	1.1
$65,000 to $74,999	0.7	0.0	0.5	1.2	1.4	0.6	0.3	0.2
$75,000 to $84,999	0.5	0.0	0.4	0.7	0.7	0.8	0.2	0.2
$85,000 to $99,999	0.3	0.1	0.2	0.5	0.5	0.4	0.1	0.0
$100,000 or more	0.6	0.1	0.3	0.9	1.0	0.8	0.3	0.4
Median income								
Women with income	$12,130	$5,310	$15,557	$17,397	$17,723	$12,381	$9,277	$9,427
Full-time, year-round workers	23,777	15,141	22,567	26,121	26,143	24,121	26,215	27,411
Percent working full-time, year-round	33.5%	15.6%	47.3%	49.5%	50.7%	31.2%	4.1%	0.9%

Source: Bureau of the Census, unpublished tables from the 1996 Current Population Survey; calculations by New Strategist

White Women Have Highest Incomes

Hispanic women have the lowest incomes—and their incomes are falling.

In 1995, white women who worked full-time had a median income of $24,264, versus $21,079 for black women and $17,855 for Hispanic women.

Between 1970 and 1995, the median income of black women rose by 26 percent, after adjusting for inflation. This was a larger increase than the 19 percent gain for white women during those years. Consequently, black women have narrowed the income gap with whites. In 1970, the median income of white women who worked full-time was 22 percent higher than that of their black counterparts. By 1995, the median income of white women was only 15 percent higher. Some of the racial disparity in incomes can be accounted for by differences in educational attainment. Typically, white women are better educated than black women, boosting their earning power.

The median income of Hispanic women who work full-time has been falling. The 1990s have been especially unkind to Hispanic women, with a 5 percent drop in their median income between 1990 and 1995, after adjusting for inflation. Hispanic women who work full-time now make only 74 percent as much as white women, down from 84 percent in 1974.

❖ One reason for the falling incomes of Hispanic women is immigration. During the past 15 years, millions of poorly-educated Hispanics have come to the United States. Their low earnings have depressed the income statistics for Hispanics overall.

Median Income by Race and Hispanic Origin, 1970 to 1995

(median income of women aged 15 or older who work year-round, full-time, by race and Hispanic origin, 1970 to 1995; percent change for selected years; in 1995 dollars)

	total	*white*	*black*	*Hispanic*
1995	$23,777	$24,264	$21,079	$17,855
1994	23,924	24,571	21,213	18,940
1993	23,697	24,235	21,425	18,047
1992	23,998	24,276	22,005	19,198
1991	23,772	24,119	21,410	18,516
1990	24,00:	24,299	21,623	18,868
1989	24,136	24,422	21,964	19,672
1988	23,890	24,248	21,729	19,583
1987	23,563	23,999	21,436	19,857
1986	23,420	23,779	20,807	19,733
1985	23,018	23,344	20,664	19,152
1984	22,621	22,846	20,588	19,108
1983	22,155	22,458	19,891	18,169
1982	21,781	22,074	19,729	18,114
1981	21,071	21,422	19,347	18,466
1980	21,464	21,671	20,212	18,309
1979	21,688	21,878	20,046	17,867
1978	21,767	21,973	20,365	18,809
1977	21,254	21,389	19,991	18,324
1976	21,326	21,490	20,092	18,290
1975	20,932	20,981	20,045	17,836
1974	21,066	21,244	19,606	17,745
1973	20,948	21,304	18,065	-
1972	20,777	21,185	18,123	-
1971	20,159	20,392	18,005	-
1970	20,074	20,428	16,738	-
Percent change				
1994 to 1995	-0.6%	-1.3%	-0.6%	-5.7%
1990 to 1995	-1.0	-0.1	-2.5	-5.4
1980 to 1995	10.8	12.0	4.3	-2.5
1970 to 1995	18.4	18.8	25.9	-

Note: (-) means data not available.
Source: Bureau of the Census, Internet web site, http://www.census.gov; *calculations by New Strategist*

Racial Disparity in Incomes Persists

White women are most likely to have high incomes.

Because many women work only part-time, the median income of women is low regardless of race or ethnicity. For white women, median income was $12,316 in 1995. For blacks, median income stood at $10,961, and for Hispanics it was $8,928.

Fully 55 percent of Hispanic women had incomes under $10,000 in 1995, compared with 42 percent of white and 47 percent of black women. Hispanic women are less likely than white or black women to work full-time, and this accounts in part for their lower incomes. Only 28 percent of Hispanic women work full-time, versus 33 percent of white and 36 percent of black women.

Few women have incomes of $50,000 or more, regardless of race or Hispanic origin. But white women are twice as likely as black women and nearly three times more likely than Hispanic women to have incomes this high.

❖ If black and Hispanic women can narrow the educational gap with white women, the income disparity by race and ethnicity will shrink.

Income Distribution of Women by Race and Hispanic Origin, 1995

(number and percent distribution of women aged 15 or older by income, race, and Hispanic origin, 1995; median income of women by work status, and percent working full-time, year-round; women in thousands as of 1996)

	total	*white*	*black*	*Hispanic*
Total, number	106,031	88,134	13,292	9,754
Without income	10,025	7,526	1,684	2,276
With income	96,007	80,608	11,607	7,478
Under $10,000	41,101	34,023	5,423	4,081
$10,000 to $19,999	24,619	20,695	3,049	1,919
$20,000 to $29,999	14,097	11,893	1,661	849
$30,000 to $39,999	7,831	6,691	821	351
$40,000 to $49,999	3,971	3,414	374	145
$50,000 to $64,999	2,456	2,176	181	90
$65,000 to $74,999	680	566	60	12
$75,000 to $84,999	433	401	16	7
$85,000 to $99,999	275	240	5	6
$100,000 or more	544	511	19	18
Total with income, percent	100.0%	100.0%	100.0%	100.0%
Under $10,000	42.8	42.2	46.7	54.6
$10,000 to $19,999	25.6	25.7	26.3	25.7
$20,000 to $29,999	14.7	14.8	14.3	11.4
$30,000 to $39,999	8.2	8.3	7.1	4.7
$40,000 to $49,999	4.1	4.2	3.2	1.9
$50,000 to $64,999	2.6	2.7	1.6	1.2
$65,000 to $74,999	0.7	0.7	0.5	0.2
$75,000 to $84,999	0.5	0.5	0.1	0.1
$85,000 to $99,999	0.3	0.3	0.0	0.1
$100,000 or more	0.6	0.6	0.2	0.2
Median income				
Women with income	$12,130	$12,316	$10,961	$8,928
Full-time, year-round workers	23,777	24,264	21,079	17,855
Percent working full-time, year-round	33.5%	33.0%	36.2%	28.4%

Note: Numbers will not add to total because Hispanics may be of any race and not all races are shown.
Source: Bureau of the Census, unpublished tables from the 1996 Current Population Survey; calculations by New Strategist

The Earnings Gap Narrows

Women now earn 71 percent as much as men.

The rallying cry of the women's movement was once "Fifty-nine cents on the dollar!" It was meant to illustrate the fact that for every dollar men earned, women earned only 59 cents. But in the past two decades, women have narrowed the gap. By 1995, women earned 71 cents for every dollar men earned.

In 1970, women who worked year-round, full-time earned a median of $19,642 versus the $33,085 earned by their male counterparts. A decade later, there had been almost no change in women's earnings as a percent of men's.

During the 1980s, however, women's earnings rose while men's earnings fell. By 1995, women working full-time earned a median of $22,497, up 15 percent since 1970 after adjusting for inflation. Men who worked full-time earned a median of $31,496, down 5 percent from what they earned in 1970, after adjusting for inflation.

❖ As the better-educated, career oriented women of the baby-boom generation entered the labor force during the 1980s, the pay gap narrowed. Entirely closing the gap may never be possible, however, because women are more likely than men to drop out of the labor force temporarily while their children are young—a practice that lowers earnings.

Median Earnings by Sex, 1980 to 1995

(median earnings of persons aged 15 or older who work year-round, full-time by sex and women's earnings as a percent of men's, 1980-95; percent change in earnings for selected years; in 1995 dollars)

	median earnings		women's earnings as
	men	women	a percent of men's
1995	$31,496	$22,497	71%
1994	31,728	22,834	72
1993	32,070	22,936	72
1992	32,801	23,219	71
1991	32,920	22,998	70
1990	32,273	23,113	72
1989	33,591	23,068	69
1988	34,339	22,681	66
1987	34,808	22,687	65
1986	35,119	22,571	64
1985	34,268	22,129	65
1984	34,057	21,679	64
1983	33,481	21,292	64
1982	33,600	20,746	62
1981	34,268	20,299	59
1980	34,465	20,734	60
1979	35,040	20,905	60
1978	35,515	21,110	59
1977	35,269	20,782	59
1976	34,521	20,780	60
1975	34,596	20,349	59
1974	34,835	20,467	59
1973	36,117	20,455	57
1972	35,018	20,261	58
1971	33,235	19,777	60
1970	33,085	19,642	59
Percent change			
1994 to 1995	-0.7%	-1.5%	
1990 to 1995	-2.4	-2.7	
1980 to 1995	-8.6	8.5	
1970 to 1995	-4.8	14.5	

Source: Bureau of the Census, Internet web site, http://www.census.gov*; calculations by New Strategist*

In Nursing, Women Earn Almost as Much as Men

Some occupations are more egalitarian than others.

Women working as nurses and therapists are closer to achieving income parity with men than are women in other occupations. Median weekly earnings for women working full time in these jobs are 97 percent as much as men's. Women working as registered nurses earned a median of $693 a week in 1995, while men in this occupation earned a median of $715 a week. Women therapists earned $665 a week, while their male counterparts earned $685. The only other occupations in which women earn at least 90 percent as much as men are cashiers and mail carriers.

Women working in securities and financial services sales earned just slightly more than half of what men earned. Among all major job categories, in fact, the greatest income disparity between men and women is found in sales occupations. Other occupations with large earnings gaps include physicians and managers in marketing, advertising, and public relations.

❖ Men's earnings exceed women's because the typical male worker is better educated and has been on the job longer than the typical female worker. The earnings gap in many fields should narrow as well-educated, career-oriented younger women gain job experience.

Median Weekly Earnings by Occupation and Sex, 1995

(median weekly earnings of full-time wage and salary workers aged 16 or older by selected occupation and sex, and women's earnings as a percent of men's, 1995)

	women	men	women's earnings as a percent of men's
Total	$406	$538	75%
Managerial and professional specialty	605	829	73
Executive, administrative, and managerial	570	833	68
Administrators & officials, public admin.	652	829	79
Financial managers	635	942	67
Managers, marketing, adv., public relations	631	1,063	59
Administrators, education and related fields	674	952	71
Managers, medicine and health	580	838	69
Mgrs., food serving & lodging estab.	376	516	73
Managers, properties and real estate	464	614	76
Accountants and auditors	548	747	73
Professional specialty	632	827	76
Engineers	806	935	86
Computer systems analysts and scientists	783	910	86
Physicians	806	1,241	65
Registered nurses	693	715	97
Therapists	665	685	97
Teachers, college and university	735	941	78
Teachers, prekindergarten and kindergarten	371	-	-
Teachers, elementary school	627	713	88
Teachers, secondary school	637	723	88
Librarians	595	-	-
Social workers	497	565	88
Lawyers	958	1,171	82
Technical, sales, and administrative support	383	556	69
Technicians and related support	480	641	75
Licensed practical nurses	443	-	-
Computer programmers	681	762	89
Legal assistants	501	582	86
Sales occupations	330	579	57
Insurance sales	453	777	58
Real estate sales	516	650	79
Securities and financial services sales	506	936	54

(continued)

(continued from previous page)

	women	men	ratio of women's earnings to men's
Sales workers, retail and personal services	$253	$365	69%
Cashiers	233	256	91
Administrative support, including clerical	384	489	79
Computer operators	392	527	74
Secretaries	395	-	-
Typists	394	-	-
Receptionists	327	-	-
File clerks	332	-	-
Bookkeepers	382	445	86
Telephone operators	380	-	-
Mail carriers	602	665	91
Bank tellers	298	-	-
Teachers' aides	267	-	-
Service Occupations	264	357	74
Child care workers, private household	182	-	-
Cleaners and servants, private household	199	-	-
Police and detectives	511	612	83
Waitresses	258	314	82
Dental assistants	338	-	-
Nursing aides	275	331	83
Maids	238	287	83
Janitors and cleaners	259	307	84
Hairdressers and cosmetologists	281	-	-
Precision production, craft, and repair	371	534	69
Operators, fabricators, and laborers	297	413	72
Transportation & material moving occupations	354	482	73
Handlers, equip. cleaners, helpers, and laborers	284	328	87
Farming, forestry, and fishing	249	294	85

Source: Bureau of Labor Statistics, Employment and Earnings, *January 1996; calculations by New Strategist*

Education Is the Key to Higher Earnings

Women with professional degrees earn the most.

Earnings rise in lock-step with education. This fact is behind the soaring college enrollment of women. Women with college degrees earn far more than those who stopped their education with a high school diploma.

Among full-time workers, the median earnings of women who went no further than high school stood at $19,649 in 1995. For those who have a college degree, median earnings were $33,399. Women with professional degrees (such as doctors and lawyers) have the highest earnings—a median of $48,111 in 1995.

Only 6 percent of all women earned $50,000 or more in 1995. But 15 percent of women with at least a bachelor's degree have earnings this high, as do 37 percent of those with professional degrees.

❖ Among women born after World War II, about one in four has a college degree. As baby-boom and younger women gain job experience, the number of women earning high incomes will rise substantially.

Earnings of Women by Education, 1995

(number and percent distribution of women aged 25 or older by earnings and education, 1995; median earnings of women by work status, and percent working year-round, full-time; women in thousands as of 1996)

					bachelor's degree or more				
	total	not a high school grad.	high school grad. only	some college/ assoc. degree	total	bachelor's degree	master's degree	professional degree	doctoral degree
Total, number	87,984	16,190	30,911	22,071	18,813	13,321	4,288	745	459
Without earnings	33,735	10,931	12,553	6,118	4,134	3,177	770	119	68
With earnings	54,249	5,259	18,357	15,953	14,679	10,144	3,519	626	391
Under $10,000	15,023	2,699	5,923	4,039	2,361	1,785	450	85	42
$10,000 to $19,999	14,931	1,862	6,367	4,468	2,235	1,817	333	59	24
$20,000 to $29,999	11,375	469	3,824	3,930	3,154	2,456	587	68	43
$30,000 to $39,999	6,382	144	1,377	2,008	2,854	1,828	828	105	93
$40,000 to $49,999	3,386	54	533	869	1,930	1,148	640	74	68
$50,000 to $64,999	1,919	10	231	409	1,268	724	418	81	45
$65,000 to $74,999	465	12	27	111	315	159	98	31	27
$75,000 to $84,999	297	6	22	46	223	103	79	31	10
$85,000 to $99,999	169	-	11	15	144	52	43	30	19
$100,000 or more	302	3	42	61	196	72	41	61	22

(continued)

(continued from previous page)

					bachelor's degree or more				
	total	not a high school grad.	high school grad. only	some college/ assoc. degree	total	bachelor's degree	master's degree	professional degree	doctoral degree
Total with earnings, percent	100.0%	100.0%	100.0%	100.0%	100.0%	100.0%	100.0%	100.0%	100.0%
Under $10,000	27.7	51.3	32.3	25.3	16.1	17.6	12.8	13.6	10.7
$10,000 to $19,999	27.5	35.4	34.7	28.0	15.2	17.9	9.5	9.4	6.1
$20,000 to $29,999	21.0	8.9	20.8	24.6	21.5	24.2	16.7	10.9	11.0
$30,000 to $39,999	11.8	2.7	7.5	12.6	19.4	18.0	23.5	16.8	23.8
$40,000 to $49,999	6.2	1.0	2.9	5.4	13.1	11.3	18.2	11.8	17.4
$50,000 to $64,999	3.5	0.2	1.3	2.6	8.6	7.1	11.9	12.9	11.5
$65,000 to $74,999	0.9	0.2	0.1	0.7	2.1	1.6	2.8	5.0	6.9
$75,000 to $84,999	0.5	0.1	0.1	0.3	1.5	1.0	2.2	5.0	2.6
$85,000 to $99,999	0.3	-	0.1	0.1	1.0	0.5	1.2	4.8	4.9
$100,000 or more	0.6	0.1	0.2	0.4	1.3	0.7	1.2	9.7	5.6
Median earnings									
Women with earnings	$17,630	$9,617	$15,017	$18,489	$28,252	$25,800	$34,148	$38,896	$38,357
Full-time, year-round workers	23,619	14,392	19,649	23,813	33,399	30,798	38,593	48,111	41,920
Percent working year-round, full-time	37.1%	15.7%	35.8%	43.8%	50.0%	48.3%	52.9%	56.5%	61.7%

Note: (-) means sample is too small to make a reliable estimate.
Source: Bureau of the Census, unpublished tables from the 1996 Current Population Survey; calculations by New Strategist

Older Householders Have Seen Incomes Grow

The youngest householders have experienced a sharp decline in income.

Household income rose by only 6 percent between 1970 and 1995, after adjusting for inflation. But this overall increase masks differing fortunes by age. Median household income rose by 48 percent for the oldest households and declined by 15 percent for the youngest households, after adjusting for inflation.

Government policy has a greater influence on the finances of these two groups than on the middle aged. Older Americans depend on Social Security benefits, which have been rising with inflation. Many of the youngest depend on the minimum wage, which has been losing value. The fortunes of the oldest age group have also been improving as a more affluent older generation enters its 60s, replacing poorer elderly Americans.

The highest incomes historically have been found among householders aged 45 to 54 because those are the peak earning years. In 1995, this age group had a median household income of $48,058, up 14 percent since 1970 after adjusting for inflation. In 1970, the median income of householders in this age group was only about $1,000 greater than that of householders aged 35 to 44. By 1995, the median income of the older group was more than $4,500 greater.

❖ Older women are becoming the most important decision makers in the consumer marketplace as their household incomes grow.

Median Income of Households by Age of Householder, 1970 to 1995

(median income of households by age of householder, 1970 to 1995; percent change for selected years; in 1995 dollars)

	total	< 25	25 to 34	35 to 44	45 to 54	55 to 64	65 or older
1995	$34,076	$20,979	$34,701	$43,465	$48,058	$38,077	$19,096
1994	33,178	19,888	34,090	42,848	48,600	36,230	18,608
1993	32,949	20,390	32,991	43,096	48,733	35,304	18,721
1992	33,278	19,186	33,933	43,290	48,268	36,925	18,613
1991	33,709	20,491	34,510	44,029	48,955	37,265	18,994
1990	34,914	20,991	35,399	44,963	48,882	37,739	19,653
1989	35,526	22,937	36,653	46,255	51,033	37,878	19,383
1988	35,073	21,952	36,597	47,091	49,228	37,234	19,225
1987	34,962	22,064	36,176	47,202	49,912	36,973	19,376
1986	34,620	21,289	36,011	45,591	49,586	37,232	19,252
1985	33,452	21,315	35,529	44,001	47,056	36,198	18,772
1984	32,878	20,576	34,814	43,687	46,228	35,341	18,774
1983	31,957	20,507	33,274	42,352	46,442	34,853	17,930
1982	32,155	22,025	33,925	42,038	44,612	35,191	17,601
1981	32,263	22,398	34,697	42,936	45,744	35,590	16,750
1980	32,795	23,538	35,808	43,752	46,518	36,196	16,260
1979	33,901	24,534	37,488	45,506	47,466	36,938	16,226
1978	34,011	24,867	37,258	44,993	47,822	36,188	15,987
1977	32,727	23,079	36,352	43,588	46,726	34,509	15,305
1976	32,548	22,737	35,906	42,900	45,320	34,411	15,296
1975	31,999	22,068	35,597	42,146	44,261	33,856	15,145
1974	32,879	23,820	36,476	43,711	45,142	33,681	15,540
1973	33,941	24,203	38,210	45,084	45,465	35,120	14,798
1972	33,284	24,236	37,335	43,551	45,051	34,441	14,310
1971	31,923	23,270	35,632	41,074	42,488	33,040	13,483
1970	32,229	24,609	35,757	41,074	42,115	32,864	12,908
Percent change							
1994 to 1995	2.7%	5.5%	1.8%	1.4%	-1.1%	5.1%	2.6%
1990 to 1995	-2.4	-0.1	-2.0	-3.3	-1.7	0.9	-2.8
1980 to 1995	3.9	-10.9	-3.1	-0.7	3.3	5.2	17.4
1970 to 1995	5.7	-14.8	-3.0	5.8	14.1	15.9	47.9

Source: Bureau of the Census, Internet web site, http://www.census.gov*; calculations by New Strategist*

Affluent Households Are Now Headed by Baby Boomers

Median incomes are highest for householders aged 35 to 54.

Households headed by people aged 45 to 54 have the highest incomes, a median of $48,058 in 1995. Ranking second in affluence are households headed by people aged 35 to 44. Their median income was $43,465 in 1995. With boomers spanning the ages of 31 to 49 in 1995, they account for a majority of householders in the affluent 35-to-54 age group.

Householders aged 35 to 54 are in their peak-earning years, which explains their affluence. Many are dual-earner couples. Fully 13 percent of householders aged 45 to 54 have incomes of $100,000 or more. As boomers entirely fill the 45-to-54 age group in the next few years, the number of households with incomes of $100,000 or more will expand substantially.

Among householders aged 55 to 64, median income drops to $38,077. Incomes are lower in this age group because many householders are retired.

❖ As boomers age into the 55-to-64 age group in the decade ahead, the household income of 55 to 64 year olds may rise relative to that of 45-to-54-year-olds. Not only will boomers be less likely to retire early, but career-oriented baby-boom women will boost household income.

Income Distribution of Households by Age, 1995

(number and percent distribution of households by household income and age of householder, 1995; households in thousands as of 1996)

	total	< 25	25 to 34	35 to 44	45 to 54	55 to 64	65 to 74	75 or older
Total, number	99,627	5,282	19,225	23,226	18,008	12,401	11,908	9,578
Under $10,000	12,190	1,158	1,937	1,632	1,366	1,463	1,983	2,651
$10,000 to $19,999	17,009	1,368	2,861	2,650	1,752	1,783	3,196	3,401
$20,000 to $29,999	14,905	1,114	3,243	3,055	2,009	1,655	2,289	1,539
$30,000 to $39,999	13,129	699	3,119	3,231	2,199	1,593	1,471	814
$40,000 to $49,999	10,565	416	2,598	2,877	2,048	1,283	943	401
$50,000 to $59,999	8,276	244	1,858	2,596	1,707	1,007	609	257
$60,000 to $69,999	6,332	114	1,169	2,089	1,577	824	405	151
$70,000 to $79,999	4,571	81	779	1,431	1,268	714	210	88
$80,000 to $89,999	3,257	36	536	1,019	959	473	150	83
$90,000 to $99,999	2,281	16	313	671	728	371	136	44
$100,000 or more	7,114	36	811	1,974	2,394	1,234	518	148
Median income	$34,076	$20,979	$34,701	$43,465	$48,058	$38,077	$23,031	$15,342
Total, percent	100.0%	100.0%	100.0%	100.0%	100.0%	100.0%	100.0%	100.0%
Under $10,000	12.2	21.9	10.1	7.0	7.6	11.8	16.7	27.7
$10,000 to $19,999	17.1	25.9	14.9	11.4	9.7	14.4	26.8	35.5
$20,000 to $29,999	15.0	21.1	16.9	13.2	11.2	13.3	19.2	16.1
$30,000 to $39,999	13.2	13.2	16.2	13.9	12.2	12.8	12.4	8.5
$40,000 to $49,999	10.6	7.9	13.5	12.4	11.4	10.3	7.9	4.2
$50,000 to $59,999	8.3	4.6	9.7	11.2	9.5	8.1	5.1	2.7
$60,000 to $69,999	6.4	2.2	6.1	9.0	8.8	6.6	3.4	1.6
$70,000 to $79,999	4.6	1.5	4.1	6.2	7.0	5.8	1.8	0.9
$80,000 to $89,999	3.3	0.7	2.8	4.4	5.3	3.8	1.3	0.9
$90,000 to $99,999	2.3	0.3	1.6	2.9	4.0	3.0	1.1	0.5
$100,000 or more	7.1	0.7	4.2	8.5	13.3	10.0	4.4	1.5

Source: Bureau of the Census, unpublished tables from the 1996 Current Population Survey; calculations by New Strategist

Married Women Are Nation's Income Elite

Middle-aged married couples make the most money.

Married couples headed by 45-to-54-year-olds have the highest median income, fully $62,576 in 1995. This was nearly double the median income of the average household. Behind the much higher incomes of married couples are two earners. Without the income provided by working wives, many couples would find it difficult to maintain a comfortable standard of living.

Most married couples have above-average incomes. Only those under age 25 or aged 65 or older have incomes below the all-household median of $34,076.

Fully 19 percent of couples aged 45 to 54 have incomes of $100,000 or more. As the enormous baby-boom generation entirely fills this age group, the number of couples with incomes of $100,000 or more will rise significantly.

❖ The earnings of wives no longer pay for family extras, but for necessities. While the two-earner lifestyle provides financial comfort, it creates extraordinary time pressures. Convenience is one of the most important product and service benefits to two-earner couples.

Income Distribution of Married Couples by Age, 1995

(number and percent distribution of married-couple households by household income and age of householder, 1995; households in thousands as of 1996)

	total	< 25	25 to 34	35 to 44	45 to 54	55 to 64	65 to 74	75 or older
Total, number	53,567	1,528	9,960	13,897	11,161	7,741	6,177	3,104
Under $10,000	1,737	112	308	320	245	352	238	162
$10,000 to $19,999	5,585	378	890	844	528	727	1,235	983
$20,000 to $29,999	7,082	415	1,412	1,273	851	863	1,432	834
$30,000 to $39,999	7,230	285	1,711	1,664	1,126	1,016	998	431
$40,000 to $49,999	6,854	176	1,701	1,921	1,229	920	668	240
$50,000 to $59,999	5,992	91	1,324	1,942	1,255	788	457	133
$60,000 to $69,999	4,890	38	856	1,665	1,280	663	299	90
$70,000 to $79,999	3,559	16	549	1,140	1,042	601	157	52
$80,000 to $89,999	2,653	6	373	866	818	396	132	61
$90,000 to $99,999	1,952	6	253	573	656	330	115	19
$100,000 or more	6,033	4	581	1,690	2,130	1,084	444	100
Median income	$47,129	$26,433	$43,800	$54,515	$62,576	$49,898	$31,614	$24,381
Total, percent	100.0%	100.0%	100.0%	100.0%	100.0%	100.0%	100.0%	100.0%
Under $10,000	3.2	7.3	3.1	2.3	2.2	4.5	3.9	5.2
$10,000 to $19,999	10.4	24.7	8.9	6.1	4.7	9.4	20.0	31.7
$20,000 to $29,999	13.2	27.2	14.2	9.2	7.6	11.1	23.2	26.9
$30,000 to $39,999	13.5	18.7	17.2	12.0	10.1	13.1	16.2	13.9
$40,000 to $49,999	12.8	11.5	17.1	13.8	11.0	11.9	10.8	7.7
$50,000 to $59,999	11.2	6.0	13.3	14.0	11.2	10.2	7.4	4.3
$60,000 to $69,999	9.1	2.5	8.6	12.0	11.5	8.6	4.8	2.9
$70,000 to $79,999	6.6	1.0	5.5	8.2	9.3	7.8	2.5	1.7
$80,000 to $89,999	5.0	0.4	3.7	6.2	7.3	5.1	2.1	2.0
$90,000 to $99,999	3.6	0.4	2.5	4.1	5.9	4.3	1.9	0.6
$100,000 or more	11.3	0.3	5.8	12.2	19.1	14.0	7.2	3.2

Source: Bureau of the Census, unpublished tables from the 1996 Current Population Survey; calculations by New Strategist

Low Incomes for Older Women Who Live Alone

But many younger women who live by themselves have substantial incomes.

The median income of the 14.6 million women who live alone was just $14,331 in 1995. This median masks sharp income difference between older and younger women who live alone.

Over half of women who live alone are aged 65 or older. Most are widows, dependent on Social Security. Because few older women spent much time in the labor force, they are not likely to have their own pension coverage.

Women aged 25 to 44 who live alone have relatively high incomes. The median income of women aged 35 to 44 who live alone stood at $27,343, with 16 percent having incomes of $50,000 or more. These are career-oriented baby-boom women, and their high incomes show their commitment to the labor force.

❖ As hard-working baby-boom women become widowed in the decades ahead, the incomes of women who live alone will rise. Many will have earned their own pension and Social Security benefits.

Income Distribution of Women Living Alone by Age, 1995

(number and percent distribution of women living alone by household income and age of householder, 1995; women in thousands as of 1996)

	total	*< 25*	*25 to 34*	*35 to 44*	*45 to 54*	*55 to 64*	*65 to 74*	*75 or older*
Total, number	14,612	498	1,487	1,485	1,756	1,852	3,137	4,397
Under $10,000	4,945	167	204	223	443	637	1,226	2,045
$10,000 to $19,999	4,579	199	350	280	371	474	1,201	1,706
$20,000 to $29,999	2,144	105	368	328	328	322	349	344
$30,000 to $39,999	1,329	21	273	260	254	160	191	170
$40,000 to $49,999	711	-	155	162	157	107	90	40
$50,000 to $59,999	371	2	66	78	81	73	22	49
$60,000 to $69,999	221	3	38	59	53	26	26	16
$70,000 to $79,999	130	-	10	52	29	29	7	5
$80,000 to $89,999	44	-	10	8	10	10	2	5
$90,000 to $99,999	38	-	2	11	10	3	9	2
$100,000 or more	99	1	11	23	24	12	13	16
Median income	$14,331	$13,616	$24,970	$27,343	$21,545	$16,164	$12,149	$10,619
Total, percent	100.0%	100.0%	100.0%	100.0%	100.0%	100.0%	100.0%	100.0%
Under $10,000	33.8	33.5	13.7	15.0	25.2	34.4	39.1	46.5
$10,000 to $19,999	31.3	40.0	23.5	18.9	21.1	25.6	38.3	38.8
$20,000 to $29,999	14.7	21.1	24.7	22.1	18.7	17.4	11.1	7.8
$30,000 to $39,999	9.1	4.2	18.4	17.5	14.5	8.6	6.1	3.9
$40,000 to $49,999	4.9	-	10.4	10.9	8.9	5.8	2.9	0.9
$50,000 to $59,999	2.5	0.4	4.4	5.3	4.6	3.9	0.7	1.1
$60,000 to $69,999	1.5	0.6	2.6	4.0	3.0	1.4	0.8	0.4
$70,000 to $79,999	0.9	-	0.7	3.5	1.7	1.6	0.2	0.1
$80,000 to $89,999	0.3	-	0.7	0.5	0.6	0.5	0.1	0.1
$90,000 to $99,999	0.3	-	0.1	0.7	0.6	0.2	0.3	0.0
$100,000 or more	0.7	0.2	0.7	1.5	1.4	0.6	0.4	0.4

Note: (-) means sample is too small to make a reliable estimate.
Source: Bureau of the Census, unpublished tables from the 1996 Current Population Survey; calculations by New Strategist

Not All Female-Headed Families Are Poor

Older female-headed families have relatively high incomes.

While the popular perception of female-headed families is that they are in or near poverty, this is true only for those headed by young adults. The median income of female-headed families with a householder aged 45 to 54 stood at $30,349 in 1995, nearly equal to the all-household median of $34,076.

Female-headed families include both single mothers raising children alone and female householders living with adult relatives such as grown children, siblings, or parents. Families headed by women under age 45 are likely to include children under age 18. Most of these households have only one earner, if any, leaving them with lower incomes than older women.

Families headed by women aged 45 or older are less likely to include young children. Frequently, a second earner is in the household—boosting incomes.

❖ Female-headed families divide into two markets—struggling young women and much more comfortable older women. Younger householders are important consumers of affordable children products, while the older market will be more interested in discretionary items such as travel.

Income Distribution of Female-Headed Families by Age, 1995

(number and percent distribution of families headed by women with no spouse present by household income and age of householder, 1995; families in thousands as of 1996)

	total	< 25	25 to 34	35 to 44	45 to 54	55 to 64	65 to 74	75 or older
Total, number	12,514	1,093	2,904	3,660	2,116	1,111	914	717
Under $10,000	2,812	510	965	681	273	174	129	82
$10,000 to $19,999	3,101	262	878	876	405	245	236	200
$20,000 to $29,999	2,212	129	446	687	367	222	202	158
$30,000 to $39,999	1,761	87	289	589	384	194	115	105
$40,000 to $49,999	1,052	53	123	324	284	104	94	71
$50,000 to $59,999	598	29	60	212	149	47	66	35
$60,000 to $69,999	372	5	58	130	84	40	29	27
$70,000 to $79,999	224	10	45	61	48	34	20	7
$80,000 to $89,999	145	6	14	28	53	27	5	11
$90,000 to $99,999	56	-	2	21	13	5	-	15
$100,000 or more	183	4	24	54	57	19	19	7
Median income	$21,348	$11,179	$14,867	$23,481	$30,349	$26,919	$24,386	$24,897
Total, percent	100.0%	100.0%	100.0%	100.0%	100.0%	100.0%	100.0%	100.0%
Under $10,000	22.5	46.7	33.2	18.6	12.9	15.7	14.1	11.4
$10,000 to $19,999	24.8	24.0	30.2	23.9	19.1	22.1	25.8	27.9
$20,000 to $29,999	17.7	11.8	15.4	18.8	17.3	20.0	22.1	22.0
$30,000 to $39,999	14.1	8.0	10.0	16.1	18.1	17.5	12.6	14.6
$40,000 to $49,999	8.4	4.8	4.2	8.9	13.4	9.4	10.3	9.9
$50,000 to $59,999	4.8	2.7	2.1	5.8	7.0	4.2	7.2	4.9
$60,000 to $69,999	3.0	0.5	2.0	3.6	4.0	3.6	3.2	3.8
$70,000 to $79,999	1.8	0.9	1.5	1.7	2.3	3.1	2.2	1.0
$80,000 to $89,999	1.2	0.5	0.5	0.8	2.5	2.4	0.5	1.5
$90,000 to $99,999	0.4	-	0.1	0.6	0.6	0.5	-	2.1
$100,000 or more	1.5	0.4	0.8	1.5	2.7	1.7	2.1	1.0

Note: (-) means sample is too small to make a reliable estimate.
Source: Bureau of the Census, unpublished tables from the 1996 Current Population Survey; calculations by New Strategist

One in Five Wives Earns More

Over 7 million women earn more than their husbands.

The number of wives who earn more than their husbands has been climbing for many years. The 7 million wives who earned more than their husbands in 1995 was 72 percent greater than the 4 million of 1981. The proportion of wives who earn more rose from 16 to 22 percent during those years.

One factor behind this long-term increase is the entry of career-oriented baby-boom women into the labor force. Another factor is the decline in the earnings of men, after adjusting for inflation. The small drop in the proportion of wives earning more than their husbands between 1994 and 1995 is due to the economic recovery following the recession of the early 1990s. As unemployed men found jobs, and as the salaries of those with jobs increased, the share of women earning more than their husbands fell slightly.

❖ The number and proportion of wives who earn more than their husbands should continue to grow in the years ahead, along with women's earnings.

Wives Who Earn More Than Their Husbands, 1981 to 1995

(number of married couples in which both husband and wife have earnings, number in which wives earn more than husbands, and percent of wives earning more than husbands, 1981-1995; families in thousands as of the following year)

	husbands and wives with earnings	wives earning more than husbands	percent of wives earning more than husbands
1995	32,030	7,028	21.9%
1994	32,093	7,218	22.5
1993	31,267	6,960	22.3
1992	31,224	6,979	22.4
1991	31,003	6,499	21.0
1987	29,079	5,266	18.1
1983	26,120	4,800	18.4
1981	25,744	4,088	15.9

Source: Bureau of the Census, Internet web site, http://www.census.gov

Most of the Nation's Poor Are Female

The poverty rate for females rose between 1970 and 1995.

In 1995, 15 percent of the nation's females were poor, up from 14 percent in 1970. The number of poor females increased from 14.6 million to 20.7 million during those years.

While poverty rates among females have fluctuated somewhat over the years—ranging from a low of 12.5 percent to a high of 16.9 percent—the female share of poor Americans has barely budged. In 1995, females accounted for 57 percent of the nation's poor—the same proportion as in 1970.

❖ Though the poverty rate among all females has changed little over the past two decades, today's poor females are more likely to be children and less likely to be elderly than the female poor of 1970.

Females in Poverty, 1970 to 1995

(total number of females, number and percent in poverty, and female percent of poor, 1970-1995; females in thousands as of the following year)

	total	below poverty number	below poverty percent	percent of poor
1995	134,880	20,742	15.4%	56.9%
1994	133,778	21,744	16.3	57.1
1993	132,610	22,365	16.9	57.0
1992	131,261	21,792	16.6	57.3
1991	128,761	20,626	16.0	57.8
1990	127,571	19,373	15.2	57.7
1989	126,288	18,162	14.4	57.6
1988	125,131	18,146	14.5	57.2
1987	123,767	18,518	15.0	56.9
1986	122,640	18,649	15.2	57.6
1985	121,624	18,923	15.6	57.2
1984	120,425	19,163	15.9	56.9
1983	119,332	20,084	16.8	57.0
1982	118,237	19,556	16.5	56.9
1981	117,147	18,462	15.8	58.0
1980	116,037	17,065	14.7	58.3
1979	112,306	14,810	13.2	58.4
1978	111,175	14,480	13.0	59.1
1977	110,238	14,381	13.0	58.2
1976	109,348	14,603	13.4	58.5
1975	108,652	14,970	13.8	57.8
1974	107,743	13,881	12.9	57.4
1973	106,898	13,316	12.5	58.0
1972	106,168	14,258	13.4	58.3
1971	105,298	14,841	14.1	58.1
1970	104,248	14,632	14.0	57.4

Source: Bureau of the Census, Internet web site, http://wwwcensus.gov*; calculations by New Strategist*

Sharp Racial Differences in Female Poverty

Blacks and Hispanics are much more likely to be poor than whites.

Only 12 percent of white females are poor. This compares with one-third of black and Hispanic females. Nevertheless, whites account for a 66 percent majority of the nation's poor females.

Among blacks and Hispanics, poverty rates are highest among children. Forty-two percent of black girls and 41 percent of Hispanic girls under age 18 are poor compared with 17 percent of white girls.

Among whites, women aged 18 to 24 have the highest poverty rate (19 percent). Least likely to be poor, regardless of race, are women aged 45 to 54. At this age, most women find it easier to maintain steady employment since their children are now old enough to fend for themselves. Among older women, disabilities become more common, making it difficult for them to work and increasing their chances of being poor.

❖ The higher poverty rates of blacks and Hispanics are due in part to their lower educational attainment. The lack of affordable daycare also makes it difficult for minority women to climb out of poverty.

Females in Poverty by Age, Race, and Hispanic Origin, 1995

(total number of females, and number and percent below poverty by age, race, and Hispanic origin, 1995; females in thousands as of 1996)

		in poverty	
	total	number	percent
Total females	134,880	20,742	15.4%
Under age 18	34,455	7,314	21.2
Aged 18 to 24	12,441	2,696	21.7
Aged 25 to 34	20,528	3,166	15.4
Aged 35 to 44	21,805	2,367	10.9
Aged 45 to 54	16,260	1,390	8.5
Aged 55 to 59	5,787	718	12.4
Aged 60 to 64	5,205	594	11.4
Aged 65 to 74	10,057	1,117	11.1
Aged 75 or older	8,341	1,379	16.5
White females	110,731	13,760	12.4
Under age 18	26,977	4,497	16.7
Aged 18 to 24	9,815	1,834	18.7
Aged 25 to 34	16,555	2,088	12.6
Aged 35 to 44	17,876	1,543	8.6
Aged 45 to 54	13,744	941	6.8
Aged 55 to 59	4,911	487	9.9
Aged 60 to 64	4,458	449	10.1
Aged 65 to 74	8,898	829	9.3
Aged 75 or older	7,497	1,091	14.6
Black females	18,001	5,829	32.4
Under age 18	5,623	2,352	41.8
Aged 18 to 24	1,949	708	36.4
Aged 25 to 34	2,941	934	31.8
Aged 35 to 44	2,872	675	23.5
Aged 45 to 54	1,848	367	19.8
Aged 55 to 59	637	178	28.0
Aged 60 to 64	554	125	22.6
Aged 65 to 74	897	234	26.1
Aged 75 or older	680	256	37.6

(continued)

(continued from previous page)

	total	in poverty	
		number	percent
Hispanic females	14,007	4,602	32.9%
Under age 18	4,961	2,050	41.3
Aged 18 to 24	1,734	603	34.8
Aged 25 to 34	2,443	694	28.4
Aged 35 to 44	2,043	545	26.7
Aged 45 to 54	1,171	245	21.0
Aged 55 to 59	440	111	25.4
Aged 60 to 64	371	108	29.2
Aged 65 to 74	551	147	26.6
Aged 75 or older	293	97	33.2

Source: Bureau of the Census, Poverty in the United States: 1995, *Current Population Reports, P160-194, 1996*

Single Mothers Have the Highest Poverty Rates

Families with children are more likely to be poor.

In 1995, 10.8 percent of all families were poor, almost identical to the 10.3 percent who were poor in 1970. The number of poor families has grown over the years, however, as the population has expanded.

Women heading families without a husband are far more likely to be poor than married couples. One-third of the nation's female-headed families are poor, compared to only 6 percent of married couples.

Families with children are more likely to be poor than those without. Forty-two percent of single-parent families headed by women are poor, as are 8 percent of married couples with children. Since 1980, there has been little change in the poverty rates of these family types.

❖ Poverty rates for single-parents will always be higher than those for couples because married-couple households are more likely to include two earners.

Families in Poverty by Type and Presence of Children, 1980 to 1995

(total number of families, and number and percent below poverty by type of family and presence of children under age 18, 1980-95; percent change in numbers and rates for selected years; families in thousands as of the following year)

	total families			married couples			female householder, no spouse present		
		in poverty			in poverty			in poverty	
	total	number	percent	total	number	percent	total	number	percent
With and without children <18									
1995	69,597	7,532	10.8%	53,570	2,982	5.6%	12,514	4,057	32.4%
1994	69,313	8,053	11.6	53,865	3,272	6.1	12,220	4,232	34.6
1993	68,506	8,393	12.3	53,181	3,481	6.5	12,411	4,424	35.6
1992	68,216	8,144	11.9	53,090	3,385	6.4	12,061	4,275	35.4
1991	67,173	7,712	11.5	52,457	3,158	6.0	11,692	4,161	35.6
1990	66,322	7,098	10.7	52,147	2,981	5.7	11,268	3,768	33.4
1989	66,090	6,784	10.3	52,137	2,931	5.6	10,890	3,504	32.2
1988	65,837	6,874	10.4	52,100	2,897	5.6	10,890	3,642	33.4
1987	65,204	7,005	10.7	51,675	3,011	5.8	10,696	3,654	34.2
1986	64,491	7,023	10.9	51,537	3,123	6.1	10,445	3,613	34.6
1985	63,558	7,223	11.4	50,933	3,438	6.7	10,211	3,474	34.0
1984	62,706	7,277	11.6	50,350	3,488	6.9	10,129	3,498	34.5
1983	62,015	7,647	12.3	50,081	3,815	7.6	9,896	3,564	36.0
1982	61,393	7,512	12.2	49,908	3,789	7.6	9,469	3,434	36.3
1981	61,019	6,851	11.2	49,630	3,394	6.8	9,403	3,252	34.6
1980	60,309	6,217	10.3	49,294	3,032	6.2	9,082	2,972	32.7
Percent change									
1990-1995	4.9%	6.1%	-	2.7%	0.0%	-	11.1%	7.7%	-
1980-1995	15.4	21.2	-	8.7	-1.6	-	37.8	36.5	-

(continued)

(continued from previous page)

	total families			married couples			female householder, no spouse present		
		in poverty			in poverty			in poverty	
	total	number	percent	total	number	percent	total	number	percent
With children <18									
1995	36,719	5,976	16.3%	26,034	1,961	7.5%	8,751	3,634	41.5%
1994	36,782	6,408	17.4	26,367	2,197	8.3	8,665	3,816	44.0
1993	36,456	6,751	18.5	26,121	2,363	9.0	8,758	4,034	46.1
1992	35,851	6,457	18.0	25,907	2,237	8.6	8,375	3,867	46.2
1991	34,861	6,170	17.7	25,357	2,106	8.3	7,991	3,767	47.1
1990	34,503	5,676	16.4	25,410	1,990	7.8	7,707	3,426	44.5
1989	34,279	5,308	15.5	25,476	1,872	7.3	7,445	3,190	42.8
1988	34,251	5,373	15.7	25,598	1,847	7.2	7,361	3,294	44.7
1987	33,996	5,465	16.1	25,464	1,963	7.7	7,216	3,281	45.5
1986	33,801	5,516	16.3	25,571	2,050	8.0	7,094	3,264	46.0
1985	33,536	5,586	16.7	25,496	2,258	8.9	6,892	3,131	45.4
1984	32,942	5,662	17.2	25,038	2,344	9.4	6,832	3,124	45.7
1983	32,787	5,871	17.9	25,216	2,557	10.1	6,622	3,122	47.1
1982	32,565	5,712	17.5	25,276	2,470	9.8	6,397	3,059	47.8
1981	32,587	5,191	15.9	25,278	2,199	8.7	6,488	2,877	44.3
1980	32,773	4,822	14.7	25,671	1,974	7.7	6,299	2,703	42.9
Percent change									
1990-1995	6.4%	5.3%	-	2.5%	-1.5%	-	13.5%	6.1%	-
1980-1995	12.0	23.9	-	1.4	-0.7	-	38.9	34.4	-

Source: Bureau of the Census, unpublished tables from the 1996 Current Population Survey; calculations by New Strategist

Fortunes Have Improved for Black Couples

Poverty rates have been rising among Hispanics.

Poverty rates declined sharply for black couples between 1980 and 1995. Only 9 percent were poor in 1995, down from 14 percent in 1980. During those years, the proportion of white couples in poverty did not change much. In 1995, only 5 percent of white couples were poor. Poverty rates for Hispanic couples have been rising. In 1995, 19 percent were poor, up from 15 percent in 1980.

Married couples with children are slightly more likely to be poor than those without. This is especially true among Hispanics. Twenty-three percent of Hispanic couples with children under age 18 are poor—up from 21 percent in 1987.

❖ Hispanic couples are more likely to be poor than white or black couples in part because many Hispanics are recent immigrants with little education or earning power. Another factor boosting poverty among Hispanics is that Hispanic women are less likely to work than white or black women.

Married Couples in Poverty by Race and Hispanic Origin, 1980 to 1995

(total number of married-couple households, and number and percent below poverty by race, Hispanic origin, and presence of children under age 18, 1980-95; percent change in numbers and rates for selected years; families in thousands as of the following year)

	white			black			Hispanic		
		in poverty			in poverty			in poverty	
	total	number	percent	total	number	percent	total	number	percent
With and without children <18									
1995	47,877	2,443	5.1%	3,713	314	8.5%	4,247	803	18.9%
1994	47,905	2,629	5.5	3,842	336	8.7	4,236	827	19.5
1993	47,452	2,757	5.8	3,715	458	12.3	4,038	770	19.1
1992	47,383	2,677	5.7	3,777	490	13.0	3,940	743	18.8
1991	47,124	2,573	5.5	3,631	399	11.0	3,532	674	19.1
1990	47,014	2,386	5.1	3,569	448	12.6	3,454	605	17.5
1989	46,981	2,329	5.0	3,750	443	11.8	3,395	549	16.2
1988	46,877	2,294	4.9	3,722	421	11.3	3,398	547	16.1
1987	46,510	2,382	5.1	3,681	439	11.9	3,196	556	17.4
1986	46,410	2,591	5.6	3,742	403	10.8	3,118	518	16.6
1985	45,924	2,815	6.1	3,680	447	12.2	2,962	505	17.0
1984	45,643	2,858	6.3	3,469	479	13.8	2,824	469	16.6
1983	45,470	3,125	6.9	3,454	535	15.5	2,752	437	17.7
1982	45,252	3,104	6.9	3,486	543	15.6	2,448	465	19.0
1981	45,007	2,712	6.0	3,535	543	15.4	2,414	366	15.1
1980	44,860	2,437	5.4	3,392	474	14.0	2,365	363	15.3
Percent change									
1990-1995	1.8%	2.4%	-	4.0%	-29.9%	-	23.0%	32.7%	-
1980-1995	6.7	0.2	-	9.5	-33.8	-	79.6	121.2	-

(continued)

(continued from previous page)

	white			black			Hispanic		
		in poverty			in poverty			in poverty	
	total	number	percent	total	number	percent	total	number	percent
With children <18									
1995	22,663	1,583	7.0%	2,119	209	9.9%	2,902	657	22.6%
1994	22,839	1,708	7.5	2,147	245	11.4	2,923	698	23.9
1993	22,670	1,868	8.2	2,147	298	13.9	2,747	652	23.7
1992	22,440	1,753	7.8	2,229	343	15.4	2,692	615	22.9
1991	22,213	1,715	7.7	2,129	263	12.4	2,445	575	23.5
1990	22,289	1,572	7.1	2,104	301	14.3	2,405	501	20.8
1989	22,271	1,457	6.5	2,179	291	13.3	2,309	453	19.6
1988	22,435	1,434	6.4	2,181	272	12.5	2,339	445	19.0
1987	22,336	1,538	6.9	2,205	290	13.2	2,197	460	20.9
1986	22,466	1,692	7.5	2,236	257	11.5	-	-	-
1985	22,399	1,827	8.2	2,185	281	12.9	-	-	-
1984	22,181	1,879	8.5	2,001	331	16.6	-	-	-
1983	22,361	2,060	9.2	2,052	369	18.0	-	-	-
1982	22,390	2,005	9.0	2,093	360	17.2	-	-	-
1981	22,334	1,723	7.7	2,202	357	16.2	-	-	-
1980	22,793	1,544	6.8	2,154	333	15.5	-	-	-
Percent change									
1990-1995	1.7%	0.7%	-	0.7%	-30.6%	-	20.7%	31.1%	-
1980-1995	-0.6	2.5	-	-1.6	-37.2	-	-	-	-

Note: (-) means data not available.
Source: Bureau of the Census, unpublished tables from the 1996 Current Population Survey; calculations by New Strategist

Little Change in Poverty Rates for Female-Headed Families

Hispanic families are most likely to be poor.

Poverty rates barely budged between 1980 and 1995 for female-headed families—regardless of race or Hispanic origin. Twenty-seven percent of white, 45 percent of black, and 49 percent of Hispanic female-headed families were poor in 1995. While rates have not changed much over the years, the number of female-headed families in poverty rose substantially because of population growth. The number of poor Hispanic female-headed families more than doubled between 1980 and 1995.

Female-headed families with children under age 18 are most likely to be poor. Among whites, 36 percent are poor. For blacks and Hispanics, a majority of female-headed families with children were poor in 1995—53 percent of those headed by blacks and 57 percent of those headed by Hispanics.

❖ Regardless of race or Hispanic origin, poverty rates for female-headed families are not likely to decline much in the future because it now takes two earners to make ends meet.

Female-Headed Families in Poverty by Race and Hispanic Origin, 1980 to 1995

(total number of female-headed families, and number and percent below poverty by race, Hispanic origin, and presence of children under age 18, 1980-95; percent change in numbers and rates for selected years; families in thousands as of the following year)

	white			black			Hispanic		
		in poverty			in poverty			in poverty	
	total	number	percent	total	number	percent	total	number	percent
With & without children <18									
1995	8,284	2,200	26.6%	3,769	1,701	45.1%	1,604	792	49.4%
1994	8,031	2,329	29.0	3,716	1,715	46.2	1,485	773	52.1
1993	8,131	2,376	29.2	3,828	1,908	49.9	1,498	772	51.6
1992	7,868	2,245	28.5	3,738	1,878	50.2	1,348	664	49.3
1991	7,726	2,192	28.4	3,582	1,834	51.2	1,261	627	49.7
1990	7,512	2,010	26.8	3,430	1,648	48.1	1,186	573	48.3
1989	7,306	1,858	25.4	3,275	1,524	46.5	1,116	530	47.5
1988	7,342	1,945	26.5	3,223	1,579	49.0	1,112	546	49.1
1987	7,297	1,961	26.9	3,089	1,577	51.1	1,082	565	52.2
1986	7,227	2,041	28.2	2,967	1,488	50.1	1,032	528	51.2
1985	7,111	1,950	27.4	2,874	1,452	50.5	980	521	53.1
1984	6,941	1,878	27.1	2,964	1,533	51.7	905	483	53.4
1983	6,796	1,926	28.3	2,871	1,541	53.7	860	454	52.8
1982	6,507	1,813	27.9	2,734	1,535	56.2	767	425	55.4
1981	6,620	1,814	27.4	2,605	1,377	52.9	750	399	53.2
1980	6,266	1,609	25.7	2,634	1,301	49.4	706	362	51.3
Percent change									
1990-1995	10.3%	9.5%	-	9.9%	3.2%	-	35.2%	38.2%	-
1980-1995	32.2	36.7	-	43.1	30.7	-	127.2	118.8	-

(continued)

(continued from previous page)

	white			black			Hispanic		
		in poverty			in poverty			in poverty	
	total	number	percent	total	number	percent	total	number	percent
With children <18									
1995	5,554	1,980	35.6%	2,884	1,533	53.2%	1,283	735	57.3%
1994	5,390	2,064	38.3	2,951	1,591	53.9	1,182	700	59.2
1993	5,361	2,123	39.6	3,084	1,780	57.7	1,167	706	60.5
1992	5,099	2,021	39.6	2,971	1,706	57.4	1,037	598	57.7
1991	4,967	1,969	39.6	2,771	1,676	60.5	972	584	60.1
1990	4,786	1,814	37.9	2,698	1,513	56.1	921	536	58.2
1989	4,627	1,671	36.1	2,624	1,415	53.9	848	491	57.9
1988	4,553	1,740	38.2	2,583	1,452	56.2	861	510	59.2
1987	4,548	1,742	38.3	2,453	1,437	58.6	865	527	60.9
1986	4,552	1,812	39.8	2,386	1,384	58.0	822	489	59.5
1985	4,470	1,730	38.7	2,269	1,336	58.9	771	493	64.0
1984	4,337	1,682	38.8	2,335	1,364	58.4	711	447	62.8
1983	4,210	1,676	39.8	2,244	1,362	60.7	660	418	63.4
1982	4,037	1,584	39.3	2,199	1,401	63.7	613	391	63.8
1981	4,237	1,564	36.9	2,118	1,261	59.5	622	374	60.0
1980	3,995	1,433	35.9	2,171	1,217	56.0	-	-	-
Percent change									
1990-1995	16.0	9.2	-	6.9	1.3	-	39.3	37.1	-
1980-1995	39.0	38.2	-	32.8	26.0	-	-	-	-

Note: (-) means data not available.
Source: Bureau of the Census, unpublished tables from the 1996 Current Population Survey; calculations by New Strategist

CHAPTER

5

Labor Force

❖ **The working woman, once an oddity, is now the norm.**

Only 38 percent of women aged 16 or older were in the labor force in 1960. By 1995, fully 59 percent of women were working or looking for work.

❖ **About three-quarters of working women have full-time jobs.**

The proportion who work full-time peaks at 77 to 79 percent among women aged 25 to 54.

❖ **Most new mothers are back at work within 12 months of the child's birth.**

More than half of women aged 15 to 44 who had a child in 1994 were in the labor force within 12 months of the child's birth.

❖ **Many women still work in pink-collar jobs.**

Forty-two percent of working women are employed in technical, sales, or administrative support positions, compared with only 20 percent of men.

❖ **The higher the educational level, the better the job.**

Forty-one percent of women working as executives, administrators, or managers have a bachelor's degree or more.

❖ **Labor force participation rates among women are projected to rise.**

Between 1995 and 2005, the percentage of women aged 16 or older who are in the labor force will rise from 59 to 62 percent.

❖ **Women may someday be a majority of workers.**

Women will account for 48 percent of the labor force in 2005, up from 46 percent in 1994.

Millions of Women Have Gone to Work

In 1960 only two out of five women were in the labor force.

The working woman, once an oddity, is now the norm. Only 38 percent of women aged 16 or older were in the labor force in 1960. By 1995, fully 59 percent of women were working or looking for work.

In 1960, women aged 45 to 54 were most likely to work—with a labor force participation rate of 50 percent. By 1995, women aged 35 to 44 were most likely to work, with 77 percent in the labor force.

The biggest increase in labor force participation has been in the 25-to-34 age group, when women are most likely to have young children. In 1960, only 36 percent of women aged 25 to 34 were in the labor force. By 1995, this figure had risen to 75 percent.

❖ Working women are now a fact of life, although many businesses have not yet fully adjusted to this new norm. Women's labor force participation drives many consumer trends, not the least of which is the demand for convenience.

Labor Force Participation, 1960 to 1995

(civilian labor force participation rates of women aged 16 or older; selected years 1960 to 1995; percentage point change, 1960-95)

	1995	***1990***	***1980***	***1970***	***1960***	***percentage point change 1960-1995***
Total	58.9%	57.5%	51.5%	43.3%	37.7%	21.2
Aged 16 to 19	52.2	51.8	52.9	44.0	39.3	12.9
Aged 20 to 24	70.3	71.6	68.9	57.7	46.1	24.2
Aged 25 to 34	74.9	73.6	65.5	45.0	36.0	38.9
Aged 35 to 44	77.2	76.5	65.5	51.1	43.4	33.8
Aged 45 to 54	74.4	71.2	59.9	54.4	49.8	24.6
Aged 55 to 64	49.2	45.3	41.3	43.0	37.2	12.0
Aged 65 or older	8.8	8.7	8.1	9.7	10.8	-2.0

Note: The civilian labor force equals the number employed plus the number unemployed.
Source: Bureau of Labor Statistics, Employment and Earnings, *January 1996 and January 1991; and* Historical Statistics of the United States: Colonial Times to 1970, *Part 1, 1975; calculations by New Strategist*

Most Women Work

Fifty-nine percent of women aged 16 or older were in the labor force in 1995.

Among women aged 25 to 49, at least three out of four are in the labor force. The highest labor force participation rate is found among women aged 40 to 44—78 percent of whom are working or looking for work.

Labor force participation rates among women fall sharply after age 54. Seventy-one percent of women in their early 50s are in the labor force, compared with just 60 percent of those aged 55 to 59 and 38 percent of women aged 60 to 64. Only 9 percent of women aged 65 or older are in the labor force.

❖ The women most likely to be in the labor force are also the ones most likely to be raising children. They need convenient service, time-saving products, and innovative ways to simply their lives.

Employment Status of Women by Age, 1995

(employment status of women aged 16 or older by age, 1995; numbers in thousands)

	civilian labor force					not in labor force	
				unemployed			
	total	percent of population	employed	number	percent	total	percent of population
Total women	60,944	58.9%	57,523	3,421	5.6%	42,462	41.1%
Aged 16 to 19	3,729	52.2	3,127	602	16.1	3,415	47.8
Aged 16 and 17	1,557	43.1	1,258	299	19.2	2,057	56.9
Aged 18 and 19	2,172	61.5	1,869	303	14.0	1,359	38.5
Aged 20 to 24	6,349	70.3	5,779	571	9.0	2,680	29.7
Aged 25 to 34	15,528	74.9	14,647	880	5.7	5,191	25.1
Aged 25 to 29	7,259	74.9	6,831	428	5.9	2,439	25.1
Aged 30 to 34	8,269	75.0	7,816	452	5.5	2,753	25.0
Aged 35 to 44	16,562	77.2	15,828	735	4.4	4,891	22.8
Aged 35 to 39	8,559	76.3	8,149	410	4.8	2,652	23.7
Aged 40 to 44	8,003	78.1	7,679	325	4.1	2,240	21.9
Aged 45 to 54	11,801	74.4	11,421	381	3.2	4,061	25.6
Aged 45 to 49	6,894	77.2	6,658	236	3.4	2,031	22.8
Aged 50 to 54	4,907	70.7	4,762	145	3.0	2,030	29.3
Aged 55 to 64	5,356	49.2	5,163	193	3.6	5,524	50.8
Aged 55 to 59	3,380	59.5	3,260	120	3.6	2,301	40.5
Aged 60 to 64	1,976	38.0	1,903	73	3.7	3,222	62.0
Aged 65 or older	1,618	8.8	1,558	60	3.7	16,699	91.2
Aged 65 to 69	930	17.5	894	37	3.9	4,371	82.5
Aged 70 to 74	448	9.3	430	18	4.0	4,390	90.7
Aged 75 or older	240	2.9	235	5	2.1	7,938	97.1

Note: The civilian labor force equals the number employed plus the number unemployed. The civilian population equals the number in the labor force plus the number not in the labor force.
Source: Bureau of Labor Statistics, Employment and Earnings, *January 1996; calculations by New Strategist*

Hispanic Women Are Least Likely to Work

But over half of Hispanic women are in the labor force.

An almost equal proportion of white and black women are in the labor force—59 and 60 percent, respectively, in 1995. Hispanic women are less likely to work, with a labor force participation rate of 53 percent.

By age, there are some differences in participation rates among blacks, Hispanics, and whites. Among women aged 16 to 24, whites are far more likely to be in the labor force than are blacks or Hispanics. For both black and white women aged 25 to 44, about three-quarters are in the labor force. The highest labor force participation rate for Hispanic women is found in the 35-to-44 age group, with 66 percent working or looking for work.

❖ Because women's incomes have become vital to maintaining a middle-class standard of living, labor force participation rates will continue to rise for women in all racial and ethnic groups.

Labor Force Participation by Age, Race, and Hispanic Origin, 1995

(civilian labor force participation rates of women aged 16 or older, by age, race, and Hispanic origin, 1995)

	total	*white*	*black*	*Hispanic*
Total	58.9%	59.0%	59.5%	52.6%
Aged 16 to 19	52.2	55.5	39.8	40.4
Aged 20 to 24	70.3	72.3	63.7	55.9
Aged 25 to 34	74.9	75.8	73.9	61.6
Aged 35 to 44	77.2	77.6	77.3	65.9
Aged 45 to 54	74.4	75.2	70.5	60.5
Aged 55 to 64	49.2	49.5	47.2	37.2
Aged 65 or older	8.8	9.0	7.7	6.6

Note: The civilian labor force equals the number employed plus the number unemployed.
Source: Bureau of Labor Statistics, Employment and Earnings, *January 1996*

Most Women Work Full-Time

About three-quarters of working women have full-time jobs.

The stereotype of the working woman is the wife who earns money for family extras at a part-time job. But this stereotype is wrong. Fully 73 percent of working women work full-time.

Those least likely to work full-time are teenagers. Among employed girls aged 16 and 17, 90 percent work part-time. Part-timers are a 64 percent majority of working women aged 18 and 19. After age 20, however, most working women have full-time jobs. The proportion who work full-time peaks at 77 to 79 percent among women aged 25 to 54.

After age 64, part-time work again becomes the norm. Only one-third of working women aged 65 or older have full-time jobs, while 64 percent are part-timers.

❖ For many women, part-time jobs do not offer enough pay or benefits to justify their time commitment. Full-time work provides more career opportunity, health insurance and other benefits, and a bigger pay check.

Women Working Full- or Part-Time, 1995

(number and percent of women aged 16 or older employed full-time or part-time, 1995; numbers in thousands)

		full-time		part-time	
	total employed	number	percent	number	percent
Total	57,597	41,743	72.5%	15,779	27.4%
Aged 16 and 17	1,257	121	9.6	1,136	90.4
Aged 18 and 19	1,870	679	36.3	1,191	63.7
Aged 20 to 24	5,844	3,842	65.7	1,936	33.1
Aged 25 to 34	14,726	11,498	78.1	3,149	21.4
Aged 35 to 44	15,904	12,240	77.0	3,587	22.6
Aged 45 to 54	11,501	9,127	79.4	2,294	19.9
Aged 55 to 64	5,235	3,699	70.7	1,464	28.0
Aged 65 or older	1,592	536	33.7	1,022	64.2

Source: Bureau of Labor Statistics, unpublished data from the 1995 Current Population Survey; calculations by New Strategist

Mothers Are More Likely to Work Than Other Women

Even most of those with preschoolers work.

Sixty-three percent of women aged 16 or older had some work experience in 1994. Those with children under age 18 were more likely to work than those without children at home. Many of those without children at home are older women who never worked.

Two-thirds of women with children under age 6 had work experience in 1994—30 percent full-time and 37 percent part-time. Among mothers of children aged 6 to 17, 44 percent worked full-time and 34 percent worked part-time.

Divorced mothers are more likely to work than those who are married, widowed, or never married. Eighty-four percent of divorced women with children under age 18 had work experience in 1994, compared with 74 percent of married mothers and 64 percent of widowed mothers. Women with children under age 18 who have never married are least likely to work. Only 61 percent of this group had work experience in 1994.

❖ With most mothers of young children in the workforce, work/family conflicts are not about to disappear. Businesses can benefit by offering workers the flexibility to manage both work and family—as long as the job gets done.

Work Experience by Presence of Children and Marital Status, 1994

(number and percent distribution of women aged 16 or older by presence of children under age 18 at home, marital status, and work experience in 1994; numbers in thousands)

	total women		worked			
	number	percent	total	full-time	part-time	did not work
Total	103,128	100.0%	62.5%	33.1%	29.4%	37.5%
No children <18	67,714	100.0	56.8	30.7	26.1	43.2
With children <18	35,413	100.0	73.3	37.7	35.7	26.7
With children 6-17 only	18,721	100.0	78.7	44.4	34.3	21.3
With children <6	16,692	100.0	67.3	30.1	37.2	32.7
Married	54,902	100.0	65.0	35.3	29.8	35.0
No children <18	29,292	100.0	57.2	33.7	23.5	42.8
With children <18	25,611	100.0	74.0	37.0	37.0	26.0
With children 6-17 only	13,396	100.0	78.9	42.2	36.7	21.1
With children <6	12,215	100.0	68.7	31.4	37.4	31.3
Never married	22,853	100.0	70.3	30.6	39.8	27.3
No children <18	19,190	100.0	72.0	31.4	40.7	28.0
With children <18	3,662	100.0	61.4	26.3	35.1	38.6
With children 6-17 only	1,159	100.0	67.9	38.7	29.2	32.0
With children <6	2,504	100.0	58.3	20.5	37.8	41.7
Divorced	10,262	100.0	76.9	51.4	25.5	23.1
No children <18	6,596	100.0	73.3	49.8	23.4	26.7
With children <18	3,666	100.0	83.5	54.3	29.2	16.5
With children 6-17 only	2,677	100.0	86.1	59.1	27.0	13.9
With children <6	989	100.0	76.3	41.4	35.0	23.7
Widowed	11,080	100.0	19.7	9.4	10.3	80.3
No children <18	10,653	100.0	17.9	8.3	9.6	82.1
With children <18	427	100.0	63.9	35.6	28.3	36.1
With children 6-17 only	347	100.0	65.1	34.6	30.5	34.9
With children <6	80	100.0	58.8	40.0	18.8	41.3

Note: The proportion of women with work experience is greater than the proportion in the labor force because work experience can occur at any time during an entire 12-month period, while labor force participation refers to work during a specific week of a year.
Source: Bureau of Labor Statistics, unpublished tables from the 1995 Current Population Survey; calculations by New Strategist

Hispanic Mothers Are Least Likely to Work

Only half of Hispanic women with preschoolers had work experience in 1994.

Among women with children under age 18 at home, 74 percent of white women and 72 percent of black women had work experience in 1994. But only 58 percent of Hispanic women with children under age 18 worked in 1994.

Similar proportions of black and white women with preschoolers had work experience in 1994 (67 percent of blacks and 68 percent of whites). But Hispanic women with young children were much less likely to work (50 percent). Black women with children under age 18 are most likely to work full-time (42 percent, compared with 37 percent of white women and 29 percent of Hispanic women).

❖ The percentage of Hispanic women with work experience is likely to rise rapidly in the years ahead, eventually closing the gap with white and black women.

Work Experience by Presence of Children, Race, and Hispanic Origin, 1994

(number and percent distribution of women aged 16 or older by presence of children under age 18 at home, race, Hispanic origin, and work experience in 1994; numbers in thousands)

	total		worked			
	number	percent	total	full-time	part-time	did not work
Total	103,128	100.0%	62.5%	33.1%	29.4%	37.5%
No children <18	67,714	100.0	56.8	30.7	26.1	43.2
With children <18	35,413	100.0	73.3	37.7	35.7	26.7
With children 6-17 only	18,721	100.0	78.7	44.4	34.3	21.3
With children <6	16,692	100.0	67.3	30.1	37.2	32.7
White	86,002	100.0	62.8	32.8	30.0	37.2
No children <18	57,466	100.0	57.1	30.6	26.4	42.9
With children <18	28,536	100.0	74.2	37.0	37.2	25.8
With children 6-17 only	15,103	100.0	79.9	43.6	36.2	20.2
With children <6	13,433	100.0	67.9	29.6	38.2	32.1
Black	12,781	100.0	61.6	35.5	26.1	38.4
No children <18	7,710	100.0	55.0	31.0	23.9	45.0
With children <18	5,070	100.0	71.6	42.3	24.0	28.4
With children 6-17 only	2,722	100.0	75.5	49.6	26.8	24.5
With children <6	2,349	100.0	67.0	33.8	33.2	33.0
Hispanic	9,210	100.0	54.6	28.0	26.6	45.4
No children <18	4,836	100.0	51.7	27.1	24.6	48.3
With children <18	4,375	100.0	57.8	29.0	28.8	42.2
With children 6-17 only	1,909	100.0	67.7	37.0	30.7	32.2
With children <6	2,466	100.0	50.0	22.8	27.2	50.0

Note: Numbers will not add to total because Hispanics may be of any race and not all races are shown. The proportion of women with work experience is greater than the proportion in the labor force because work experience can occur at any time during an entire 12-month period, while labor force participation refers to work during a specific week of a year.
Source: Bureau of Labor Statistics, unpublished tables from the 1995 Current Population Survey; calculations by New Strategist

New Mothers Soon Go Back to Work

Only the youngest are likely to stay home.

More than half of women aged 15 to 44 who had a child in 1994 were in the labor force within 12 months of the child's birth. Only the youngest new mothers, under age 20, were not likely to work—39 percent were in the labor force within 12 months of giving birth.

It's much easier to work with only one child to worry about. Fifty-nine percent of women who had their first child in 1994 were in the labor force within 12 months, compared with 49 percent of those who gave birth to their second or subsequent children.

The more education a woman has, the more likely she is to return to work within a year of giving birth. Sixty-six percent of women with at least some college experience were back at work within a year of having a child. Among women who went no further than high school, only 48 percent went back to work that soon.

❖ The more educated the woman, the more she has to lose from dropping out of the labor force while her children are young.

New Mothers in the Labor Force, 1994

(number and percent of women aged 15 to 44 in the labor force in June 1994 who had a child in the past year, by selected characteristics; numbers in thousands)

	number	percent
Total	3,890	53.1%
Aged 15 to 19	397	39.3
Aged 20 to 24	938	51.0
Aged 25 to 29	1,054	54.5
Aged 30 to 44	1,501	57.1
Birth order and age		
First birth	1,647	59.0
Aged 15 to 19	319	40.1
Aged 20 to 24	544	56.5
Aged 25 to 29	429	67.5
Aged 30 to 44	355	69.2
Second or higher birth	2,242	48.9
Aged 15 to 19	78	36.1
Aged 20 to 24	394	43.4
Aged 25 to 29	624	45.6
Aged 30 to 44	1,146	53.4
Educational attainment		
Less than high school	832	33.5
High school graduate only	1,303	48.1
College, 1 or more years	1,754	66.2
No degree	679	59.9
Associate's degree	302	71.1
Bachelor's degree or more	773	69.7
Race		
White	3,107	55.4
Black	567	47.0
Asian	112	37.7
Hispanic origin		
Hispanic	644	37.7
Non-Hispanic	3,245	56.2
Marital status		
Married, husband present	2,798	54.5
Widowed, divorced, separated	199	52.0
Never married	892	49.0

Source: Bureau of the Census, Fertility of American Women: June 1994, *Current Population Reports, P20-482, 1995*

Most Children Have Working Parents

The proportion has grown substantially since 1980.

In 1994, 66 percent of children lived in households where all parents (the custodial parent or both parents) were in the labor force, up from 53 percent in 1980. Preschoolers are almost as likely to have all parents in the household working as are school-aged children (60 compared with 69 percent). In 1980, 44 percent of children under age 6 and 57 percent of those aged 6 to 17 had all parents in the labor force.

The percentage of children with working parents varies only slightly by marital status. In 1980, only 50 percent of children living with married parents had both parents working. By 1994, that proportion had grown to 64 percent—almost equal to the 67 percent of children with single mothers who work.

Labor force participation of white parents has risen more than that of black or Hispanic parents. Black and white children are now about equally likely to have both parents in the labor force (66 percent). Children of Hispanic parents are less likely to have both parents working (52 percent).

❖ The children of working parents are often more independent than those with stay-at-home mothers. They are consumers in their own right, making purchasing decisions and influencing many family expenditures.

Children with Working Parents, 1980 and 1994

(percent of children under age 18 with all parents in the household in the labor force, by age, race, Hispanic origin, and family type of child, 1980 and 1994; percentage point change, 1980-94)

	1994	*1980*	*percentage point change, 1980-94*
Total children	66%	53%	13
Under age 6	60	44	16
Aged 6 to 17	69	57	12
Race and Hispanic origin			
White	66	53	13
Under age 6	60	43	17
Aged 6 to 17	69	57	12
Black	66	58	8
Under age 6	62	53	9
Aged 6 to 17	68	60	8
Hispanic	52	44	8
Under age 6	47	39	8
Aged 6 to 17	56	47	9
Family type			
Married couple	64	50	14
Under age 6	58	42	16
Aged 6 to 17	68	54	14
Single mother	67	64	3
Under age 6	62	55	7
Aged 6 to 17	70	67	3

Source: U.S. Department of Health and Human Services, Trends in the Well-Being of America's Children and Youth: 1996*; calculations by New Strategist*

A Majority of Couples Are Dual Earners

In 56 percent of the nation's married couples, both husband and wife are in the labor force.

Only 22 percent of the nation's married couples are traditional—with only the husband in the labor force. In another 17 percent of couples, neither husband nor wife is in the labor force—most of them retirees. In 6 percent of couples only the wife works.

The dual-earner share peaks at 72 percent among couples aged 30 to 49. It drops to 66 percent among couples aged 50 to 54 and to 54 percent among couples aged 55 to 59. The dual-earner share declines not only because many older women never worked, but also because early retirement begins to affect the statistics.

The greatest diversity is found among couples aged 60 to 64, an age group experiencing the transition from work to retirement. Thirty percent of couples in this age group are dual earners, while 23 percent are traditional. In 16 percent of these couples, only the woman works (in most cases, her husband has retired). In the largest share, 32 percent, neither husband nor wife work.

❖ With dual earners accounting for nearly three out of four couples aged 30 to 49—many of whom also have children—time pressure is intense. These busy couples need ways to save time and simplify their lives.

Married Couples by Labor Force Status of Husbands and Wives, 1995

(number and percent distribution of married-couple households by age of householder and labor force status of husband and wife, 1995; numbers in thousands)

	total married couples	husband and wife in labor force	husband only in labor force	wife only in labor force	husband and wife not in labor force
Total number	53,858	29,999	11,777	3,043	9,039
Under age 20	79	35	42	1	-
Aged 20 to 24	1,553	1,007	476	36	34
Aged 25 to 29	3,959	2,712	1,081	84	82
Aged 30 to 34	6,357	4,561	1,564	143	89
Aged 35 to 39	7,131	5,117	1,730	163	121
Aged 40 to 44	6,788	4,903	1,533	228	124
Aged 45 to 49	6,128	4,429	1,300	241	158
Aged 50 to 54	5,025	3,331	1,185	314	195
Aged 55 to 59	3,934	2,106	1,074	375	379
Aged 60 to 64	3,618	1,082	825	574	1,138
Aged 65 or older	9,286	717	968	884	6,719
Percent	100.0%	55.7%	21.9%	5.7%	16.8%
Under age 20	100.0	44.3	53.2	1.3	-
Aged 20 to 24	100.0	64.8	30.7	2.3	2.2
Aged 25 to 29	100.0	68.5	27.3	2.1	2.1
Aged 30 to 34	100.0	71.7	24.6	2.2	1.4
Aged 35 to 39	100.0	71.8	24.3	2.3	1.7
Aged 40 to 44	100.0	72.2	22.6	3.4	1.8
Aged 45 to 49	100.0	72.3	21.2	3.9	2.6
Aged 50 to 54	100.0	66.3	23.6	6.2	3.9
Aged 55 to 59	100.0	53.5	27.3	9.5	9.6
Aged 60 to 64	100.0	29.9	22.8	15.9	31.5
Aged 65 or older	100.0	7.7	10.4	9.5	72.4

Source: Bureau of the Census, unpublished tables from the 1995 Current Population Survey; calculations by New Strategist

Job Tenure Is Stable for Women

But tenure fell sharply for men.

Job tenure has changed little for women since 1983, while it has plummeted for men, according to the Employee Benefit Research Institute. The number of years working women have been with their current employer has been stable because of women's increasing attachment to the labor force. Women are less likely to quit working after having children, boosting their years on the job. And as more women regard their work as a career rather than "just a job," they are likely to remain with their employers longer.

In contrast to women, job tenure has dropped sharply for men. Since 1983, when job tenure peaked for all but the youngest men, the steepest declines in job tenure have been among the oldest male workers. Men aged 55 to 64 had been with their current employer a median of 17 years in 1983. By 1996, job tenure for this age group had fallen to 12 years—a 29 percent drop. Job tenure fell by more than three years for men aged 45 to 54, and by nearly two years for men aged 25 to 34.

❖ Job tenure can decline when workers switch jobs or when they are laid off and forced to find new jobs. The fact that job tenure has declined the most among older men points toward involuntary lay-offs as the biggest factor.

❖ Working women have also faced lay-offs. But while some have been forced to leave their jobs, others have been on the job longer because of women's growing commitment to the labor force. Consequently, women's job tenure has been stable.

Job Tenure by Age and Sex, 1983 to 1996

(median number of years workers aged 25 to 64 have been with their current employer by sex and age; and change in years 1983 to 1996)

	1996	1991	1987	1983	change 1983-96
Women					
Aged 25 to 34	2.7	3.2	3.1	3.1	-0.4
Aged 35 to 44	5.0	5.0	4.9	4.6	0.4
Aged 45 to 54	7.0	7.3	7.3	6.9	0.1
Aged 55 to 64	10.0	10.4	10.3	10.5	-0.5
Men					
Aged 25 to 34	3.0	3.7	3.7	3.4	-0.4
Aged 35 to 44	6.0	7.2	7.6	7.7	-1.7
Aged 45 to 54	10.0	12.2	12.3	13.4	-3.4
Aged 55 to 64	12.0	15.5	15.7	17.0	-5.0

Source: Employee Benefit Research Institute, 1996 Data on the Mobility of American Workers, *1997*

Women's Occupations Differ from Men's

Many women still work in pink-collar jobs.

Although women are in the labor force in larger numbers than ever before, they are still concentrated in pink-collar jobs. Forty-two percent of working women are employed in technical, sales, or administrative support positions, compared with only 20 percent of men. One-quarter of women, but only 6 percent of men, are administrative support workers.

Men still dominate the skilled trades. Eighteen percent of men, but only 2 percent of women, work in precision production, craft, and repair occupations. Twenty percent of men are operators, fabricators, or laborers, compared with only 8 percent of women.

Women are slightly more likely than men to work in managerial or professional specialty occupations (29 percent of women, compared with 27 percent of men). They are somewhat less likely than men to work in executive, administrative, or management positions. Fifteen percent of men hold these jobs, compared with 13 percent of women.

❖ The earnings gap between men and women is due in part to their different occupations. Women are clustered in low-paying support and service jobs, while men are more likely to hold jobs in the skilled trades or upper-level management.

Occupation by Sex, 1995

(total number and percent distribution of employed persons aged 16 or older, by occupation and sex, 1995; numbers in thousands)

	total	*women*	*men*
Total employed, number	124,900	57,523	67,377
Total employed, percent	100.0%	100.0%	100.0%
Managerial and professional specialty	28.3	29.4	27.3
Executive, administrative, and managerial	13.8	12.8	14.6
Professional specialty	14.5	16.7	12.7
Technical, sales, and administrative support	30.0	41.9	19.8
Technicians and related support	3.1	3.5	2.8
Sales occupations	12.1	13.0	11.3
Administrative support, including clerical	14.7	25.4	5.6
Service occupations	13.6	17.7	10.1
Private household	0.7	1.4	0.1
Protective service	1.8	0.6	2.8
Service, except private household and protective	11.1	15.7	7.2
Precision production, craft, and repair	10.8	2.1	18.3
Operators, fabricators, and laborers	14.5	7.6	20.3
Machine operators, assemblers, and inspectors	6.3	5.1	7.4
Transportation and material moving occupations	4.1	0.9	6.9
Handlers, equipment cleaners, helpers, and laborers	4.0	1.7	6.0
Farming, forestry, and fishing	2.9	1.3	4.3

Source: Bureau of Labor Statistics, Employment and Earnings, *January 1996; calculations by New Strategist*

One-Third of Women Managers Are Aged 35 to 44

Women managers aged 25 to 34 outnumber those aged 45 to 54, but not for long.

Of the nation's 58 million working women, 7 million are executives, administrators, or managers. But the largest number (15 million) are still found in support occupations—such as secretaries and clerks.

Among women under age 20, one in five is a cashier and 22 percent are in food service. These are the entry-level jobs common to high school and college students. Women aged 20 to 24 are most likely to be in administrative support jobs (27 percent).

A large portion of women aged 25 to 54 are in managerial or professional specialty occupations. From 18 to 20 percent work in professional specialty jobs such as nursing or teaching. From 14 to 15 percent are executives, administrators, or managers.

Women aged 35 to 44 account for one-third of all women in executive, administrative, or managerial jobs. This is largely an artifact of demographics: there are more women in this age group than in any other. But it also reflects the higher education and career orientation of baby-boom women.

❖ As baby-boom women age, the number of women executives and managers in the 45-to-54 age group will far surpass those in the 25-to-34 age group.

Women's Occupations by Age, 1995

(number of employed women aged 16 or older by selected occupation and age, 1995; numbers in thousands)

	total	16 to 19	20 to 24	25 to 34	35 to 44	45 to 54	55 to 64	65 or older
Total employed women	57,523	3,127	5,779	14,647	15,828	11,421	5,163	1,558
Managerial & professional specialty	16,940	150	983	4,592	5,468	3,975	1,429	342
Executive, administrative & managerial	7,346	49	391	1,974	2,362	1,742	663	166
Professional specialty	9,593	101	593	2,619	3,106	2,233	766	176
Health assessment & treating	2,369	4	94	649	857	531	202	31
Registered nurses	1,841	1	59	437	699	448	169	28
Teachers, except postsecondary	3,365	45	220	828	1,018	928	271	54
Elementary school	1,461	3	76	349	441	450	124	19
Technicians, sales & administrative support	24,107	1,567	2,887	6,134	6,186	4,525	2,118	692
Technicians & related support	2,009	20	204	617	664	366	124	15
Health technologists & technicians	1,314	11	120	381	456	249	84	12
Sales	7,485	1,026	1,100	1,738	1,590	1,182	600	249
Supervisors & proprietors	1,741	22	182	497	487	377	136	41
Sales workers, retail & personal services	4,336	976	815	833	703	524	333	152
Cashiers	2,160	635	429	406	308	206	123	51
Administrative support, including clerical	14,613	521	1,584	3,779	3,931	2,977	1,394	427
Secretaries, stenographers & typists	4,015	100	348	1,012	1,083	911	443	117
Information clerks	1,648	130	270	418	341	265	162	62
Financial records processing	2,083	26	147	521	564	457	255	113

(continued)

(continued from previous page)

	total	16 to 19	20 to 24	25 to 34	35 to 44	45 to 54	55 to 64	65 or older
Service	10,155	1,133	1,323	2,400	2,362	1,634	958	344
Private household	784	97	87	141	170	124	111	54
Protective services	356	31	43	102	91	51	28	10
Other service	9,015	1,006	1,193	2,157	2,101	1,459	820	279
Food preparation and service	3,381	701	567	745	589	414	264	100
Health services	2,043	80	268	513	528	393	208	54
Nurse aides, orderlies, & attendants	1,571	51	199	367	406	324	176	49
Precision production, craft and repair	1,201	30	91	295	393	259	111	23
Mechanics and repairers	175	3	12	50	64	36	9	1
Construction trades	120	9	11	29	39	23	8	2
Extractive occupations	5	0	-	1	2	2	-	-
Precision production	902	18	68	215	288	198	95	20
Operators, fabricators & laborers	4,393	203	447	1,091	1,231	883	448	89
Machine operators, assemblers & inspectors	2,949	87	292	729	843	634	312	51
Transport and material moving	490	12	30	122	152	113	47	14
Handlers, equipment cleaners, helpers & laborers	955	103	126	241	235	137	88	25
Farming, forestry & fishing	726	44	47	135	188	145	99	68
Farm operators & managers	366	6	5	44	98	87	71	55
Other agricultural & related occupations	351	37	41	89	89	55	27	12
Forestry and logging	5	0	1	1	1	1	0	1
Fishing, hunting, and trapping	4	0	0	1	0	2	0	-

Note: Numbers will not add to total because not all occupations are shown. (-) means sample is too small to make a reliable estimate.
Source: Bureau of Labor Statistics, unpublished tables from the 1995 Current Population Survey

Distribution of Women by Occupation and Age, 1995

(percent distribution of employed women aged 16 or older by selected occupation and age, 1995)

	total	16 to 19	20 to 24	25 to 34	35 to 44	45 to 54	55 to 64	65 or older
Total employed women	100.0%	100.0%	100.0%	100.0%	100.0%	100.0%	100.0%	100.0%
Managerial & professional specialty	29.4	4.8	17.0	31.4	34.5	34.8	27.7	22.0
Executive, administrative & managerial	12.8	1.6	6.8	13.5	14.9	15.3	12.8	10.7
Professional specialty	16.7	3.2	10.3	17.9	19.6	19.6	14.8	11.3
Health assessment & treating	4.1	0.1	1.6	4.4	5.4	4.6	3.9	2.0
Registered nurses	3.2	-	1.0	3.0	4.4	3.9	3.3	1.8
Teachers, except postsecondary	5.8	1.4	3.8	5.7	6.4	8.1	5.2	3.5
Elementary school	2.5	0.1	1.3	2.4	2.8	3.9	2.4	1.2
Technicians, sales & administrative support	41.9	50.1	50.0	41.9	39.1	39.6	41.0	44.4
Technicians & related support	3.5	0.6	3.5	4.2	4.2	3.2	2.4	1.0
Health technologists & technicians	2.3	0.4	2.1	2.6	2.9	2.2	1.6	0.8
Sales	13.0	32.8	19.0	11.9	10.0	10.3	11.6	16.0
Supervisors & proprietors	3.0	0.7	3.1	3.4	3.1	3.3	2.6	2.6
Sales workers, retail & personal services	7.5	31.2	14.1	5.7	4.4	4.6	6.4	9.8
Cashiers	3.8	20.3	7.4	2.8	1.9	1.8	2.4	3.3
Administrative support, including clerical	25.4	16.7	27.4	25.8	24.8	26.1	27.0	27.4
Secretaries, stenographers & typists	7.0	3.2	6.0	6.9	6.8	8.0	8.6	7.5
Information clerks	2.9	4.2	4.7	2.9	2.2	2.3	3.1	4.0
Financial records processing	3.6	0.8	2.5	3.6	3.6	4.0	4.9	7.3

(continued)

(continued from previous page)

	total	16 to 19	20 to 24	25 to 34	35 to 44	45 to 54	55 to 64	65 or older
Service	17.7%	36.2%	22.9%	16.4%	14.9%	14.3%	18.6%	22.1%
Private household	1.4	3.1	1.5	1.0	1.1	1.1	2.1	3.5
Protective services	0.6	1.0	0.7	0.7	0.6	0.4	0.5	0.6
Other service	15.7	32.2	20.6	14.7	13.3	12.8	15.9	17.9
Food preparation and service	5.9	22.4	9.8	5.1	3.7	3.6	5.1	6.4
Health services	3.6	2.6	4.6	3.5	3.3	3.4	4.0	3.5
Nurse aides, orderlies, & attendants	2.7	1.6	3.4	2.5	2.6	2.8	3.4	3.1
Precision production, craft and repair	2.1	1.0	1.6	2.0	2.5	2.3	2.1	1.5
Mechanics and repairers	0.3	0.1	0.2	0.3	0.4	0.3	0.2	0.1
Construction trades	0.2	0.3	0.2	0.2	0.2	0.2	0.2	0.1
Extractive occupations	-	-	-	-	-	-	-	-
Precision production	1.6	0.6	1.2	1.5	1.8	1.7	1.8	1.3
Operators, fabricators & laborers	7.6	6.5	7.7	7.4	7.8	7.7	8.7	5.7
Machine operators, assemblers & inspectors	5.1	2.8	5.1	5.0	5.3	5.6	6.0	3.3
Transport and material moving	0.9	0.4	0.5	0.8	1.0	1.0	0.9	0.9
Handlers, equip. cleaners, helpers & laborers	1.7	3.3	2.2	1.6	1.5	1.2	1.7	1.6
Farming, forestry & fishing	1.3	1.4	0.8	0.9	1.2	1.3	1.9	4.4
Farm operators & managers	0.6	0.2	0.1	0.3	0.6	0.8	1.4	3.5
Other agricultural & related occupations	0.6	1.2	0.7	0.6	0.6	0.5	0.5	0.8
Forestry and logging	-	-	-	-	-	-	-	0.1
Fishing, hunting, and trapping	-	-	-	-	-	-	-	-

Note: Numbers will not add to total because not all occupations are shown. (-) means sample is too small to make a reliable estimate or share is below 0.5 percent.
Source: Bureau of Labor Statistics, unpublished tables from the 1995 Current Population Survey; calculations by New Strategist

Age Distribution of Women by Occupation, 1995

(percent distribution of employed women aged 16 or older by selected occupation and age, 1995)

	total	16 to 19	20 to 24	25 to 34	35 to 44	45 to 54	55 to 64	65+
Total employed women	100.0%	5.4%	10.0%	25.5%	27.5%	19.9%	9.0%	2.7%
Managerial & professional specialty	100.0	0.9	5.8	27.1	32.3	23.5	8.4	2.0
Executive, administrators & managerial	100.0	0.7	5.3	26.9	32.2	23.7	9.0	2.3
Professional specialty	100.0	1.1	6.2	27.3	32.4	23.3	8.0	1.8
Health assessment & treating	100.0	0.2	4.0	27.4	36.2	22.4	8.5	1.3
Registered nurses	100.0	0.1	3.2	23.7	38.0	24.3	9.2	1.5
Teachers, except postsecondary	100.0	1.3	6.5	24.6	30.3	27.6	8.1	1.6
Elementary school	100.0	0.2	5.2	23.9	30.2	30.8	8.5	1.3
Technicians, sales & administrative support	100.0	6.5	12.0	25.4	25.7	18.8	8.8	2.9
Technicians & related support	100.0	1.0	10.2	30.7	33.1	18.2	6.2	0.7
Health technologists & technicians	100.0	0.8	9.1	29.0	34.7	18.9	6.4	0.9
Sales	100.0	13.7	14.7	23.2	21.2	15.8	8.0	3.3
Supervisors & proprietors	100.0	1.3	10.5	28.5	28.0	21.7	7.8	2.4
Sales workers, retail & personal services	100.0	22.5	18.8	19.2	16.2	12.1	7.7	3.5
Cashiers	100.0	29.4	19.9	18.8	14.3	9.5	5.7	2.4
Administrative support, including clerical	100.0	3.6	10.8	25.9	26.9	20.4	9.5	2.9
Secretaries, stenographers & typists	100.0	2.5	8.7	25.2	27.0	22.7	11.0	2.9
Information clerks	100.0	7.9	16.4	25.4	20.7	16.1	9.8	3.8
Financial records processing	100.0	1.2	7.1	25.0	27.1	21.9	12.2	5.4

(continued)

(continued from previous page)

	total	16 to 19	20 to 24	25 to 34	35 to 44	45 to 54	55 to 64	65 or older
Service	100.0%	11.2%	13.0%	23.6%	23.3%	16.1%	9.4%	3.4%
Private household	100.0	12.4	11.1	18.0	21.7	15.8	14.2	6.9
Protective services	100.0	8.7	12.1	28.7	25.6	14.3	7.9	2.8
Other service	100.0	11.2	13.2	23.9	23.3	16.2	9.1	3.1
Food preparation and service	100.0	20.7	16.8	22.0	17.4	12.2	7.8	3.0
Health services	100.0	3.9	13.1	25.1	25.8	19.2	10.2	2.6
Nurse aides, orderlies, & attendants	100.0	3.2	12.7	23.4	25.8	20.6	11.2	3.1
Precision production, craft and repair	100.0	2.5	7.6	24.6	32.7	21.6	9.2	1.9
Mechanics and repairers	100.0	1.7	6.9	28.6	36.6	20.6	5.1	0.6
Construction trades	100.0	7.5	9.2	24.2	32.5	19.2	6.7	1.7
Extractive occupations	100.0	-	-	20.0	40.0	40.0	-	-
Precision production	100.0	2.0	7.5	23.8	31.9	22.0	10.5	2.2
Operators, fabricators & laborers	100.0	4.6	10.2	24.8	28.0	20.1	10.2	2.0
Machine operators, assemblers & inspectors	100.0	3.0	9.9	24.7	28.6	21.5	10.6	1.7
Transport and material moving	100.0	2.4	6.1	24.9	31.0	23.1	9.6	2.9
Handlers, equipment cleaners, helpers & laborers	100.0	10.8	13.2	25.2	24.6	14.3	9.2	2.6
Farming, forestry & fishing	100.0	6.1	6.5	18.6	25.9	20.0	13.6	9.4
Farm operators & managers	100.0	1.6	1.4	12.0	26.8	23.8	19.4	15.0
Other agricultural & related occupations	100.0	10.5	11.7	25.4	25.4	15.7	7.7	3.4
Forestry and logging	100.0	-	20.0	20.0	20.0	20.0	-	20.0
Fishing, hunting, and trapping	100.0	-	-	25.0	-	50.0	-	-

Note: (-) means sample is too small to make a reliable estimate or share is below 0.5 percent.
Source: Bureau of Labor Statistics, unpublished tables from the 1995 Current Population Survey; calculations by New Strategist

Educated Women Have Better Jobs

College is the ticket into management and professional jobs.

Among employed women aged 25 to 64, 27 percent have a bachelor's degree, 20 percent have some college but no degree, 34 percent went no further than high school, and 9 percent did not graduate from high school.

The higher the educational level, the better the job. Among women working as executives, administrators, and managers, 41 percent have a bachelor's degree or more. Among those in professional specialty jobs (including teaching and nursing), 40 percent have a bachelor's degree and another 32 percent have an advanced degree.

In most occupations, younger women have higher levels of education than do older women. Among women working in administrative support occupations, for example, 11 percent of those aged 45 to 64 compared with 14 percent of those aged 25 to 34 have a bachelor's degree.

❖ Now that more than half of women who graduate from high school attend college, the pool of college-educated women is growing. Well-educated women will push those with less education into lower-paying jobs.

Occupation by Age and Education, 1995

(total number and percent distribution of employed women aged 25 to 64 by age, occupation, and educational attainment, 1995; numbers in thousands)

	total								
	number	percent	less than high school	high school graduate only	some college, no degree	associate's degree	bachelor's degree only	advanced degree	bachelor's degree or more
Total employed, aged 25 to 64	46,925	100.0%	8.7%	34.0%	20.1%	10.1%	18.4%	8.8%	27.1%
Executive, administrative, and managerial	6,496	100.0	2.5	24.3	21.5	10.7	28.8	12.2	41.0
Professional specialty	8,916	100.0	0.8	7.0	7.9	12.1	40.3	31.9	72.2
Technicians and related support	1,787	100.0	1.0	19.5	26.0	25.9	24.0	3.8	27.7
Sales	4,895	100.0	8.0	42.7	21.4	8.2	17.1	2.7	19.7
Administrative support, including clerical	12,102	100.0	3.1	43.5	29.8	11.5	10.6	1.5	12.1
Private household	564	100.0	38.8	41.3	8.5	5.9	4.6	0.9	5.6
Other service	6,994	100.0	20.8	46.4	20.2	6.6	5.2	0.8	5.9
Farming, forestry, and fishing	517	100.0	21.9	42.6	18.8	4.4	9.7	2.9	12.4
Precision production, craft, and repair	1,052	100.0	18.3	51.7	18.2	5.8	4.3	1.8	6.1
Machine operators, assemblers, and inspectors	2,482	100.0	32.6	50.9	10.3	3.1	3.1	0.1	3.2
Transportation and material moving	469	100.0	16.6	51.6	19.6	7.5	4.5	-	4.5
Handlers, equipment cleaners, helpers, laborers	650	100.0	28.5	48.5	16.0	2.6	2.9	1.4	4.3
Aged 25 to 34	14,580	100.0	7.3	31.7	20.4	11.0	23.3	6.2	29.6
Executive, administrative, and managerial	1,940	100.0	1.8	19.5	17.7	11.2	41.2	8.6	49.8
Professional specialty	2,627	100.0	0.9	6.9	6.4	11.5	50.6	23.8	74.4
Technicians and related support	634	100.0	1.1	17.7	24.9	26.2	26.8	3.3	30.2
Sales	1,689	100.0	8.6	35.3	22.9	8.6	22.4	2.2	24.7

(continued)

(continued from previous page)

	total		less than high school	high school graduate only	some college, no degree	associate's degree	bachelor's degree only	advanced degree	bachelor's degree or more
	number	percent							
Administrative support, including clerical	3,764	100.0%	2.4%	40.0%	29.8%	13.3%	13.3%	1.2%	14.4%
Private household	160	100.0	36.9	35.0	11.9	7.5	8.8	1.3	9.6
Other service	2,272	100.0	16.5	44.6	23.8	8.3	6.5	0.2	6.7
Farming, forestry, and fishing	123	100.0	26.8	45.5	16.3	2.4	8.9	0.0	8.6
Precision production, craft, and repair	292	100.0	11.6	52.1	20.9	6.8	7.2	1.4	8.5
Machine operators, assemblers, and inspectors	710	100.0	28.5	52.1	12.8	4.1	2.4	0.1	2.5
Transportation and material moving	126	100.0	7.1	58.7	24.6	4.8	4.0	-	3.9
Handlers, equipment cleaners, helpers, laborers	242	100.0	22.3	52.1	17.4	4.1	3.3	0.8	4.3
Aged 35 to 44	15,756	100.0	7.4	32.9	20.7	11.2	18.1	9.8	27.9
Executive, administrative, and managerial	2,192	100.0	2.2	24.6	22.5	10.3	27.7	12.6	40.3
Professional specialty	3,225	100.0	0.5	6.2	8.8	12.5	38.9	33.0	71.9
Technicians and related support	691	100.0	0.3	16.2	23.0	31.4	24.3	4.8	29.1
Sales	1,468	100.0	7.0	43.4	21.2	9.1	15.8	3.5	19.3
Administrative support, including clerical	3,990	100.0	2.7	41.3	31.7	12.9	9.7	1.8	11.5
Private household	165	100.0	36.4	50.3	6.1	4.8	-	2.4	2.3
Other service	2,260	100.0	18.1	46.6	21.4	7.7	5.0	1.2	6.2
Farming, forestry, and fishing	181	100.0	17.7	42.0	15.5	7.7	14.9	1.7	16.6
Precision production, craft, and repair	392	100.0	11.7	57.4	19.6	6.6	2.0	2.6	4.6
Machine operators, assemblers, and inspectors	816	100.0	31.3	51.8	8.3	3.7	4.8	-	4.7
Transportation and material moving	184	100.0	16.8	48.9	21.7	8.7	3.8	-	4.0
Handlers, equipment cleaners, helpers, laborers	192	100.0	26.0	47.9	19.8	-	2.6	3.6	6.1

(continued)

(continued from previous page)

	total		less than high school	high school graduate only	some college, no degree	associate's degree	bachelor's degree only	advanced degree	bachelor's degree or more
	number	percent							
Aged 45 to 64	16,590	100.0%	11.1%	37.1%	19.2%	8.3%	14.3%	10.0%	24.3%
Executive, administrative, and managerial	2,363	100.0	3.2	27.9	23.7	10.7	19.7	14.8	34.5
Professional specialty	3,064	100.0	1.0	7.8	8.2	12.3	33.0	37.6	70.7
Technicians and related support	462	100.0	1.7	27.1	31.8	17.3	19.3	3.0	22.2
Sales	1,737	100.0	8.3	49.2	20.3	6.9	12.8	2.4	15.2
Administrative support, including clerical	4,349	100.0	4.0	48.5	28.0	8.7	9.2	1.6	10.8
Private household	239	100.0	41.8	39.3	7.9	5.4	5.0	-	5.1
Other service	2,463	100.0	27.3	47.9	15.8	4.1	4.1	0.9	4.9
Farming, forestry, and fishing	214	100.0	21.5	41.1	22.9	2.8	5.6	5.1	11.1
Precision production, craft, and repair	367	100.0	30.2	45.5	14.4	3.8	4.6	1.4	5.7
Machine operators, assemblers, and inspectors	957	100.0	36.5	49.0	10.1	1.9	2.3	0.1	2.4
Transportation and material moving	159	100.0	24.5	49.1	13.2	8.2	5.7	-	5.4
Handlers, equipment cleaners, helpers, laborers	216	100.0	38.4	44.4	10.6	3.2	2.8	-	2.8

Note: (-) means sample is too small to make a reliable estimate or share is less than 0.5 percent.
Source: Bureau of the Census, Educational Attainment in the United States: March 1995, *PPL-48, 1996; calculations by New Strategist*

Few Women Are Self-Employed

Only 7 percent of working women work for themselves.

Of the 53 million women working in nonagricultural occupations, only 3 million—or 7 percent—are self-employed.

The proportion of working women who are self-employed rises with age. Among workers under age 25, only about 2 percent are self-employed. This share rises to 17 percent among working women aged 65 or older.

❖ As technology allows workers to do more from home, expect to see an increase in the proportion of women who are self-employed.

Self-Employment by Age, 1995

(total number of employed women aged 16 or older in nonagricultural industries, number and percent whose longest job was self-employment, 1995; numbers in thousands)

	total employed	self-employed number	self-employed percent
Total	53,115	3,440	6.5%
Aged 16 to 19	3,019	51	1.7
Aged 20 to 24	5,607	112	2.0
Aged 25 to 34	13,740	716	5.2
Aged 35 to 44	14,529	1,039	7.2
Aged 45 to 54	10,381	846	8.1
Aged 55 to 64	4,581	458	10.0
Aged 65 or older	1,258	219	17.4

Source: Bureau of Labor Statistics, Employment and Earnings, *January 1996; calculations by New Strategist*

Over 4 Million Women Are Alternative Workers

Eight percent of employed women do not work at traditional jobs.

In the first survey of what it terms "alternative" work arrangements, the Bureau of Labor Statistics finds 1 in 12 working women in nontraditional jobs—defined as independent contractors, on-call workers, workers for temporary-help agencies, or workers provided by a contract firm. These workers are considered alternative because they are not employees of the organization for whom they perform their services, nor do they necessarily work standard schedules.

Most alternative workers are independent contractors—freelancers, consultants, real estate agents, and others who obtain customers on their own for whom they provide a product or service. Many independent contractors are self-employed. Among women, the likelihood of being an independent contractor increases with age, to a peak of 10 percent among women aged 65 or older. Among employed men, independent contracting peaks at 20 percent for those aged 65 or older.

❖ Although many think the number of alternative workers is increasing, trend data to support this claim will not be available until the bureau again surveys alternative workers.

Women in Alternative Work Arrangements, 1995

(total number of alternative workers aged 16 or older, number of women alternative workers, and percent of employed women who are alternative workers by age and type of alternative work, 1995; numbers in thousands)

	total alternative workers	independent contractors	on-call workers	temporary-help agency workers	workers provided by contract firms
Total, number	12,110	8,309	1,968	1,181	652
Total women, number	4,542	2,717	1,015	624	186
Percent with alternative jobs					
Total women	8.0%	4.8%	1.8%	1.1%	0.3%
Aged 16 to 19	5.8	1.9	2.7	1.0	0.2
Aged 20 to 24	5.1	1.1	1.6	1.7	0.7
Aged 25 to 34	7.6	4.1	1.7	1.4	0.4
Aged 35 to 44	7.8	5.1	1.5	1.0	0.2
Aged 45 to 54	9.1	6.3	1.6	0.8	0.4
Aged 55 to 64	9.6	6.5	2.2	0.7	0.2
Aged 65 or older	15.0	10.1	4.3	0.6	-

Note: Independent contractors are wage and salary workers who obtain customers on their own to provide a product or service. The self-employed are included, except those who are incorporated. On-call workers are in a pool of workers who are only called to work as needed, such as substitute teachers and construction workers supplied by a union hiring hall. Temporary help agency workers are those who said they are paid by a temporary help agency. Workers provided by contract firms are those employed by a company that provides employees or their services to others under contract, such as security, landscaping and computer programming.
Source: Bureau of Labor Statistics, Monthly Labor Review, *October 1996*

Few Women Are in Labor Unions

Unions are most popular among 45-to-54-year-olds.

Fourteen percent of employed women wage and salary workers are represented by unions. Twelve percent say they are union members.

Union representation is most common among women aged 45 to 54. One out of five wage and salary workers in this age group is represented by a union. Among women aged 35 to 44 and those aged 55 to 64, 17 percent are represented by unions.

Only 12 percent of women aged 25 to 34 are represented by unions. Women aged 16 to 24 are least likely to be represented by unions, at just 6 percent.

❖ Few employed women are unionized because traditional labor unions are concentrated in male-dominated industries and have ignored many of women's concerns, such as flexitime and family leave.

Union Membership by Age, 1995

(number and percent of employed women wage and salary workers aged 16 or older by age and union affiliation, 1995; numbers in thousands)

	total employed	represented by unions*		members of unions**	
		number	percent	number	percent
Total	52,369	7,479	14.3%	6,430	12.3%
Aged 16 to 24	8,673	478	5.5	382	4.4
Aged 25 to 34	13,667	1,621	11.9	1,377	10.1
Aged 35 to 44	14,295	2,423	16.9	2,085	14.6
Aged 45 to 54	10,101	2,078	20.6	1,804	17.9
Aged 55 to 64	4,423	771	17.4	685	15.5
Aged 65 or older	1,210	108	8.9	98	8.1

**Members of a labor union or an employee association similar to a union as well as workers who report no union affiliation but whose jobs are covered by a union or an employee association contract.*
*** Members of a labor union or an employee association similar to a union.*
Source: Bureau of Labor Statistics, Employment and Earnings, *January 1996*

More Women Will Be Going to Work

Labor force participation rates among women are projected to rise.

Women's labor force participation rates, which have been rising for decades, are projected to continue upward. Between 1995 and 2005, the percentage of women aged 16 or older who are in the labor force will rise by an additional 3 percentage points, from 59 to 62 percent.

The largest increases in labor force participation will be found among women aged 45 to 64. As the baby-boom generation fills this age group, the participation rate will rise by 6 to 7 percentage points. In 1995, a 49 percent minority of women aged 55 to 64 were in the labor force. The share will rise to a 57 percent majority by 2005.

The smallest increase in labor force participation rates is projected for women aged 16 to 24 because an increasing proportion will be going to college.

❖ Women's labor force participation rates are close to peaking—especially in the age groups already filled with baby boomers.

Labor Force Participation, 1995 and 2005

(labor force participation rates for women aged 16 or older by age, 1995 and 2005; percentage point change, 1995 to 2005)

	1995	2005	percentage point change 1995 to 2005
Total	58.9%	61.7%	2.8
Aged 16 to 19	52.2	50.7	-1.5
Aged 20 to 24	70.3	70.7	0.4
Aged 25 to 34	74.9	76.4	1.5
Aged 35 to 44	77.2	80.0	2.8
Aged 45 to 54	74.4	80.7	6.3
Aged 55 to 64	49.2	56.6	7.4
Aged 65 or older	8.8	10.2	1.4

Source: Bureau of Labor Statistics, Monthly Labor Review, *November 1995; and* Employment and Earnings, *January 1996; calculations by New Strategist*

Women Will Be Nearly Half of Workers in 2005

Woman may someday be a majority of workers.

Between 1994 and 2005, new entrants to the labor force will be almost evenly divided between men and women. But men will be leaving the labor force in greater numbers. Consequently, women will account for 48 percent of the labor force in 2005, up from 46 percent in 1994.

Non-Hispanic white women made up 35 percent of the labor force in 1994, a proportion that will remain about the same through 2005. Non-Hispanic white men will account for only 38 percent of workers in 2005, down from 41 percent in 1994 as minority workers gain share.

❖ As women's presence in the work force grows, employers must accommodate their needs. Women workers want the chance to advance in their careers, as well as flexible schedules, health insurance, and pension benefits.

Workers Entering and Leaving the Labor Force, 1994 to 2005

(number of persons aged 16 or older in the civilian labor force and projected entrants and leavers, by sex, race, and Hispanic origin, 1994 and 2005; numbers in thousands)

	total labor force, 1994	entrants 1994-2005	leavers 1994-2005	total labor force, 2005
TOTAL NUMBER	131,051	39,343	23,289	147,106
Men	70,814	19,720	13,691	76,842
Women	60,238	19,624	9,598	70,263
White, non-Hispanic	100,463	26,058	18,177	108,345
Men	54,306	12,937	10,814	56,429
Women	46,157	13,122	7,363	51,916
Black, non-Hispanic	14,304	4,871	2,783	16,392
Men	6,981	2,314	1,512	7,783
Women	7,323	2,557	1,271	8,609
Hispanic	11,974	6,085	1,729	16,330
Men	7,210	3,321	1,039	9,492
Women	4,764	2,765	690	6,838
Asian and other, non-Hispanic	4,310	2,329	600	6,039
Men	2,317	1,148	326	3,139
Women	1,994	1,180	274	2,900
TOTAL PERCENT	100.0%	100.0%	100.0%	100.0%
Men	54.0	50.1	58.8	52.2
Women	46.0	49.9	41.2	47.8
White, non-Hispanic	76.7	66.2	78.0	73.7
Men	41.4	32.9	46.4	38.4
Women	35.2	33.4	31.6	35.3
Black, non-Hispanic	10.9	12.4	12.0	11.1
Men	5.3	5.9	6.5	5.3
Women	5.6	6.5	5.5	5.9
Hispanic	9.1	15.5	7.4	11.1
Men	5.5	8.4	4.5	6.5
Women	3.6	7.0	3.0	4.6
Asian and other, non-Hispanic	3.3	5.9	2.6	4.1
Men	1.8	2.9	1.4	2.1
Women	1.5	3.0	1.2	2.0

Note: Hispanics may be of any race.
Source: Bureau of Labor Statistics, Monthly Labor Review, *November 1995*

Few Women Want to Work Full-Time

But most men don't want full-time jobs, either.

Women are almost evenly divided between those who want to work for pay and those who would prefer unpaid work as homemakers or volunteers—if they didn't need the money their job provides. Most men (61 percent) say they would prefer paid work. But men are not that much more ambitious than women. Only one-third say they would want to work full-time if they didn't need to. Among women, 15 percent would prefer full-time work. The youngest women, aged 18 to 24, are most likely to say they would prefer full-time work (22 percent).

The women who would most like to devote themselves to caring for the family are those aged 25 to 34 (39 percent). A majority of these women have young children at home. Among women aged 45 to 54, only 25 percent would prefer to be homemakers.

❖ Today's women are ambitious. Most want to do something more than stay at home and care for the family. Even among those who would rather not work for pay, substantial percentages would prefer volunteer work.

Preferences for Full- or Part-Time Work, 1995

"If you had enough money to live as comfortably as you'd like, would you prefer to work full time, work part time, do volunteer-type work, or work at home caring for the family?"

(percent of persons aged 18 to 55 responding by sex, and percent of women responding by age, 1995)

	prefer paid work			prefer unpaid work		
	total	full-time	part-time	total	volunteer	care for family
Total men	61%	33%	28%	38%	17%	21%
Total women	48	15	33	51	20	31
Aged 18 to 24	51	22	29	49	17	32
Aged 25 to 34	45	17	28	55	16	39
Aged 35 to 44	50	11	39	50	22	28
Aged 45 to 55	50	14	36	49	24	25

Source: Women: The New Providers, *Whirlpool Foundation Study Part One, Families and Work Institute, 1995*

Women Are Split Between Careers and Jobs

College graduates pursue careers, while others just have jobs.

Sixty percent of working men say they consider their current job to be a career, compared with 43 percent of working women. Most employed women consider their work to be "just a job," according to the Virginia Slims Opinion Poll.

Younger women, many of whom have low-paying, entry-level jobs, are least likely to consider their work a career. Only 32 percent of women aged 18 to 29 say their job is a career, compared with 44 to 49 percent of women aged 30 or older.

More than three out of four employed women with college degrees consider their work a career. But among those with only a high school diploma, only 27 percent say their work is a career.

Half of women with household incomes of $35,000 or more say their work is a career. Most of those with lower incomes say their work is just a job.

❖ As younger, better-educated women replace older, less-educated women in the work force, the proportion of women who say their work is a career will rise.

Career or Just a Job? 1995

(percent of employed women who consider their work to be a career or "just a job" by selected characteristics, 1995)

	career	just a job
Total employed women	43%	55%
Age		
Aged 18 to 29	32	65
Aged 30 to 39	49	49
Aged 40 to 49	47	52
Aged 50 or older	44	54
Education		
Not a high school graduate	19	80
High school graduate only	27	71
Some college	44	54
College graduate or more	77	21
Household income		
Under $15,000	22	77
$15,000 to $24,999	33	65
$25,000 to $34,999	46	53
$35,000 to $49,999	52	47
$50,000 or more	50	47
Employment status		
Employed full-time	50	48
Employed part-time	25	72
Race		
White	44	54
Black	36	62
Total employed men	60	37

Source: The 1995 Virginia Slims Opinion Poll, Roper Starch Worldwide, Inc., New York

Job Satisfaction Rises with Age

Women in their 50s report the highest job satisfaction.

Most women say they are very or moderately satisfied with their jobs. Women aged 50 to 59 are most likely to say they are very satisfied, with a majority of 51 percent reporting this level of satisfaction. Among women aged 30 to 49 or aged 60 or older, 42 to 46 percent are very satisfied with their jobs. Only 36 percent of women under age 30 say they are very satisfied, however.

Nineteen percent of women aged 18 to 29 and 15 percent of those aged 30 to 39 are a little or very dissatisfied with their job. These age groups have the highest levels of dissatisfaction. Only 7 percent of working women aged 60 or older are a little or very dissatisfied with their job. It's likely that most older women who dislike their work choose to retire.

❖ As today's young women advance in their careers, job satisfaction will increase—but only if employers offer opportunities to advance and ways to resolve work and family conflicts.

Job Satisfaction by Age, 1994

"How satisfied are you with your job? "

(percent of women responding by age, 1994)

	very satisfied	*moderately satisfied*	*a little dissatisfied*	*very dissatisfied*
Total	43.3%	37.2%	9.8%	3.0%
Aged 18 to 29	35.8	42.0	14.0	5.1
Aged 30 to 39	42.9	40.2	11.2	3.5
Aged 40 to 49	45.5	40.7	8.1	3.6
Aged 50 to 59	50.7	36.4	8.3	0.9
Aged 60 or older	42.2	21.5	6.3	0.9

Note: Asked only of those currently working. Numbers may not add to 100 because "don't know" and no answer are not included.
Source: 1994 General Social Survey, National Opinion Research Center, University of Chicago

CHAPTER

6

Living Arrangements

❖ **Most women are married.**

The proportion of women who are married tops 50 percent in the 25-to-29 age group and doesn't fall below this level until the 75-or-older age group.

❖ **More women than ever are postponing marriage.**

The percentage of women aged 20 to 24 who have never married rose from 36 to 67 percent between 1970 and 1995.

❖ **A growing proportion of marriages are remarriages.**

In 1970, only 19 percent of brides were previously divorced. In 1990, more than one-third of brides were marrying for the second (or more) time.

❖ **Only one-third of black children live with both parents.**

Although 76 percent of white children and 63 percent of Hispanic children live in two-parent homes, the share is only 33 percent among black children.

❖ **Young women are postponing leaving home.**

In 1995, only 28 percent of 18-to-24-year-old women were heading their own families, down 17 percentage points since 1970.

❖ **After age 74, most women live alone.**

Most women aged 65 to 74 live with their husband. But among women aged 75 or older, 54 percent live alone.

❖ **Over half of householders aged 45 to 54 still have children at home.**

Among households headed by 45-to-54-year-olds, 33 percent include children under age 18, while another 20 percent include children aged 18 or older.

❖ **Hispanics head more than one in ten married-couple families with children.**

Hispanic couples with children under age 18 outnumber black couples with young children, although there are more blacks than Hispanics in the U.S.

Most Women Are Married

The never-married rank second in importance.

In 1995, 56 percent of American women aged 15 or older were married. Twenty-four percent of women had never been married, while 10 percent were currently divorced and 11 percent were currently widowed.

The proportion of women who are married tops 50 percent in the 25-to-29 age group. It remains above 50 percent well into old age, falling below this level only among women aged 75 or older. The never-married share drops below 10 percent among women aged 40 or older. The proportion of women who are divorced is greater than the share who are still single by the 35-to-39 age group. The divorced share peaks at 16 percent among women aged 40 to 54. This figure does not include women who have been divorced but are now remarried.

Widowhood is the norm for elderly women for two reasons. Most women marry men who are slightly older, and men die at a younger age than women. One-third of women aged 65 to 74 are widowed. The widowed proportion rises to 60 percent among women aged 75 to 84, and to 81 percent among those aged 85 or older.

❖ Many women are on their own (never-married, divorced, or widowed) for a substantial portion of their adult lives, making it more important than ever for businesses to target women as individuals rather than as wives.

Marital Status of Women by Age, 1995

(number and percent distribution of women aged 15 or older by age and marital status, 1995; numbers in thousands)

	total	*never married*	*married*	*divorced*	*widowed*
Total number	105,028	24,693	58,984	10,270	11,082
Under age 20	8,934	8,582	330	17	4
Aged 20 to 24	9,119	6,087	2,769	247	17
Aged 25 to 29	9,712	3,429	5,576	689	17
Aged 30 to 34	11,088	2,111	7,758	1,150	69
Aged 35 to 39	11,200	1,408	8,103	1,569	120
Aged 40 to 44	10,163	881	7,519	1,604	159
Aged 45 to 54	15,672	959	11,617	2,441	655
Aged 55 to 64	10,878	467	7,543	1,463	1,405
Aged 65 to 74	10,117	408	5,571	786	3,352
Aged 75 to 84	6,122	255	1,961	264	3,641
Aged 85 or older	2,025	105	235	41	1,643
Total percent	100.0%	23.5%	56.2%	9.8%	10.6%
Under age 20	100.0	96.1	3.7	0.2	0.0
Aged 20 to 24	100.0	66.8	30.4	2.7	0.2
Aged 25 to 29	100.0	35.3	57.4	7.1	0.2
Aged 30 to 34	100.0	19.0	70.0	10.4	0.6
Aged 35 to 39	100.0	12.6	72.3	14.0	1.1
Aged 40 to 44	100.0	8.7	74.0	15.8	1.6
Aged 45 to 54	100.0	6.1	74.1	15.6	4.2
Aged 55 to 64	100.0	4.3	69.3	13.4	12.9
Aged 65 to 74	100.0	4.0	55.1	7.8	33.1
Aged 75 to 84	100.0	4.2	32.0	4.3	59.5
Aged 85 or older	100.0	5.2	11.6	2.0	81.1

Source: Bureau of the Census, Marital Status and Living Arrangements: March 1995, *Current Population Reports, P20-491, 1996*

Marital Status Varies by Race

The differences between black and white women are dramatic.

White women are much more likely to be married than are black women. While 59 percent of white women aged 15 or older in 1995 were married, the proportion was only 38 percent among blacks. Hispanic women were almost as likely as white women to be married, at 57 percent.

While just 21 percent of white women had never married, the share among blacks was fully 40 percent. Hispanics were also more likely to have never married than whites, with 28 percent of Hispanic women still single. Divorce is slightly more common among blacks, while widowhood is more common among whites.

❖ The sharp differences in marital status by race and ethnicity create lifestyle differences affecting consumer behavior. These differences must be taken into account before targeting white, black, or Hispanic women.

Marital Status of Women by Age, Race, and Hispanic Origin, 1995

(percent distribution of women aged 15 or older by marital status, by age, race, and Hispanic origin, 1995)

	never married			married		
	white	black	Hispanic	white	black	Hispanic
Total	20.9%	40.1%	28.4%	58.8%	37.7%	56.9%
Under age 20	95.6	98.9	91.2	4.2	1.0	8.4
Aged 20 to 24	63.7	83.9	51.8	33.1	13.3	44.8
Aged 25 to 29	30.8	58.3	30.9	61.5	35.1	63.9
Aged 30 to 34	15.7	40.1	19.0	73.4	47.6	71.8
Aged 35 to 39	9.7	30.6	13.4	75.5	50.1	70.2
Aged 40 to 44	6.7	21.8	10.9	77.1	52.5	72.1
Aged 45 to 54	5.1	14.2	8.1	76.4	56.2	73.6
Aged 55 to 64	3.8	9.3	6.6	71.5	52.8	66.4
Aged 65 to 74	3.7	7.5	8.8	56.8	38.3	47.7
Aged 75 to 84	4.0	4.6	6.2	33.1	20.3	26.2
Aged 85 or older	5.3	5.2	-	12.1	6.8	-

	divorced			widowed		
	white	black	Hispanic	white	black	Hispanic
Total	9.7%	11.6%	8.6%	10.7%	10.5%	6.2%
Under age 20	0.2	0.1	0.2	-	-	0.2
Aged 20 to 24	3.0	1.6	3.1	0.2	0.2	0.3
Aged 25 to 29	7.5	6.6	4.9	0.2	-	0.2
Aged 30 to 34	10.5	11.1	8.3	0.5	1.2	0.8
Aged 35 to 39	13.8	17.9	14.5	1.0	1.4	1.8
Aged 40 to 44	15.0	22.1	14.7	1.2	3.6	2.3
Aged 45 to 54	15.0	21.3	13.0	3.5	8.3	5.2
Aged 55 to 64	13.3	14.0	12.6	11.4	24.0	14.5
Aged 65 to 74	7.4	12.5	11.8	32.2	41.7	31.8
Aged 75 to 84	4.3	5.1	5.0	58.7	69.9	62.6
Aged 85 or older	1.9	3.2	-	80.7	84.7	-

Note: (-) means sample is too small to make a reliable estimate.
Source: Bureau of the Census, Marital Status and Living Arrangements: March 1995, *Current Population Reports, P20-491, 1996*

More Older Women Will Be Divorced

The baby-boom generation will have an impact on the marital status of older women.

A growing share of older women will have never married or will be divorced a half century from now, while a shrinking share will be widowed, according to Census Bureau projections. The proportion of older women who are married is not projected to change much, however, as more women divorce or remain single throughout their lives.

While only 5 percent of women aged 65 or older had never married in 1990, this share should rise to 8 percent by 2050 as younger generations of Americans who are less likely to marry enter the older age groups.

The proportion of elderly women who are divorced will rise even more than the never-married between 1990 and 2050, from 5 to 14 percent, as the divorce-prone younger generations replace duty-bound older Americans.

The share of women aged 65 or older who are widows will fall from 49 to 37 percent between 1990 and 2050 as the life expectancy of men increases.

❖ In the future, proportionately fewer elderly women will have been traumatized by the death of a husband and more will have been on their own for years. Consequently, older women will be more independent and active than ever before.

Marital Status of Women Aged 65 or Older, 1990 to 2050

(percent distribution of women aged 65 or older by marital status, 1990 to 2050)

	total	*never married*	*married*	*divorced*	*widowed*
Aged 65 or older					
1990	100.0%	4.9%	41.5%	5.1%	48.6%
2000	100.0	4.8	39.5	6.7	49.0
2010	100.0	4.5	40.8	10.3	44.3
2020	100.0	5.0	43.6	14.3	37.1
2030	100.0	6.5	44.0	15.1	34.5
2040	100.0	7.4	42.1	14.2	36.4
2050	100.0	7.9	41.5	13.6	36.9
Aged 65 to 74					
1990	100.0	4.6	53.2	6.2	36.1
2000	100.0	4.4	53.9	8.6	33.1
2010	100.0	4.7	55.6	13.2	26.6
2020	100.0	5.6	55.4	16.6	22.4
2030	100.0	7.7	56.0	15.5	20.8
2040	100.0	8.4	57.0	13.5	21.2
2050	100.0	8.7	57.5	13.7	20.1
Aged 75 or older					
1990	100.0	5.4	25.4	3.6	65.6
2000	100.0	5.1	26.0	4.9	64.0
2010	100.0	4.3	26.2	7.5	62.1
2020	100.0	4.3	28.3	11.2	56.2
2030	100.0	5.1	30.8	14.6	49.5
2040	100.0	6.6	30.7	14.7	48.0
2050	100.0	7.4	29.3	13.6	49.8

Source: Bureau of the Census, 65+ in the United States, *Current Population Reports, P23-190, 1996*

A Growing Share of Women Are Single

More women than ever are postponing marriage.

The percentage of women who have never married is dramatically higher in 1995 than it was in 1970. Over the quarter century, the proportion of never-married women grew in all but the oldest age groups. The percentage of women aged 20 to 24 who have never been married rose most sharply, from 36 to 67 percent between 1970 and 1995.

The increase in the percentage of never-marrieds is even greater among black women. In 1960, 44 percent of black women in their early 20s had never married. This figure nearly doubled by 1995, to 84 percent. Among black women in their late 30s, 31 percent are still single compared with only 10 percent of their white counterparts.

Hispanic women are more likely than black or white women to marry while in their early 20s. Only 52 percent of Hispanic women aged 20 to 24 have not been married. Many Hispanics are immigrants from countries where early marriage is common.

❖ While most of the increase in singlehood among women is a postponement and not a rejection of marriage, social scientists predict that the percentage of women who never marry will be higher among boomers and Generation Xers than among older generations of women.

Never-Married Women by Age, Race, and Hispanic Origin, 1970 and 1995

(percent of women who have never married by age, race, and Hispanic origin, 1970 and 1995; and percentage point change 1970-1995)

	1995	1970	percentage point change 1970 to 1995
Total women			
Aged 20 to 24	66.8%	35.8%	31.0
Aged 25 to 29	35.3	10.5	24.8
Aged 30 to 34	19.0	6.2	12.8
Aged 35 to 39	12.6	5.4	7.2
Aged 40 to 44	8.7	4.9	3.8
Aged 45 to 54	6.1	4.9	1.2
Aged 55 to 64	4.3	6.8	-2.5
Aged 65 or older	4.2	7.7	-3.5
White women			
Aged 20 to 24	63.7	34.6	29.1
Aged 25 to 29	30.8	9.2	21.6
Aged 30 to 34	15.7	5.5	10.2
Aged 35 to 39	9.7	4.6	5.1
Aged 40 to 44	6.7	4.8	1.9
Aged 45 to 54	5.1	4.9	0.2
Aged 55 to 64	3.8	7.0	-3.2
Aged 65 or older	4.0	8.0	-4.0
Black women			
Aged 20 to 24	83.9	43.5	40.4
Aged 25 to 29	58.3	18.8	39.5
Aged 30 to 34	40.1	10.8	29.3
Aged 35 to 39	30.6	12.1	18.5
Aged 40 to 44	21.8	6.9	14.9
Aged 45 to 54	14.2	4.4	9.8
Aged 55 to 64	9.3	4.7	4.6
Aged 65 or older	6.4	4.2	2.2

(continued)

(continued from previous page)

	1995	*1970*	*percentage point change 1970 to 1995*
Hispanic women			
Aged 20 to 24	51.8%	33.4%	18.4
Aged 25 to 29	30.9	13.7	17.2
Aged 30 to 34	19.0	8.4	10.6
Aged 35 to 39	13.4	6.9	6.5
Aged 40 to 44	10.9	6.3	4.6
Aged 45 to 54	8.1	6.1	2.0
Aged 55 to 64	6.6	6.7	-0.1
Aged 65 or older	7.6	7.7	-0.1

Source: Bureau of the Census, Marital Status and Living Arrangements: March 1995, *Current Population Reports, P20-491, 1996; and* Marital Status and Living Arrangements: March 1994*: Current Population Reports, P20-484, 1996; calculations by New Strategist*

A Return to Later Marriage

Median age at first marriage fell, then rose, since the turn of the century.

Over a century ago in 1890, half of women married for the first time at age 22 or older. The median age at first marriage for men was 26 in that year.

Age at first marriage fell during the first half of the century, however. In the early 1950s, nearly half of women married while they were still in their teens. These are the mothers of the baby-boom generation.

In 1963, median age at first marriage began to rise. As the women of the baby-boom generation came of age, many chose to postpone marriage while they went to college and started careers. In the late 1970s, median age at first marriage for women again reached age 22. By 1995, it was at a record 24.5 years of age, a level reached in 1993.

❖ Like the women of 100 years ago, today's young women are waiting to marry—but their reasons for doing so are different. Women today are pursuing education and career before committing themselves to marriage and family, enjoying an independent lifestyle their great-grandmothers could only dream about.

Median Age at First Marriage, 1890 to 1995

(median age at first marriage for persons by sex, 1890-1995; in years)

	women	men
1995	24.5	26.9
1994	24.5	26.7
1993	24.5	26.5
1992	24.4	26.5
1991	24.1	26.3
1990	23.9	26.1
1989	23.8	26.2
1988	23.6	25.9
1987	23.6	25.8
1986	23.1	25.7
1985	23.3	25.5
1984	23.0	25.4
1983	22.8	25.4
1982	22.5	25.2
1981	22.3	24.8
1980	22.0	24.7
1979	22.1	24.4
1978	21.8	24.2
1977	21.6	24.0
1976	21.3	23.8
1975	21.1	23.5
1974	21.1	23.1
1973	21.0	23.2
1972	20.9	23.3
1971	20.9	23.1
1970	20.8	23.2
1969	20.8	23.2
1968	20.8	23.1
1967	20.6	23.1
1966	20.5	22.8
1965	20.6	22.8
1964	20.5	23.1
1963	20.5	22.8
1962	20.3	22.7
1961	20.3	22.8

(continued)

(continued from previous page)

	women	*men*
1960	20.3	22.8
1959	20.2	22.5
1958	20.2	22.6
1957	20.3	22.6
1956	20.1	22.5
1955	20.2	22.6
1954	20.3	23.0
1953	20.2	22.8
1952	20.2	23.0
1951	20.4	22.9
1950	20.3	22.8
1949	20.3	22.7
1948	20.4	23.3
1947	20.5	23.7
1940	21.5	24.3
1930	21.3	24.3
1920	21.2	24.6
1910	21.6	25.1
1900	21.9	25.9
1890	22.0	26.1

Source: Bureau of the Census, Marital Status and Living Arrangements: March 1995*, PPL-52, 1996*

Here Comes the Bride—Again

A growing proportion of marriages are remarriages.

If tradition was strictly adhered to, today's brides would be wearing white at only two out of three weddings. In 1990, more than one-third of brides were making a second (or more) trip down the aisle. While a tiny 3 percent of brides were widows, fully 32 percent were divorcees.

In 1970, only 19 percent of brides were previously divorced, while 76 percent were marrying for the first time. Today, only 65 percent of brides are marrying for the first time.

The older the bride, the more likely she has been married before. While fewer than 10 percent of women under age 25 who married in 1990 had been married before, the share was above 50 percent among brides aged 30 or older. Among brides aged 45 or older, over 90 percent had been married before.

❖ Although etiquette once dictated a small, low-key affair for second or subsequent weddings, many women are spending lavishly the second or third time around.

Marital Status of Brides, 1970 to 1990

(percent distribution of brides by previous marital status, 1970-90)

	total	single	divorced	widowed
1990	100.0%	64.9%	32.0%	3.1%
1989	100.0	65.7	31.3	3.1
1988	100.0	65.6	31.2	3.2
1987	100.0	65.7	31.1	3.3
1986	100.0	65.7	30.9	3.3
1985	100.0	66.1	30.5	3.4
1984	100.0	66.5	30.3	3.4
1983	100.0	66.4	30.2	3.5
1982	100.0	66.8	29.9	3.4
1981	100.0	66.7	29.7	3.5
1980	100.0	67.7	28.5	3.6
1979	100.0	68.0	27.9	4.2
1978	100.0	68.5	27.5	4.0
1977	100.0	68.6	27.1	4.2
1976	100.0	69.6	26.1	4.4
1975	100.0	70.4	24.9	4.6
1974	100.0	72.3	22.7	4.9
1973	100.0	73.5	21.7	4.6
1972	100.0	75.3	20.0	4.7
1971	100.0	76.1	19.0	4.9
1970	100.0	76.4	18.5	5.1

Source: National Center for Health Statistics, Advance Report of Final Marriage Statistics, 1989 and 1990, *Vol. 43, No. 12 Supplement, 1995*

First Marriages and Remarriages by Age of Bride, 1990

(total number of marriages and percent that are remarriages for brides, by age of bride, 1990)

	total	percent remarriages
Total marriages	1,869,892	34.9%
Under age 20	203,854	1.8
Aged 20 to 24	547,411	9.6
Aged 25 to 29	459,064	27.9
Aged 30 to 34	265,661	53.3
Aged 35 to 39	158,856	73.4
Aged 40 to 44	101,889	85.8
Aged 45 to 49	56,132	90.2
Aged 50 to 54	28,865	91.3
Aged 55 to 59	16,206	93.0
Aged 60 to 64	13,088	92.7
Aged 65 or older	18,866	94.7

Note: Remarriages exclude those in Iowa, Michigan, Ohio, and South Carolina.
Source: National Center for Health Statistics, Advance Report of Final Marriage Statistics, 1989 and 1990, *Vol. 43, No. 12 Supplement, 1995; calculations by New Strategist*

Youngest Women Are Most Happily Married

Three out of four wives aged 18-to-24 say they are very happily married.

Most married women say their marriage is very happy. In 1994, 59 percent described their marriage this way. Another 36 percent of wives say their marriage is "pretty happy," while only 4 percent describe their marriage as "not too happy." Many unhappy couples divorce, which limits the proportion of couples who report being in unhappy marriages.

Marital happiness varies by age. Young women—who are more likely to have been married only a short time—have the happiest marriages. Many have not yet had children and experienced the stresses associated with childrearing.

Women in their 30s and 40s face conflicting work and family demands. This may be why the proportion of wives who say they are very happily married falls to about 58 percent in the 25-to-44 age group.

Women aged 55 to 64 are least likely to report their marriage as being very happy, at 54 percent. They are most likely to say their marriage is only "pretty happy." The stresses of retirement may account for this drop. Those who manage the transition to retirement can look forward to an improving relationship. The proportion of wives reporting very happy marriages climbs to 62 percent among women aged 65 or older.

❖ The large proportion of women at all ages who admit their marriage is only "pretty happy" reveals the struggle to keep relationships going in these complex times. Couples need relief from stress and opportunities to enjoy one another.

Marital Happiness, 1994

"Taking things all together, how would describe your marriage? Would you say that your marriage is very happy, pretty happy, or not too happy?"

(percent of women responding by age, 1994)

	very happy	*pretty happy*	*not too happy*
Total	59.1%	36.4%	4.2%
Aged 18 to 24	75.0	25.0	0.0
Aged 25 to 34	58.6	34.8	6.2
Aged 35 to 44	58.4	37.3	3.8
Aged 45 to 54	60.4	36.0	3.7
Aged 55 to 64	53.5	42.6	3.0
Aged 65 or older	61.7	34.6	3.7

Note: Percentages are based on respondents who were married or living as married.
Source: 1994 General Social Survey, National Opinion Research Center, University of Chicago

Majority of Americans Who Live Alone Are Women

At younger ages, men are more likely to live alone.

Women are more likely to live alone today than ever before. This fact reflects the increasing independence of both younger and older women due to their greater economic well-being.

Overall, 15 percent of women lived alone in 1995, up from 9 percent in 1970. The proportion of women who live alone grew in every age group during those years. Among women aged 75 or older, a 54 percent majority lived alone in 1995—up from 37 percent in 1970. The increase in the proportion of older women who live alone is due to their growing affluence, allowing more to maintain an independent household following the death of a husband.

Between 1995 and 2005 the number of women who live alone will increase by 10 percent, according to Census Bureau projections. The largest increase will be among women aged 45 to 64. By 2005, there will be 35 percent more women living alone in this age group because of the aging of the baby-boom generation.

❖ Women who live alone are a unique market for a wide range of goods and services, from housing and food to travel and entertainment.

Women Living Alone, 1970 and 1995

(number and percent of women aged 18 or older living alone by age, 1970 and 1995; women as a percent of total persons living alone, 1995; numbers in thousands)

	1995		1970		women as % of total persons living alone, 1995
	number	percent	number	percent	
Total	14,640	14.7%	7,319	9.4%	59.0%
Under age 25	591	4.7	282	1.4	48.6
Aged 25 to 34	1,448	7.0	358	2.8	39.5
Aged 35 to 44	1,400	6.6	313	2.6	38.2
Aged 45 to 64	3,594	13.5	790	6.6	56.3
Aged 65 to 74	3,247	32.1	2,204	31.6	74.1
Aged 75 or older	4,360	53.5	1,693	37.0	79.5

Source: Bureau of the Census, Internet web site, http://www.census.gov*; and* Marital Status and Living Arrangements: 1994, *Current Population Reports, P20-484, 1996; calculations by New Strategist*

Projections of Women Living Alone, 1995 to 2005

(number of women aged 18 or older living alone by age, 1995 and 2005; percent change in number, 1995-2005; numbers in thousands)

	1995	2005	percent change 1995-2005
Total	14,640	16,093	9.9%
Under age 25	591	613	3.7
Aged 25 to 34	1,448	1,443	-0.3
Aged 35 to 44	1,400	1,539	9.9
Aged 45 to 64	3,594	4,855	35.1
Aged 65 to 74	3,247	2,888	-11.1
Aged 75 or older	4,360	4,754	9.0

Source: Bureau of the Census, unpublished tables from the 1995 Current Population Survey; and Projections of the Number of Households and Families in the United States: 1995 to 2010, *Current Population Reports, P25-1129, 1996; calculations by New Strategist*

More Children Live with Their Mother Only

Only one-third of black children live with both parents.

The proportion of children who live with only one parent was far higher in 1995 than in 1970. While the number of children living with their father only has also increased since 1970, the overwhelming majority of children who live with only one parent are with their mother.

In 1970, 12 percent of children under age 18 lived with just one parent. By 1995 the proportion had more than doubled, rising to 27 percent.

White children are most likely to live with both parents (76 percent). A majority of Hispanic children also live in two-parent homes (63 percent), but among black families, single parents are the norm. Over half of black children live in single-parent families, almost always with their mother. Only 33 percent live in two-parent homes, down from 59 percent in 1970.

❖ While most women report having little free time, single mothers are especially squeezed. With both time and money in short supply, price and convenience are important selling points to these women.

Living Arrangements of Children by Race and Hispanic Origin, 1970 and 1995

(number and percent distribution of children under age 18 by race, Hispanic origin, and living arrangement of child, 1970 and 1995; numbers in thousands)

	1995		1970	
	number	*percent*	*number*	*percent*
Total children	70,254	100.0%	69,162	100.0%
Two parents	48,276	69.2	58,939	85.2
One parent	18,938	26.7	8,199	11.9
Mother only	16,477	23.5	7,452	10.8
Father only	2,461	3.2	748	1.1
Other relatives	2,352	3.1	1,547	2.2
Nonrelatives only	688	1.0	477	0.7
White children	55,327	100.0	58,790	100.0
Two parents	41,946	76.2	52,624	89.5
One parent	11,719	20.9	5,109	8.7
Mother only	9,827	17.7	4,581	7.8
Father only	1,892	3.1	528	0.9
Other relatives	1,212	2.1	696	1.2
Nonrelatives only	450	0.9	362	0.6
Black children	11,301	100.0	9,422	100.0
Two parents	3,746	33.3	5,508	58.5
One parent	6,339	57.1	2,996	31.8
Mother only	5,881	53.4	2,783	29.5
Father only	458	3.7	213	2.3
Other relatives	1,012	8.0	820	8.7
Nonrelatives only	204	1.5	97	1.0
Hispanic children	9,843	100.0	4,006	100.0
Two parents	6,191	63.4	3,111	77.7
One parent	3,215	31.8	-	-
Mother only	2,798	27.9	-	-
Father only	417	3.9	-	-
Other relatives	318	3.4	-	-
Nonrelatives only	120	1.3	-	-

Note: Numbers by race and Hispanic origin will not add to total because Hispanics may be of any race and not all races are shown. (-) means data not available.
Source: Bureau of the Census, Marital Status and Living Arrangements: March 1995, *PPL-52, 1996; calculations by New Strategist*

Many Young Adults Live with Parents

Young women are postponing leaving their parents' home.

Between 1970 and 1995 a significant shift occurred in the living arrangements of young adults. In 1970, a plurality of women aged 18 to 24 (45 percent) headed their own families. A slightly smaller percentage (41 percent) still lived with their parents, while just 4 percent were heading nonfamily households (living by themselves or with nonrelatives).

By 1995, only 28 percent of 18-to-24-year-old women were heading their own families, down 17 percentage points since 1970. Behind this decline is the postponement of marriage by young women. During those years, young women have been increasingly likely to live with their parents or head nonfamily households.

Young women are much less likely than young men to live with their parents. Fifty-eight percent of men aged 18 to 24 are in their parents' home, versus 47 percent of women in this age group. Young women are less likely to live with their parents than young men because women marry at an earlier age than men.

❖ Later marriage has changed the lifestyles of young adults as well as that of their middle-aged parents, making multi-generational activities important for both young and middle-aged women.

Living Arrangements of Young Adults by Sex, 1970 and 1995

(number and percent distribution of persons aged 18 to 24 by sex and living arrangement, 1970 and 1995; numbers in thousands)

	1995		1970	
	number	percent	number	percent
Total persons aged 18 to 24	25,158	100.0%	22,357	100.0%
Child of householder	13,224	52.6	10,582	47.3
Family householder or spouse	5,252	20.9	8,470	37.9
Nonfamily householder	2,346	9.3	1,066	4.8
Other	4,336	17.2	2,239	10.0
Women aged 18 to 24	12,613	100.0	11,959	100.0
Child of householder	5,896	46.7	4,941	41.3
Family householder or spouse	3,568	28.3	5,351	44.7
Nonfamily householder	1,100	8.7	503	4.2
Other	2,049	16.2	1,164	9.7
Men aged 18 to 24	12,545	100.0	10,398	100.0
Child of householder	7,328	58.4	5,641	54.3
Family householder or spouse	1,684	13.4	3,119	30.0
Nonfamily householder	1,246	9.9	563	5.4
Other	2,287	18.2	1,075	10.3

Source: Bureau of the Census, Marital Status and Living Arrangements: March 1995, *PPL-52, 1996; and* Marital Status and Living Arrangements: March 1994, *Current Population Reports, P20-484, 1996*

Living Arrangements Differ Among Older Women

After age 74, most women live alone.

Most women aged 65 to 74 live with their husband. But among women aged 75 or older, 54 percent live alone.

The lifestyles of older women are very different from those of older men because few older men live alone. Among men aged 65 to 74, 14 percent live by themselves. This proportion rises to just 23 percent among men aged 75 or older. Most older men live with their wives.

Older women are more likely than men to live in the home of a relative, usually with grown children. While 8 percent of women aged 65 or older live in a relative's home, this is true for only 4 percent of men aged 65 or older.

❖ The 8 million elderly women who live alone represent a unique market. Many are healthy and active, enjoying entertainment and leisure activities. They worry about crime, however, and prefer to travel in groups and take advantage of daytime entertainment.

Living Arrangements of the Elderly, 1995

(number and percent distribution of persons aged 65 or older by age, living arrangement, and sex, 1995; numbers in thousands)

	total	*women*	*men*
NUMBER			
Total, aged 65 or older	31,267	18,264	13,003
Alone	9,862	7,607	2,255
Family householder or spouse	18,810	8,846	9,964
Other, with relatives	2,030	1,509	521
Other, with nonrelatives	567	302	265
Aged 65 to 74	18,214	10,117	8,097
Alone	4,381	3,247	1,134
Family householder or spouse	12,684	6,156	6,528
Other, with relatives	804	565	239
Other, with nonrelatives	345	149	196
Aged 75 or older	13,053	8,147	4,906
Alone	5,481	4,360	1,121
Family householder or spouse	6,126	2,690	3,436
Other, with relatives	1,226	944	282
Other, with nonrelatives	222	153	69
PERCENT			
Total, aged 65 or older	100.0%	100.0%	100.0%
Alone	31.5	41.7	17.3
Family householder or spouse	60.2	48.4	76.6
Other, with relatives	6.5	8.3	4.0
Other, with nonrelatives	1.8	1.7	2.0
Aged 65 to 74	100.0	100.0	100.0
Alone	24.1	32.1	14.0
Family householder or spouse	69.6	60.8	80.6
Other, with relatives	4.4	5.6	3.0
Other, with nonrelatives	1.9	1.5	2.4
Aged 75 or older	100.0	100.0	100.0
Alone	42.0	53.5	22.8
Family householder or spouse	46.9	33.0	70.0
Other, with relatives	9.4	11.6	5.7
Other, with nonrelatives	1.7	1.9	1.4

Source: Bureau of the Census, Marital Status and Living Arrangements: March 1995, *Current Population Reports, P20-491, 1996; calculations by New Strategist*

Fewer Family Households

Families fell from 89 to 70 percent of households between 1950 and 1995.

In the "Leave It to Beaver" era, the overwhelming majority of American households were made up of families. Over three-quarters were married couples, most of which included children. Only 11 percent of households were people living alone or unrelated people living together (nonfamily households).

By 1995, American households were dramatically different. Married couples were a much smaller share of households, while single-parent and nonfamily households were a much larger share.

In 1950, 8 percent of households were headed by single mothers. This figure rose to 12 percent by 1995. The share of single-father households tripled since 1950, but is still a tiny 1.5 percent.

The percentage of nonfamily households grew from 11 to 30 percent between 1950 and 1995. Behind this increase is the rising share of older women who live alone. Nonfamily households headed by women accounted for only 7 percent of all households in 1950, but for 17 percent by 1995.

❖ As lifestyles diversify, women can no longer be reached with a single advertising image, particularly if that image resembles a 1950's housewife.

Households by Type, 1950 to 1995

(number and percent distribution of households by household type, 1950 to 1995; numbers in thousands)

	1995	1990	1980	1970	1960	1950
Total number	98,990	93,347	80,776	63,401	52,799	43,554
Family households	69,305	66,090	59,550	51,456	44,905	38,838
Married couples	53,858	52,317	49,112	44,728	39,254	34,075
With children <18	25,241	24,537	24,961	25,541	23,358	18,824
Without children <18	28,617	27,780	24,151	19,187	15,896	15,251
Female hh, no spouse present	12,220	10,890	8,705	5,500	4,422	3,594
With children <18	7,615	6,599	5,445	2,971	2,099	1,272
Without children <18	4,605	4,291	3,260	2,529	2,323	2,322
Male hh, no spouse present	3,226	2,884	1,733	1,228	1,228	1,169
With children <18	1,440	1,153	616	345	232	229
Without children <18	1,786	1,731	1,117	883	996	940
Nonfamily households	29,686	27,257	21,226	11,945	7,895	4,716
Female householder	16,496	15,651	12,419	7,882	5,179	3,048
Male householder	13,190	11,606	8,807	4,063	2,716	1,668
Total percent	100.0%	100.0%	100.0%	100.0%	100.0%	100.0%
Family households	70.0	70.8	73.7	81.2	85.0	89.2
Married couples	54.4	56.0	60.8	70.5	74.3	78.2
With children <18	25.5	26.3	30.9	40.3	44.2	43.2
Without children <18	28.9	29.8	29.9	30.3	30.1	35.0
Female hh, no spouse present	12.3	11.7	10.8	8.7	8.4	8.3
With children <18	7.7	7.1	6.7	4.7	4.0	2.9
Without children <18	4.7	4.6	0.8	4.0	4.4	5.3
Male hh, no spouse present	3.3	3.1	2.1	1.9	2.3	2.7
With children <18	1.5	1.2	0.8	0.5	0.4	0.5
Without children <18	1.8	1.9	1.4	1.4	1.9	2.2
Nonfamily households	30.0	29.2	26.3	18.8	15.0	10.8
Female householder	16.7	16.8	15.4	12.4	9.8	7.0
Male householder	13.3	12.4	10.9	6.4	5.1	3.8

Source: Bureau of the Census, Internet web site, http://www.census.gov; *calculations by New Strategist*

Married Couples Are Most Common in Middle-Age

Nearly two-thirds of households headed by 45-to-54-year-olds are married couples.

Slightly more than half (54 percent) of American households were headed by married couples in 1995. Couples account for just 30 percent of households headed by people under age 25, rising to more than half in the 25-to-34 age group. The married-couple share of households remains above 50 percent until the 65-or-older age group.

Households headed by people under age 25 are the most diverse. One-fifth of the youngest householders are women heading families without a spouse, while another one-fifth are women heading nonfamily households. Household diversity is also great among the oldest householders. One-third of householders aged 65 or older are women who live alone.

❖ Because of the increasing diversity of households, businesses must look beyond married couples when marketing products and services. Even among the most married of householders, those aged 45 to 54, a substantial 37 percent are not married couples.

Households by Type and Age of Householder, 1995

(number and percent distribution of households by household type and age of householder, 1995; numbers in thousands)

	total	under 25	25 to 34	35 to 44	45 to 54	55 to 64	65 or older
Total number	98,990	5,444	19,452	22,914	17,590	12,224	21,365
Family households	69,305	3,079	14,077	18,273	13,746	8,894	11,237
Married couples	53,858	1,632	10,316	13,919	11,153	7,552	9,286
Female hh, no spouse present	12,220	1,124	2,965	3,502	2,037	1,056	1,536
Male hh, no spouse present	3,226	323	796	852	556	285	414
Nonfamily households	29,686	2,365	5,376	4,641	3,845	3,330	10,128
Female householder	16,496	1,107	2,031	1,713	1,896	2,008	7,741
Living alone	14,592	573	1,440	1,400	1,676	1,913	7,591
Male householder	13,190	1,258	3,345	2,928	1,949	1,322	2,388
Living alone	10,140	623	2,213	2,263	1,650	1,137	2,253
Total percent	100.0%	100.0%	100.0%	100.0%	100.0%	100.0%	100.0%
Family households	70.0	56.6	72.4	79.7	78.1	72.8	52.6
Married couples	54.4	30.0	53.0	60.7	63.4	61.8	43.5
Female hh, no spouse present	12.3	20.6	15.2	15.3	11.6	8.6	7.2
Male hh, no spouse present	3.3	5.9	4.1	3.7	3.2	2.3	1.9
Nonfamily households	30.0	43.4	27.6	20.3	21.9	27.2	47.4
Female householder	16.7	20.3	10.4	7.5	10.8	16.4	36.2
Living alone	14.7	10.5	7.4	6.1	9.5	15.6	35.5
Male householder	13.3	23.1	17.2	12.8	11.1	10.8	11.2
Living alone	10.2	11.4	11.4	9.9	9.4	9.3	10.5

Source: Bureau of the Census, Internet web site, http://www.census.gov; *and unpublished tables from the 1995* Current Population Survey; *calculations by New Strategist*

Households Vary Sharply by Race and Ethnicity

Black households are more diverse than white or Hispanic households.

Only one-third of black households are headed by married couples, while an almost equal proportion are female-headed families. In contrast, over half of white and Hispanic households are headed by married couples.

Hispanic households are more likely to include nuclear families (husband, wife, and children) than either white or black households. In 1995, 36 percent of Hispanic households were headed by married couples with children under age 18 at home. This compared with only 26 percent of white and 17 percent of black households. Though blacks are still the largest minority in the U.S. and will be until after the turn of the century, Hispanics already outnumber blacks among couples with children.

Single-parent families headed by women account for only 6 percent of white households, but for 14 percent of Hispanic and 21 percent of black households. Overall, blacks account for one in three female-headed single-parent families.

Women living alone account for a much larger share of black and white households than of Hispanic households. Fifteen percent of black and white households are women living alone, versus only 8 percent of Hispanic households.

❖ As consumers, women's needs differ depending on their living arrangements. The diversity of household types by race and ethnicity mean that white, black, and Hispanic women have different needs.

Households by Type, Race, and Hispanic Origin of Householder, 1995

(number and percent distribution of households by household type, race, and Hispanic origin of householder, 1995; numbers in thousands)

	total	*white*	*black*	*Hispanic*
Total number	98,990	83,737	11,655	7,735
Family households	69,305	58,437	8,093	6,200
Married couples	53,858	47,899	3,842	4,235
With children < 18	25,241	22,005	1,926	2,743
Without children <18	28,617	25,894	1,916	1,492
Female hh, no spouse present	12,220	8,031	3,716	1,485
With children < 18	7,615	4,841	2,489	1,048
Without children <18	4,606	3,191	1,227	437
Male hh, no spouse present	3,226	2,507	536	479
With children < 18	1,440	1,105	267	192
Without children <18	1,786	1,401	268	287
Nonfamily households	29,686	25,300	3,562	1,535
Female householder	16,496	14,207	1,909	745
Living alone	14,592	12,547	1,728	615
Male householder	13,190	11,093	1,653	790
Living alone	10,140	8,453	1,381	541
Total percent	100.0%	100.0%	100.0%	100.0%
Family households	70.0	69.8	69.4	80.2
Married couples	54.4	57.2	33.0	54.8
With children < 18	25.5	26.3	16.5	35.5
Without children <18	28.9	30.9	16.4	19.3
Female hh, no spouse present	12.3	9.6	31.9	19.2
With children < 18	7.7	5.8	21.4	13.5
Without children <18	4.7	3.8	10.5	5.6
Male hh, no spouse present	3.3	3.0	4.6	6.2
With children < 18	1.5	1.3	2.3	2.5
Without children <18	1.8	1.7	2.3	3.7
Nonfamily households	30.0	30.2	30.6	19.8
Female householder	16.7	17.0	16.4	9.6
Living alone	14.7	15.0	14.8	8.0
Male householder	13.3	13.2	14.2	10.2
Living alone	10.2	10.1	11.8	7.0

Note: Numbers will not add to total because Hispanics may be of any race and not all races are shown.
Source: Bureau of the Census, Household and Family Characteristics: March 1995, *PPL-46, 1996; calculations by New Strategist*

Most Middle-Aged Householders Have Children at Home

The proportion peaks at 85 percent among 35-to-39-year-olds.

Householders aged 30 to 44 have one thing in common: they are likely to be raising children. A majority of households in this age group include children under age 18. But for households headed by younger and older people, those with children are in the minority.

Overall, just 35 percent of American households include children, a proportion that has fallen with family size over the past few decades. Even among married couples, a 47 percent minority have children under age 18 at home. Most couples between the ages of 20 and 44 have children under age 18 at home, however.

Nearly two-thirds of female-headed families include children under age 18, with about 90 percent of those aged 20 to 44 raising children.

❖ Women can be divided into two consumer groups—those with and those without dependent children. Women under age 45 are likely to be harried parents, while those aged 45 or older have more time and money to spend on themselves.

Households with Children by Age of Householder and Type of Household, 1995

(total number of households, and number and percent with children under age 18, by age of householder and type of household, 1995; numbers in thousands)

	total households		married-couple families		female-headed families	
	total	with children	total	with children	total	with children
Total number	98,990	34,296	53,858	25,241	12,220	7,615
Under age 20	537	165	79	33	161	124
Aged 20 to 24	4,907	1,804	1,553	866	963	839
Aged 25 to 29	8,400	3,870	3,959	2,541	1,234	1,130
Aged 30 to 34	11,052	6,893	6,357	4,987	1,731	1,639
Aged 35 to 39	11,947	8,152	7,131	6,068	1,901	1,779
Aged 40 to 44	10,967	6,770	6,788	5,315	1,601	1,204
Aged 45 to 54	17,590	5,752	11,153	4,712	2,037	798
Aged 55 to 64	12,224	743	7,552	602	1,057	88
Aged 65 or older	21,365	147	9,286	118	1,536	13
Total percent	100.0%	34.6%	100.0%	46.9%	100.0%	62.3%
Under age 20	100.0	30.7	100.0	41.8	100.0	77.0
Aged 20 to 24	100.0	36.8	100.0	55.8	100.0	87.1
Aged 25 to 29	100.0	46.1	100.0	64.2	100.0	91.6
Aged 30 to 34	100.0	62.4	100.0	78.4	100.0	94.7
Aged 35 to 39	100.0	68.2	100.0	85.1	100.0	93.6
Aged 40 to 44	100.0	61.7	100.0	78.3	100.0	75.2
Aged 45 to 54	100.0	32.7	100.0	42.2	100.0	39.2
Aged 55 to 64	100.0	6.1	100.0	8.0	100.0	8.3
Aged 65 or older	100.0	0.7	100.0	1.3	100.0	0.8

Source: Bureau of the Census, Household and Family Characteristics: March 1995, *PPL-46, 1996; calculations by New Strategist*

Many Older Householders Live with Adult Children

Over half of householders aged 45 to 54 still have children at home.

Among households headed by 45 to 54 year olds, 33 percent include children under age 18, while another 20 percent include children aged 18 or older. Even among householders aged 55 to 64, a significant 28 percent still live with children—most of them aged 18 or older. Behind this statistic is the growing propensity of young adults to live with their parents.

The households most likely to include preschoolers are those headed by people aged 30 to 34—41 percent of householders in this age group have children under age 6 at home. Children of elementary school age are most likely to be found among households headed by 35-to-39-year-olds (42 percent). Teens are most likely to be found in households headed by 40 to 44 year olds—42 percent of householders in this age group live with children aged 12 to 17.

❖ Although many women have delayed their childbearing until they are in their 30s, marketers can safely assume that most infants and preschoolers have mothers under age 35.

Households with Children by Age of Householder and Age of Children, 1995

(total number of households, and number and percent distribution of those with children at home, by age of householder and age of children, 1995; numbers in thousands)

		with children				
	total households	*of any age*	*< age 18*	*12 to 17*	*6 to 11*	*< age 6*
Total number	98,990	44,233	34,296	15,385	16,495	15,609
Under age 20	537	177	165	2	5	159
Aged 20 to 24	4,907	1,810	1,804	16	246	1,718
Aged 25 to 29	8,400	3,882	3,870	203	1,669	3,210
Aged 30 to 34	11,052	6,912	6,893	1,597	3,896	4,517
Aged 35 to 39	11,947	8,291	8,152	3,782	5,046	3,657
Aged 40 to 44	10,967	7,570	6,770	4,562	3,447	1,645
Aged 45 to 54	17,590	9,596	5,752	4,506	1,958	639
Aged 55 to 64	12,224	3,444	743	611	187	49
Aged 65 or older	21,365	2,551	147	106	42	15
Total percent	100.0%	44.7%	34.6%	15.5%	16.7%	15.8%
Under age 20	100.0	33.0	30.7	0.4	0.9	29.6
Aged 20 to 24	100.0	36.9	36.8	0.3	5.0	35.0
Aged 25 to 29	100.0	46.2	46.1	2.4	19.9	38.2
Aged 30 to 34	100.0	62.5	62.4	14.4	35.3	40.9
Aged 35 to 39	100.0	69.4	68.2	31.7	42.2	30.6
Aged 40 to 44	100.0	69.0	61.7	41.6	31.4	15.0
Aged 45 to 54	100.0	54.6	32.7	25.6	11.1	3.6
Aged 55 to 64	100.0	28.2	6.1	5.0	1.5	0.4
Aged 65 or older	100.0	11.9	0.7	0.5	0.2	0.1

Source: Bureau of the Census, Household and Family Characteristics: March 1995, *PPL-46, 1996; calculations by New Strategist*

Nest Is Slow to Empty for Married Couples

A 58 percent majority of married couples have children of any age at home.

Though only 47 percent of all married couples have children under age 18 at home, this proportion rises to 58 percent when children of any age are considered.

Married-couple households are fairly evenly split by the age of the children in the home. Twenty-two percent of all couples have children under age 6, 23 percent have children aged 6-to-11, and 21 percent have children aged 12 to 17. As the children of baby boomers grow up, the proportion of households with teenagers at home should increase, while the proportion with preschoolers is likely to decline.

By age of householder, there are large differences in the proportions of couples with preschoolers, elementary-aged children, or teens. Over half of couples aged 20 to 34 have preschoolers. A majority of couples aged 35 to 39 have elementary-school-aged children, and over half of couples aged 40 to 44 have teenagers at home.

❖ Until age 55, most married women have children under their roof. Even if those children are adults, mothers continue to feel responsible for their well-being.

Married Couples with Children by Age of Householder and Age of Children, 1995

(total number of married couples, and number and percent distribution of those with children at home, by age of householder and age of children, 1995; numbers in thousands)

		with children				
	total couples	of any age	< age 18	12 to 17	6 to 11	< age 6
Total number	53,858	31,233	25,241	11,185	12,333	11,950
Under age 20	79	33	33	2	2	30
Aged 20 to 24	1,553	866	866	12	86	828
Aged 25 to 29	3,959	2,541	2,541	113	904	2,224
Aged 30 to 34	6,357	5,001	4,987	859	2,663	3,692
Aged 35 to 39	7,131	6,133	6,068	2,471	3,918	3,089
Aged 40 to 44	6,788	5,724	5,315	3,498	2,867	1,458
Aged 45 to 54	11,153	7,361	4,712	3,654	1,692	580
Aged 55 to 64	7,552	2,388	602	491	163	41
Aged 65 or older	9,286	1,186	118	85	39	8
Total percent	100.0%	58.0%	46.9%	20.8%	22.9%	22.2%
Under age 20	100.0	41.8	41.8	2.5	2.5	38.0
Aged 20 to 24	100.0	55.8	55.8	0.8	5.5	53.3
Aged 25 to 29	100.0	64.2	64.2	2.9	22.8	56.2
Aged 30 to 34	100.0	78.7	78.4	13.5	41.9	58.1
Aged 35 to 39	100.0	86.0	85.1	34.7	54.9	43.3
Aged 40 to 44	100.0	84.3	78.3	51.5	42.2	21.5
Aged 45 to 54	100.0	66.0	42.2	32.8	15.2	5.2
Aged 55 to 64	100.0	31.6	8.0	6.5	2.2	0.5
Aged 65 or older	100.0	12.8	1.3	0.9	0.4	0.1

Source: Bureau of the Census, Household and Family Characteristics: March 1995, *PPL-46, 1996; calculations by New Strategist*

Among Couples with Children, Hispanics Outnumber Blacks

Hispanics head more than one in ten married-couple families with children.

The nation's 2.7 million Hispanic couples with children under age 18 outnumber the 1.9 million black couples with young children, although there are more blacks than Hispanics in the U.S. Behind the significant presence of Hispanics among nuclear families is their earlier marriage and higher fertility. Many Hispanics are immigrants from countries such as Mexico where early marriage and large families are common.

Forty-five percent of Hispanic couples with children under age 18 have a householder younger than age 35, versus only 30 percent of white and 37 percent of black couples with children. Conversely, 43 percent of white couples with children under age 18 are aged 40 or older, versus 40 percent of black and just 35 percent of Hispanic couples with children.

❖ Hispanic women are less likely to work than white or black women. For businesses targeting traditional housewives—married women with children under age 18 who do not work—Hispanics are an important and growing share of this market.

Married Couples with Children by Age, Race, and Hispanic Origin of Householder, 1995

(number and percent distribution of married couples with children under age 18 at home, by age, race, and Hispanic origin of householder, 1995; numbers in thousands)

	total	*white*	*black*	*Hispanic*
Total number	25,241	22,005	1,926	2,743
Under age 20	33	28	-	12
Aged 20 to 24	866	766	55	164
Aged 25 to 29	2,541	2,177	229	428
Aged 30 to 34	4,987	4,323	422	617
Aged 35 to 39	6,068	5,340	446	553
Aged 40 to 44	5,315	4,720	347	443
Aged 45 to 54	4,712	4,039	357	443
Aged 55 to 64	602	516	54	71
Aged 65 or older	118	97	17	12
Total percent	100.0%	100.0%	100.0%	100.0%
Under age 20	0.1	0.1	-	0.4
Aged 20 to 24	3.4	3.5	2.9	6.0
Aged 25 to 29	10.1	9.9	11.9	15.6
Aged 30 to 34	19.8	19.6	21.9	22.5
Aged 35 to 39	24.0	24.3	23.2	20.2
Aged 40 to 44	21.1	21.4	18.0	16.2
Aged 45 to 54	18.7	18.4	18.5	16.2
Aged 55 to 64	2.4	2.3	2.8	2.6
Aged 65 or older	0.5	0.4	0.9	0.4

Note: Numbers by race and Hispanic origin will not add to total because Hispanics may be of any race and not all races are shown. (-) means sample is too small to make a reliable estimate.
Source: Bureau of the Census, Household and Family Characteristics: March 1995, *PPL-46, 1996; calculations by New Strategist*

Most Female-Headed Families Are Single Parents

Few female householders share homes with relatives other than children.

Although some female-headed families do not include young children, most do. Of the nation's 12 million female-headed families, nearly 8 million are single-parents with children under age 18. Among families headed by women aged 25 to 40, over 90 percent include children under age 18. Female-headed families without children under age 18 include either adult children or other relatives such as siblings or elderly parents.

Most families headed by women under age 30 have children under age 6 in the home. A majority of single mothers aged 25 to 39 include children aged 6 to 11, while teenagers are found most often in families headed by women aged 35 to 44.

After age 45, most female-headed families include adult children. While 40 percent of female householders aged 45 to 54 have children under age 18 at home, another 50 percent have children aged 18 or older living with them.

❖ Female-headed families tend to have low incomes because rarely is there more than one earner in the home. These householders are pressed for money and time, making both convenience and cost important benefits to them.

Female-Headed Families with Children by Age of Householder and Age of Children, 1995

(total number of female-headed families, and number and percent distribution of those with children at home, by age of householder and age of children, 1995; numbers in thousands)

		with children				
	total families	of any age	< age 18	12 to 17	6 to 11	< age 6
Total number	12,220	10,832	7,615	3,586	3,614	3,092
Under age 20	161	130	124	-	2	122
Aged 20 to 24	963	836	839	4	154	797
Aged 25 to 29	1,234	1,139	1,130	86	715	812
Aged 30 to 34	1,731	1,642	1,639	686	1,078	708
Aged 35 to 39	1,901	1,829	1,779	1,179	968	457
Aged 40 to 44	1,601	1,536	1,204	890	485	147
Aged 45 to 54	2,037	1,814	798	661	195	38
Aged 55 to 64	1,057	851	88	73	16	7
Aged 65 or older	1,536	1,053	13	9	1	4
Total percent	100.0%	88.6%	62.3%	29.3%	29.6%	25.3%
Under age 20	100.0	80.7	77.0	-	1.2	75.8
Aged 20 to 24	100.0	86.8	87.1	0.4	16.0	82.8
Aged 25 to 29	100.0	92.3	91.6	7.0	57.9	65.8
Aged 30 to 34	100.0	94.9	94.7	39.6	62.3	40.9
Aged 35 to 39	100.0	96.2	93.6	62.0	50.9	24.0
Aged 40 to 44	100.0	95.9	75.2	55.6	30.3	9.2
Aged 45 to 54	100.0	89.1	39.2	32.4	9.6	1.9
Aged 55 to 64	100.0	80.5	8.3	6.9	1.5	0.7
Aged 65 or older	100.0	68.6	0.8	0.6	0.1	0.3

Source: Bureau of the Census, Household and Family Characteristics: March 1995, *PPL-46, 1996; calculations by New Strategist*

Single Mothers Are Mostly White

Whites account for 64 percent of female-headed single-parent families.

Although the stereotype of the single mother is a black woman, blacks account for just 33 percent of such families. Hispanics account for another 14 percent. The black and Hispanic share of these families is greater than their share of all households, however.

Most single mothers, regardless of race or ethnicity, are aged 25 to 39. Only 13 percent are under age 25—with teenagers accounting for fewer than 2 percent. Another 28 percent of single mothers are aged 40 or older. Black single mothers are younger than their white or Hispanic counterparts, with 16 percent under age 25. In contrast, 30 percent of white single mothers are aged 40 or older, a larger share than among blacks or Hispanics.

❖ Female-headed families with children are more racially diverse than other household markets. Targeting this group requires an understanding of the unique wants and needs of both black and Hispanic women.

Female-Headed Families with Children by Age, Race, and Hispanic Origin of Householder, 1995

(number and percent distribution of female-headed families with children under age 18 at home, by age, race, and Hispanic origin of householder, 1995; numbers in thousands)

	total	*white*	*black*	*Hispanic*
Total number	7,615	4,841	2,489	1,048
Under age 20	124	74	47	18
Aged 20 to 24	839	466	347	108
Aged 25 to 29	1,130	655	427	170
Aged 30 to 34	1,639	1,033	550	228
Aged 35 to 39	1,779	1,188	525	235
Aged 40 to 44	1,204	817	345	162
Aged 45 to 54	798	543	216	99
Aged 55 to 64	88	61	25	26
Aged 65 or older	13	3	7	1
Total percent	100.0%	100.0%	100.0%	100.0%
Under age 20	1.6	1.5	1.9	1.7
Aged 20 to 24	11.0	9.6	13.9	10.3
Aged 25 to 29	14.8	13.5	17.2	16.2
Aged 30 to 34	21.5	21.3	22.1	21.8
Aged 35 to 39	23.4	24.5	21.1	22.4
Aged 40 to 44	15.8	16.9	13.9	15.5
Aged 45 to 54	10.5	11.2	8.7	9.4
Aged 55 to 64	1.2	1.3	1.0	2.5
Aged 65 or older	0.2	0.1	0.3	0.1

Note: Numbers will not add to total because Hispanics may be of any race and not all races are shown.
Source: Bureau of the Census, Household and Family Characteristics: March 1995, *PPL-46, 1996; calculations by New Strategist*

Rapid Growth in Households Headed by 55-to-64-Year-Olds

Forty-two percent increase in households headed by 55-to-64-year-olds is forecast as boomers enter this age group.

The number of households in the U.S. will increase by 10 percent between 1995 and 2005, according to Census Bureau projections. By age of householder, however, growth will vary sharply.

The number of householders aged 30 to 34 is projected to decline by 19 percent between 1995 and 2005, as the small, baby-bust generation (or Generation X) fills this age group. The number of married couples aged 30 to 34 is projected to decline by 25 percent.

In contrast, rapid growth is forecast for householders aged 45 to 64 as boomers enter their 50s. Among householders aged 45 to 64, especially rapid growth is forecast for female-headed families as today's single-parents get older and as aging boomers divorce.

❖ More women will be independent consumers as the number who head their own household expands by 2.7 million between 1995 and 2005.

Projections of Households by Type and Age of Householder, 1995 and 2005

(number and percent distribution of households by age of householder and type of household, 1995 and 2005; percent change in number, 1995-2005; numbers in thousands)

	1995		2005		% change
	number	percent	number	percent	1995-2005
ALL AGES					
Total households	98,990	100.0%	108,819	100.0%	9.9%
Family households	69,305	70.0	74,733	68.7	7.8
Married couples	53,858	54.4	57,371	52.7	6.5
Female householder, no spouse present	12,220	12.3	13,084	12.0	7.1
Male householder, no spouse present	3,226	3.3	4,278	3.9	32.6
Nonfamily households	29,686	30.0	34,085	31.3	14.8
Female householder	16,496	16.7	18,301	16.8	10.9
Male householder	13,190	13.3	15,784	14.5	19.7
UNDER AGE 25					
Total households	5,444	100.0	5,399	100.0	-0.8
Family households	3,079	56.6	2,660	49.3	-13.6
Married couples	1,632	30.0	1,468	27.2	-10.0
Female householder, no spouse present	1,124	20.6	864	16.0	-23.1
Male householder, no spouse present	323	5.9	328	6.1	1.5
Nonfamily households	2,365	43.4	2,738	50.7	15.8
Female householder	1,107	20.3	1,216	22.5	9.8
Male householder	1,258	23.1	1,522	28.2	21.0
AGED 25 TO 29					
Total households	8,400	100.0	7,551	100.0	-10.1
Family households	5,575	66.4	4,739	62.8	-15.0
Married couples	3,959	47.1	3,297	43.7	-16.7
Female householder, no spouse present	1,234	14.7	1,088	14.4	-11.8
Male householder, no spouse present	382	4.5	354	4.7	-7.3
Nonfamily households	2,825	33.6	2,812	37.2	-0.5
Female householder	1,117	13.3	1,092	14.5	-2.2
Male householder	1,708	20.3	1,720	22.8	0.7

(continued)

(continued from previous page)

	1995		2005		% change
	number	percent	number	percent	1995-2005
AGED 30 TO 34					
Total households	11,052	100.0%	8,996	100.0%	-18.6%
Family households	8,502	76.9	6,484	72.1	-23.7
Married couples	6,357	57.5	4,782	53.2	-24.8
Female householder, no spouse present	1,731	15.7	1,320	14.7	-23.7
Male householder, no spouse present	414	3.7	382	4.2	-7.7
Nonfamily households	2,551	23.1	2,512	27.9	-1.5
Female householder	914	8.3	892	9.9	-2.4
Male householder	1,637	14.8	1,620	18.0	-1.0
AGED 35 TO 44					
Total households	22,914	100.0	22,560	100.0	-1.5
Family households	18,273	79.7	17,203	76.3	-5.9
Married couples	13,919	60.7	12,714	56.4	-8.7
Female householder, no spouse present	3,502	15.3	3,391	15.0	-3.2
Male householder, no spouse present	852	3.7	1,098	4.9	28.9
Nonfamily households	4,641	20.3	5,357	23.7	15.4
Female householder	1,713	7.5	1,874	8.3	9.4
Male householder	2,928	12.8	3,483	15.4	19.0
AGED 45 TO 54					
Total households	17,590	100.0	23,924	100.0	36.0
Family households	13,746	78.1	18,570	77.6	35.1
Married couples	11,153	63.4	14,494	60.6	30.0
Female householder, no spouse present	2,037	11.6	3,070	12.8	50.7
Male householder, no spouse present	556	3.2	1,006	4.2	80.9
Nonfamily households	3,844	21.9	5,353	22.4	39.3
Female householder	1,896	10.8	2,584	10.8	36.3
Male householder	1,948	11.1	2,769	11.6	42.1
AGED 55 TO 64					
Total households	12,224	100.0	17,331	100.0	41.8
Family households	8,894	72.8	12,374	71.4	39.1
Married couples	7,552	61.8	10,097	58.3	33.7
Female householder, no spouse present	1,057	8.6	1,666	9.6	57.6
Male householder, no spouse present	285	2.3	611	3.5	114.4
Nonfamily households	3,330	27.2	4,956	28.6	48.8
Female householder	2,008	16.4	2,794	16.1	39.1
Male householder	1,322	10.8	2,162	12.5	63.5

(continued)

(continued from previous page)

	1995		2005		% change
	number	percent	number	percent	1995-2005
AGED 65 TO 74					
Total households	11,803	100.0%	11,597	100.0%	-1.7%
Family households	7,268	61.6	7,357	63.4	1.2
Married couples	6,169	52.3	6,229	53.7	1.0
Female householder, no spouse present	853	7.2	852	7.3	-0.1
Male householder, no spouse present	246	2.1	276	2.4	12.2
Nonfamily households	4,535	38.4	4,240	36.6	-6.5
Female householder	3,311	28.1	2,985	25.7	-9.8
Male householder	1,224	10.4	1,255	10.8	2.5
AGED 75 OR OLDER					
Total households	9,562	100.0	11,462	100.0	19.9
Family households	3,969	41.5	5,346	46.6	34.7
Married couples	3,117	32.6	4,291	37.4	37.7
Female householder, no spouse present	683	7.1	833	7.3	22.0
Male householder, no spouse present	168	1.8	222	1.9	32.1
Nonfamily households	5,593	58.5	6,116	53.4	9.4
Female householder	4,430	46.3	4,864	42.4	9.8
Male householder	1,164	12.2	1,252	10.9	7.6

Source: Bureau of the Census, Household and Family Characteristics: March 1995, *PPL-52, 1996; and* Projections of the Number of Households and Families in the United States: 1995 to 2010, *Current Population Reports, P25-1129, 1996; calculations by New Strategist*

CHAPTER

7

Population

❖ **At older ages, women outnumber men by a wide margin.**

Despite medical advances and lifestyle changes, women still outlive men. Females, it appears, are biologically sturdier than males.

❖ **The number of women aged 55 to 59 will grow by 43 percent between 1997 and 2005.**

The number of women aged 35 to 39 will decline by 12 percent during those years.

❖ **Blacks and Hispanics are a growing segment of the women's market.**

Hispanics will become the largest minority early in the next century. Already, Hispanics outnumbers blacks among girls under age 5.

❖ **Middle-aged women are a growing share of all racial and ethnic groups.**

The greatest gains between 1997 and 2005 in the number of women aged 18 to 44 will be for Asians (up 23 percent) and Hispanics (up 20 percent).

❖ **Women's population gains will be greatest in the West.**

The number of women in the West will grow by 14 percent between 1995 and 2005, while the gain will be just 2 percent in the Northeast.

❖ **The female population is growing fastest in Nevada.**

Four Western states will see the fastest increase in the female population between 1995 and 2005: Nevada, Idaho, Arizona, and Utah.

More Women Than Men

At older ages, women outnumber men by a wide margin.

There are more females than males in America, despite the fact that in any given year more boys are born than girls. Males continue to outnumber females until they are in their mid-20s, when parity is reached. After that age, women begin to outnumber men by a growing margin. Fifty-one percent of all Americans are females. But the proportion ranges from a low of 49 percent among children under age 5 to a high of 72 percent among Americans aged 85 or older.

The reason for the numerical superiority of women lies in the differing death rates of males and females. Simply put, women outlive men. This continues to be true despite medical advances and lifestyle changes that might, in theory, bring greater equality to life expectancy. Females, it appears, are biologically sturdier than males.

❖ With 6 million more females than males in the United States, women account for a majority of consumers. The women's market becomes increasingly important with age.

Population by Age and Sex, 1997

(number of persons by age and sex, and percent female, 1997; numbers in thousands)

	total	females	males	percent female
Total	267,645	136,933	130,712	51.2%
Aged 0 to 4	19,229	9,389	9,839	48.8
Aged 5 to 9	19,854	9,691	10,163	48.8
Aged 10 to 14	19,205	9,370	9,835	48.8
Aged 15 to 19	19,013	9,268	9,745	48.7
Aged 20 to 24	17,287	8,515	8,772	49.3
Aged 25 to 29	18,848	9,419	9,430	50.0
Aged 30 to 34	20,775	10,431	10,344	50.2
Aged 35 to 39	22,607	11,347	11,260	50.2
Aged 40 to 44	21,323	10,775	10,548	50.5
Aged 45 to 49	18,442	9,398	9,044	51.0
Aged 50 to 54	15,149	7,784	7,366	51.4
Aged 55 to 59	11,754	6,111	5,642	52.0
Aged 60 to 64	10,062	5,315	4,747	52.8
Aged 65 to 69	9,758	5,305	4,454	54.4
Aged 70 to 74	8,753	4,941	3,812	56.4
Aged 75 to 79	7,072	4,157	2,914	58.8
Aged 80 to 84	4,652	2,945	1,707	63.3
Aged 85 or older	3,862	2,773	1,089	71.8
Aged 18 to 24	24,689	12,140	12,549	49.2
Aged 18 or older	197,747	102,840	94,907	52.0
Aged 65 or older	34,097	20,121	13,976	59.0

Source: Bureau of the Census, Population Projections of the United States, by Age, Sex, Race, and Hispanic Origin: 1995 to 2050, Current Population Reports, *P25-1130, 1996; calculations by New Strategist*

Age Structure Determines Many Trends

Like a pig in a python, the baby-boom generation is easy to spot.

Differences in the sizes of generations are clear when the female population is viewed by single year of age. In 1997, the large baby-boom generation spanned the ages of 33 to 51. Those born during the peak year of the baby boom, 1957, turn 40 this year. More than 2 million women are now crossing an important threshold into midlife.

The impact of the aging of the generations is also easily seen in the opposite table. As the small, baby-bust generation (or Generation X) gets older, the number of people in their 20s and 30s is shrinking. Between 1997 and 2000, the number of 26-year-old women will fall by 14 percent. In contrast, the number of 51-year-old women will increase by 29 percent.

The aging of the large baby-boom generation greatly influences our perceptions of America's problems and passions. When boomers were teens and young adults, youth issues commanded the nation's attention. Now that boomers are reaching middle age, the issues of midlife—menopause, college costs, and retirement planning—are taking center stage.

❖ As the share of middle-aged women in the population expands, businesses that have long targeted young women will have to rethink their products, services, and marketing messages to appeal to forty and fiftysomething customers.

Females by Single Year of Age, 1997, 2000, and 2005

(number of females by single year of age, 1997, 2000, and 2005; percent change 1997-2000 and 2000-2005; numbers in thousands)

	1997	2000	2005	percent change 1997-2000	percent change 2000-2005
Aged 0	1,863	1,855	1,895	-0.4%	2.2%
Aged 1	1,852	1,836	1,862	-0.9	1.4
Aged 2	1,866	1,842	1,854	-1.3	0.7
Aged 3	1,878	1,852	1,852	-1.4	0.0
Aged 4	1,930	1,890	1,877	-2.1	-0.7
Aged 5	1,969	1,902	1,876	-3.4	-1.4
Aged 6	1,982	1,911	1,878	-3.6	-1.7
Aged 7	1,979	1,942	1,889	-1.9	-2.7
Aged 8	1,836	1,908	1,827	3.9	-4.2
Aged 9	1,925	2,059	1,969	7.0	-4.4
Aged 10	1,906	2,060	1,993	8.1	-3.3
Aged 11	1,878	1,965	1,982	4.6	0.9
Aged 12	1,873	1,926	2,012	2.8	4.5
Aged 13	1,835	1,917	2,073	4.5	8.1
Aged 14	1,879	1,917	2,095	2.0	9.3
Aged 15	1,893	1,926	2,104	1.7	9.2
Aged 16	1,856	1,873	2,034	0.9	8.6
Aged 17	1,894	1,946	2,029	2.7	4.3
Aged 18	1,786	1,924	1,979	7.7	2.9
Aged 19	1,839	1,996	2,089	8.5	4.7
Aged 20	1,810	1,981	2,063	9.4	4.1
Aged 21	1,695	1,848	1,961	9.0	6.1
Aged 22	1,674	1,751	1,947	4.6	11.2
Aged 23	1,627	1,727	1,933	6.1	11.9
Aged 24	1,709	1,694	1,937	-0.9	14.3
Aged 25	1,798	1,703	1,924	-5.3	13.0
Aged 26	1,937	1,668	1,838	-13.9	10.2
Aged 27	1,942	1,721	1,800	-11.4	4.6
Aged 28	1,793	1,733	1,699	-3.3	-2.0
Aged 29	1,948	2,055	1,800	5.5	-12.4
Aged 30	1,954	2,013	1,791	3.0	-11.0
Aged 31	1,963	1,917	1,720	-2.3	-10.3
Aged 32	2,087	1,900	1,772	-9.0	-6.7
Aged 33	2,163	1,940	1,874	-10.3	-3.4
Aged 34	2,264	2,048	2,073	-9.5	1.2

(continued)

(continued from previous page)

	1997	2000	2005	percent change 1997-2000	percent change 2000-2005
Aged 35	2,292	2,153	2,057	-6.1%	-4.5%
Aged 36	2,256	2,186	1,960	-3.1	-10.3
Aged 37	2,293	2,246	1,954	-2.0	-13.0
Aged 38	2,138	2,158	1,882	0.9	-12.8
Aged 39	2,369	2,395	2,133	1.1	-10.9
Aged 40	2,301	2,346	2,195	2.0	-6.4
Aged 41	2,174	2,269	2,225	4.4	-1.9
Aged 42	2,145	2,264	2,251	5.5	-0.6
Aged 43	2,078	2,241	2,275	7.8	1.5
Aged 44	2,077	2,220	2,342	6.9	5.5
Aged 45	2,000	2,160	2,313	8.0	7.1
Aged 46	1,868	2,052	2,224	9.9	8.4
Aged 47	1,876	2,022	2,256	7.8	11.6
Aged 48	1,750	1,883	2,135	7.6	13.4
Aged 49	1,904	1,970	2,247	3.5	14.1
Aged 50	1,987	1,904	2,168	-4.2	13.9
Aged 51	1,399	1,799	2,038	28.6	13.3
Aged 52	1,425	1,787	1,973	25.4	10.4
Aged 53	1,438	1,928	1,949	34.1	1.1
Aged 54	1,535	1,432	1,898	-6.7	32.5
Aged 55	1,313	1,427	1,834	8.7	28.5
Aged 56	1,267	1,448	1,822	14.3	25.8
Aged 57	1,225	1,529	1,826	24.8	19.4
Aged 58	1,130	1,252	1,822	10.8	45.5
Aged 59	1,176	1,258	1,409	7.0	12.0
Aged 60	1,102	1,190	1,416	8.0	19.0
Aged 61	1,068	1,143	1,376	7.0	20.4
Aged 62	1,081	1,124	1,441	4.0	28.2
Aged 63	1,013	1,068	1,263	5.4	18.3
Aged 64	1,051	1,090	1,230	3.7	12.8
Aged 65 to 69	5,305	5,089	5,383	-4.1	5.8
Aged 70 to 74	4,941	4,867	4,578	-1.5	-5.9
Aged 75 to 79	4,157	4,323	4,229	4.0	-2.2
Aged 80 to 84	2,945	3,055	3,364	3.7	10.1
Aged 85 to 89	1,695	1,828	1,993	7.8	9.0
Aged 90 to 94	789	860	1,007	9.0	17.1
Aged 95 to 99	238	283	341	18.9	20.5
Aged 100 or older	50	60	85	20.0	41.7

Source: Bureau of the Census, Population Projections of the United States by Age, Sex, Race, and Hispanic Origin: 1995 to 2050, *Current Population Report, P25-1130, 1996*

More Older Women

The number of women aged 55 to 59 will grow by 43 percent between 1997 and 2005.

Overall, the number of females in the U.S. population will grow by 7 percent between 1997 and 2005, from 137 million to 146 million. But growth will vary sharply by age. The number of women in their 30s will decline as the small baby-bust generation (or Generation X) enters that age group. Meanwhile, the number of women in their 50s and early 60s will expand rapidly as the large baby-boom generation ages.

The number of females under age 10 is expected to fall slightly between 1997 and 2005 as the baby boomlet comes to an end. But the children of the baby-boom generation, now in their teens, will inflate the young-adult population during the next decade. The number of women aged 20 to 24 should grow by 16 percent between 1997 and 2005.

The number of older women will grow, but not nearly as fast as the number of women in middle-age. Overall, the number of women aged 65 or older should increase by just 4 percent between 1997 and 2005. But the number aged 85 or older will grow by 24 percent during those years.

❖ The aging of American women is good news for many businesses. Older women spend more than younger women on most products and services including clothing, travel, and entertainment.

Distribution of Females by Age, 1997 and 2005

(number and percent distribution of females by age, 1997 and 2005; percent change in number, 1997-2005; numbers in thousands)

	1997		2005		percent change
	number	percent	number	percent	1997-2005
Total	136,933	100.0%	146,196	100.0%	6.8
Under age 5	9,389	6.9	9,341	6.4	-0.5
Aged 5 to 9	9,691	7.1	9,439	6.5	-2.6
Aged 10 to 14	9,370	6.8	10,154	6.9	8.4
Aged 15 to 19	9,268	6.8	10,235	7.0	10.4
Aged 20 to 24	8,515	6.2	9,841	6.7	15.6
Aged 25 to 29	9,419	6.9	9,062	6.2	-3.8
Aged 30 to 34	10,431	7.6	9,229	6.3	-11.5
Aged 35 to 39	11,347	8.3	9,986	6.8	-12.0
Aged 40 to 44	10,775	7.9	11,287	7.7	4.8
Aged 45 to 49	9,398	6.9	11,176	7.6	18.9
Aged 50 to 54	7,784	5.7	10,027	6.9	28.8
Aged 55 to 59	6,111	4.5	8,714	6.0	42.6
Aged 60 to 64	5,315	3.9	6,726	4.6	26.5
Aged 65 to 69	5,305	3.9	5,383	3.7	1.5
Aged 70 to 74	4,941	3.6	4,578	3.1	-7.3
Aged 75 to 79	4,157	3.0	4,229	2.9	1.7
Aged 80 to 84	2,945	2.2	3,364	2.3	14.2
Aged 85 or older	2,773	2.0	3,426	2.3	23.5
Aged 18 to 24	12,140	8.9	13,909	9.5	14.6
Aged 18 or older	102,840	75.1	111,095	76.0	8.0
Aged 65 or older	20,121	14.7	20,979	14.3	4.3

Source: Bureau of the Census, Population Projections of the United States, by Age, Sex, Race, and Hispanic Origin: 1995 to 2050, Current Population Reports, *P25-1130, 1996; calculations by New Strategist*

Diversity Is Greatest Among Young Women

Blacks and Hispanics are a growing segment of the women's market.

Racial and ethnic diversity has been increasing among Americans as multi-cultural younger generations replace less diverse older ones. Overall, 73 percent of American females are non-Hispanic white. The share ranges from fully 88 percent among women aged 85 or older to only 63 percent among girls under age 5. This 25-percentage-point gap creates a cultural divide that businesses must bridge.

Although blacks are still the largest minority in the U.S., Hispanics will overtake them early in the next century. Already, Hispanics outnumber blacks among girls under age 5—16 percent are Hispanic while 15 percent are non-Hispanic black. Among all females, 10 percent are Hispanic while 13 percent are non-Hispanic black.

Hispanics may be of any race, and most white. But the nonwhite share of Hispanics is slightly larger in the younger age groups.

❖ Regardless of race or ethnicity, women share many of the same wants and needs. But increasingly, marketers must consider the cultural, lifestyle, and even language differences among women.

Females by Age, Race, and Hispanic Origin, 1997

(number and percent distribution of females by age, race, and Hispanic origin, 1997; numbers in thousands)

		non-Hispanic				
	total	*white*	*black*	*Native American*	*Asian*	*Hispanic*
Total, number	136,933	99,727	17,076	1,008	4,932	14,190
Under age 5	9,389	5,943	1,435	87	394	1,530
Aged 5 to 9	9,691	6,306	1,465	94	368	1,459
Aged 10 to 14	9,370	6,263	1,373	100	374	1,260
Aged 15 to 19	9,268	6,226	1,384	92	359	1,207
Aged 20 to 24	8,515	5,700	1,241	77	352	1,145
Aged 25 to 29	9,419	6,445	1,292	76	427	1,179
Aged 30 to 34	10,431	7,278	1,389	76	445	1,243
Aged 35 to 39	11,347	8,243	1,445	79	443	1,137
Aged 40 to 44	10,775	8,015	1,316	74	416	954
Aged 45 to 49	9,398	7,156	1,083	61	354	745
Aged 50 to 54	7,784	6,115	793	48	258	571
Aged 55 to 59	6,111	4,796	651	37	191	437
Aged 60 to 64	5,315	4,208	553	29	162	363
Aged 65 to 69	5,305	4,305	512	24	145	319
Aged 70 to 74	4,941	4,151	409	19	112	250
Aged 75 to 79	4,157	3,575	322	15	71	175
Aged 80 to 84	2,945	2,572	210	10	38	115
Aged 85 or older	2,773	2,431	204	11	25	103
Aged 18 to 24	12,140	8,138	1,787	111	486	1,618
Aged 18 or older	102,840	77,428	11,965	669	3,571	9,207
Aged 65 or older	20,121	17,034	1,656	80	390	962

(continued)

(continued from previous page)

		non-Hispanic				
	total	white	black	Native American	Asian	Hispanic
Total, percent	100.0%	72.8%	12.5%	0.7%	3.6%	10.4%
Under age 5	100.0	63.3	15.3	0.9	4.2	16.3
Aged 5 to 9	100.0	65.1	15.1	1.0	3.8	15.1
Aged 10 to 14	100.0	66.8	14.7	1.1	4.0	13.4
Aged 15 to 19	100.0	67.2	14.9	1.0	3.9	13.0
Aged 20 to 24	100.0	66.9	14.6	0.9	4.1	13.4
Aged 25 to 29	100.0	68.4	13.7	0.8	4.5	12.5
Aged 30 to 34	100.0	69.8	13.3	0.7	4.3	11.9
Aged 35 to 39	100.0	72.6	12.7	0.7	3.9	10.0
Aged 40 to 44	100.0	74.4	12.2	0.7	3.9	8.9
Aged 45 to 49	100.0	76.1	11.5	0.6	3.8	7.9
Aged 50 to 54	100.0	78.6	10.2	0.6	3.3	7.3
Aged 55 to 59	100.0	78.5	10.7	0.6	3.1	7.2
Aged 60 to 64	100.0	79.2	10.4	0.5	3.0	6.8
Aged 65 to 69	100.0	81.1	9.7	0.5	2.7	6.0
Aged 70 to 74	100.0	84.0	8.3	0.4	2.3	5.1
Aged 75 to 79	100.0	86.0	7.7	0.4	1.7	4.2
Aged 80 to 84	100.0	87.3	7.1	0.3	1.3	3.9
Aged 85 or older	100.0	87.7	7.4	0.4	0.9	3.7
Aged 18 to 24	100.0	67.0	14.7	0.9	4.0	13.3
Aged 18 or older	100.0	75.3	11.6	0.7	3.5	9.0
Aged 65 or older	100.0	84.7	8.2	0.4	1.9	4.8

Note: Hispanics may be of any race.
Source: Bureau of the Census, Population Projections of the United States, by Age, Sex, Race, and Hispanic Origin: 1995 to 2050, Current Population Reports, *P25-1130, 1996; calculations by New Strategist*

Hispanic Origin of Females by Age and Race, 1997

(number and percent distribution of females by Hispanic origin, age, and race, 1997; numbers in thousands)

		Hispanic				
	total	*white*	*black*	*Native American*	*Asian*	*non-Hispanic*
Total, number	136,933	12,884	840	158	309	122,743
Under age 5	9,389	1,396	90	15	29	7,859
Aged 5 to 9	9,691	1,326	84	17	30	8,232
Aged 10 to 14	9,370	1,140	73	18	29	8,110
Aged 15 to 19	9,268	1,095	70	16	27	8,061
Aged 20 to 24	8,515	1,041	66	13	25	7,370
Aged 25 to 29	9,419	1,065	71	13	29	8,240
Aged 30 to 34	10,431	1,126	76	13	28	9,188
Aged 35 to 39	11,347	1,030	70	12	25	10,210
Aged 40 to 44	10,775	862	60	10	22	9,821
Aged 45 to 49	9,398	674	45	8	17	8,653
Aged 50 to 54	7,784	518	34	5	12	7,213
Aged 55 to 59	6,111	397	27	4	9	5,674
Aged 60 to 64	5,315	330	23	4	7	4,952
Aged 65 to 69	5,305	290	20	3	6	4,986
Aged 70 to 74	4,941	228	13	3	6	4,691
Aged 75 to 79	4,157	161	9	1	4	3,982
Aged 80 to 84	2,945	107	5	1	2	2,830
Aged 85 or older	2,773	96	4	1	1	2,670
Aged 18 to 24	12,140	1,470	93	19	36	10,522
Aged 18 or older	102,840	8,356	550	97	204	93,633
Aged 65 or older	20,121	882	51	8	19	19,159

(continued)

(continued from previous page)

	total	Hispanic white	Hispanic black	Hispanic Native American	Hispanic Asian	non-Hispanic
Total, percent	100.0%	9.4%	0.6%	0.1%	0.2%	89.6%
Under age 5	100.0	14.9	1.0	0.2	0.3	83.7
Aged 5 to 9	100.0	13.7	0.9	0.2	0.3	84.9
Aged 10 to 14	100.0	12.2	0.8	0.2	0.3	86.6
Aged 15 to 19	100.0	11.8	0.8	0.2	0.3	87.0
Aged 20 to 24	100.0	12.2	0.8	0.2	0.3	86.6
Aged 25 to 29	100.0	11.3	0.8	0.1	0.3	87.5
Aged 30 to 34	100.0	10.8	0.7	0.1	0.3	88.1
Aged 35 to 39	100.0	9.1	0.6	0.1	0.2	90.0
Aged 40 to 44	100.0	8.0	0.6	0.1	0.2	91.1
Aged 45 to 49	100.0	7.2	0.5	0.1	0.2	92.1
Aged 50 to 54	100.0	6.7	0.4	0.1	0.2	92.7
Aged 55 to 59	100.0	6.5	0.4	0.1	0.1	92.8
Aged 60 to 64	100.0	6.2	0.4	0.1	0.1	93.2
Aged 65 to 69	100.0	5.5	0.4	0.1	0.1	94.0
Aged 70 to 74	100.0	4.6	0.3	0.1	0.1	94.9
Aged 75 to 79	100.0	3.9	0.2	0.0	0.1	95.8
Aged 80 to 84	100.0	3.6	0.2	0.0	0.1	96.1
Aged 85 or older	100.0	3.5	0.1	0.0	0.0	96.3
Aged 18 to 24	100.0	12.1	0.8	0.2	0.3	86.7
Aged 18 or older	100.0	8.1	0.5	0.1	0.2	91.0
Aged 65 or older	100.0	4.4	0.3	0.0	0.1	95.2

Note: Hispanics may be of any race.
Source: Bureau of the Census, Population Projections of the United States, by Age, Sex, Race, and Hispanic Origin: 1995 to 2050, Current Population Reports, *P25-1130, 1996; calculations by New Strategist*

Middle-Aging Will Affect All Markets

Middle-aged women are a growing percentage of all racial and ethnic groups.

The number of women aged 45 to 64 will increase in every racial and ethnic group between 1997 and 2005 as the baby-boom generation ages. Growth in the 45-to-64 age group will be fastest for Asians, with an increase of more than 50 percent from 1997 to 2005. Growth in this age group will be slowest for non-Hispanic whites, with a gain of just 24 percent.

The number of women aged 18 to 44 will decline nationally as the baby-bust generation enters its 30s. But some racial and ethnic groups will see growth in this age group. The greatest gains in the number of women aged 18 to 44 will be for Asians (up 23 percent) and Hispanics (up 20 percent).

❖ Because of the aging of the baby boom, the female population will be older in 2005 than in 1997. While this aging will be more pronounced for non-Hispanic whites than for other racial or ethnic groups, it will affect most consumer markets.

Projections of Females by Race, Hispanic Origin, and Age, 1997 and 2005

(number and percent distribution of females by race, Hispanic origin, and age, 1997-2005; percent change in number, 1997-2005; numbers in thousands)

	1997		2005		percent change
	number	percent	number	percent	1997-2005
Total females	136,933	100.0%	146,196	100.0%	6.8%
Under age 18	34,093	24.9	35,101	24.0	3.0
Aged 18 to 44	54,112	39.5	53,473	36.6	-1.2
Aged 45 to 64	28,608	20.9	36,643	25.1	28.1
Aged 65 or older	20,121	14.7	20,979	14.3	4.3
White	112,611	100.0	118,113	100.0	4.9
Under age 18	26,827	23.8	27,029	22.9	0.8
Aged 18 to 44	43,672	38.8	42,238	35.8	-3.3
Aged 45 to 64	24,194	21.5	30,486	25.8	26.0
Aged 65 or older	17,916	15.9	18,359	15.5	2.5
Non-Hispanic white	99,727	100.0	101,856	100.0	2.1
Under age 18	22,299	22.4	21,506	21.1	-3.6
Aged 18 to 44	38,119	38.2	35,583	34.9	-6.7
Aged 45 to 64	22,275	22.3	27,612	27.1	24.0
Aged 65 or older	17,034	17.1	17,156	16.8	0.7
Black	17,916	100.0	19,860	100.0	10.9
Under age 18	5,400	30.1	5,785	29.1	7.1
Aged 18 to 44	7,599	42.4	7,805	39.3	2.7
Aged 45 to 64	3,209	17.9	4,381	22.1	36.5
Aged 65 or older	1,707	9.5	1,886	9.5	10.5
Non-Hispanic black	17,076	100.0	18,725	100.0	9.7
Under age 18	5,112	29.9	5,409	28.9	5.8
Aged 18 to 44	7,229	42.3	7,339	39.2	1.5
Aged 45 to 64	3,080	18.0	4,171	22.3	35.4
Aged 65 or older	1,656	9.7	1,805	9.6	9.0
Asian	5,241	100.0	6,918	100.0	32.0
Under age 18	1,466	28.0	1,868	27.0	27.4
Aged 18 to 44	2,357	45.0	2,907	42.0	23.3
Aged 45 to 64	1,010	19.3	1,522	22.0	50.7
Aged 65 or older	409	7.8	621	9.0	51.8

(continued)

(continued from previous page)

	1997		2005		percent change
	number	percent	number	percent	1997-2005
Non-Hispanic Asian	4,932	100.0%	6,526	100.0%	32.3%
Under age 18	1,361	27.6	1,743	26.7	28.1
Aged 18 to 44	2,217	45.0	2,738	42.0	23.5
Aged 45 to 64	965	19.6	1,455	22.3	50.8
Aged 65 or older	390	7.9	590	9.0	51.3
Native American	1,166	100.0	1,306	100.0	12.0
Under age 18	400	34.3	416	31.9	4.0
Aged 18 to 44	483	41.4	522	40.0	8.1
Aged 45 to 64	196	16.8	253	19.4	29.1
Aged 65 or older	88	7.5	113	8.7	28.4
Non-Hispanic Native American	1,008	100.0	1,113	100.0	10.4
Under age 18	339	33.6	353	31.7	4.1
Aged 18 to 44	416	41.3	439	39.4	5.5
Aged 45 to 64	175	17.4	223	20.0	27.4
Aged 65 or older	80	7.9	99	8.9	23.8
Hispanic	14,190	100.0	17,975	100.0	26.7
Under age 18	4,983	35.1	6,088	33.9	22.2
Aged 18 to 44	6,131	43.2	7,375	41.0	20.3
Aged 45 to 64	2,116	14.9	3,183	17.7	50.4
Aged 65 or older	962	6.8	1,328	7.4	38.0

Note: Hispanics may be of any race.
Sources: Bureau of the Census, Population Projections of the United States, by Age, Sex, Race, and Hispanic Origin: 1995 to 2050, *Current Population Reports, P25-1130, 1996; calculations by New Strategist*

Slow Growth in the Northeast

Population gains will be greatest in the West

The female population will grow by about 9 percent between 1995 and 2005 in the U.S. as a whole. But not all regions of the country will experience this rate of growth.

Growth will be greatest in the West (up 14 percent), followed by the South (12 percent). The number of females will grow by only 5 percent in the Midwest and by just 2 percent in the Northeast.

The number of girls under age 18 will decline in the Midwest between 1995 and 2005. Preschoolers are projected to decline in the Northeast and South. The greatest growth is projected for women aged 18 to 24 in the West. This group will increase by 27 percent between 1995 and 2005 as the children of boomers grow up.

❖ By 2005, only 19 percent of the nation's females will live in the Northeast. The South will continue to be the largest region, home to 36 percent of the nation's women and girls.

Projections of Females by Region and Age, 1995 and 2005

(number of females by region and age, 1995 and 2005; percent change, 1995-2005; numbers in thousands)

	1995	*2005*	*percent change 1995-2005*
Total	134,440	146,198	8.7%
Under age 5	9,568	9,338	-2.4
Aged 5 to 17	23,954	25,764	7.6
Aged 18 to 24	12,230	13,915	13.8
Aged 25 to 64	68,839	76,204	10.7
Aged 65 or older	19,849	20,977	5.7
Northeast, total	26,652	27,218	2.1
Under age 5	1,766	1,617	-8.4
Aged 5 to 17	4,392	4,585	4.4
Aged 18 to 24	2,250	2,440	8.4
Aged 25 to 64	13,851	14,401	4.0
Aged 65 or older	4,393	4,175	-3.0
Midwest, total	31,708	33,168	4.6
Under age 5	2,145	2,078	-3.1
Aged 5 to 17	5,756	5,738	-0.3
Aged 18 to 24	2,917	3,157	8.2
Aged 25 to 64	16,069	17,269	7.5
Aged 65 or older	4,821	4,926	2.2
South, total	47,219	52,806	11.8
Under age 5	3,313	3,234	-2.4
Aged 5 to 17	8,371	9,136	9.1
Aged 18 to 24	4,447	4,998	12.4
Aged 25 to 64	24,164	27,673	14.5
Aged 65 or older	6,924	7,765	12.1
West, total	28,861	33,006	14.4
Under age 5	2,344	2,409	2.8
Aged 5 to 17	5,435	6,305	16.0
Aged 18 to 24	2,616	3,320	26.9
Aged 25 to 64	14,755	16,861	14.3
Aged 65 or older	3,711	4,111	10.8

Source: Bureau of the Census, Internet web site, http://www.census.gov; *calculations by New Strategist*

Diversity Greater in Some Regions Than in Others

Females in the West are most diverse.

Non-Hispanic whites accounted for fewer than two-thirds of females living in the West in 1995. This proportion should fall to 59 percent by 2005. Black females in the West are outnumbered by both Asian and Hispanic females. Twenty-one percent of females in the West are Hispanic, a proportion that should rise to 25 percent by 2005. Asians account for 9 percent of females living in the West, a share that should increase to 11 percent by 2005.

The Midwest is the least diverse region. Eighty-five percent of midwestern females are non-Hispanic white. This proportion is projected to fall slightly—to 82 percent—by 2005.

Blacks account for the largest minority in every region but the West. They will continue to be the largest minority in the Northeast, Midwest, and South through 2005.

❖ Businesses marketing to women nationally must take into account their differing racial and ethnic composition by region. Marketing messages directed at consumers in the West, for example, must be far more multi-cultural than those directed at consumers in the Midwest.

Projections of Females by Region, Race, and Hispanic Origin, 1995 and 2005

(number and percent distribution of females by race, Hispanic origin, and region, 1995 and 2005; percent change in number, 1995-2005; numbers in thousands)

	1995		2005		percent change
	number	percent	number	percent	1995-2005
Total	134,433	100.0%	146,196	100.0%	8.8%
White	111,058	82.6	118,112	80.8	6.4
Black	17,416	13.0	19,863	13.6	14.1
Asian	4,831	3.6	6,920	4.7	43.2
Native American	1,128	0.8	1,301	0.9	15.3
Hispanic	13,283	9.9	17,976	12.3	35.3
Non-Hispanic white	98,975	73.6	101,855	69.7	2.9
Northeast, total	26,652	100.0	27,219	100.0	2.1
White	22,390	84.0	22,167	81.4	-1.0
Black	3,313	12.4	3,669	13.5	10.7
Asian	877	3.3	1,300	4.8	48.2
Native American	72	0.3	83	0.3	15.3
Hispanic	2,241	8.4	2,883	10.6	28.6
Non-Hispanic white	20,615	77.3	19,908	73.1	-3.4
Midwest, total	31,705	100.0	33,173	100.0	4.6
White	27,742	87.5	28,573	86.1	3.0
Black	3,272	10.3	3,632	10.9	11.0
Asian	507	1.6	744	2.2	46.7
Native American	184	0.6	224	0.7	21.7
Hispanic	1,008	3.2	1,372	4.1	36.1
Non-Hispanic white	26,817	84.6	27,323	82.4	1.9
South, total	47,212	100.0	52,800	100.0	11.8
White	36,852	78.1	40,486	76.7	9.9
Black	9,245	19.6	10,779	20.4	16.6
Asian	804	1.7	1,179	2.2	46.6
Native American	311	0.7	356	0.7	14.5
Hispanic	4,102	8.7	5,565	10.5	35.7
Non-Hispanic white	32,987	69.9	35,316	66.9	7.1

(continued)

(continued from previous page)

	1995		2005		percent change
	number	percent	number	percent	1995-2005
West, total	28,864	100.0%	33,004	100.0%	14.3%
White	24,074	83.4	26,886	81.5	11.7
Black	1,586	5.5	1,783	5.4	12.4
Asian	2,643	9.2	3,697	11.2	39.9
Native American	561	1.9	638	1.9	13.7
Hispanic	5,932	20.6	8,156	24.7	37.5
Non-Hispanic white	18,556	64.3	19,308	58.5	4.1

Note: Numbers by race and Hispanic origin will not sum to total because Hispanics may be of any race.
Source: Bureau of the Census, Internet web site, http://www.census.gov*; calculations by New Strategist*

California Is the Most Populous State

But the population is growing fastest in Nevada.

The female population of Nevada is projected to grow by 38 percent between 1995 and 2005, according to projections by the Census Bureau. Even after this rapid growth, however, Nevada's female population will remain relatively small—just over 1 million.

The number of females in California is projected to increase by only 10 percent between 1995 and 2005. Although this growth rate is only slightly higher than the national rate, California will continue to have the largest population by far. In 1995, nearly 16 million women and girls lived in California. No other state had more than 10 million.

Four western states will see the fastest increase in the female population between 1995 and 2005. After Nevada's 38 percent increase come Idaho with a 27 percent gain, Arizona with a 24 percent increase, and Utah with a 23 percent rise. In contrast, the number of females in New York and Connecticut will increase by less than 1 percent between 1995 and 2005.

• One-fourth of the nation's women and girls live in just three states: California, Texas, and New York.

Projections of Females by State, 1995 and 2005

(number of females by state, 1995 and 2005; percent change 1995-2005; numbers in thousands)

	1995	2005	percent change 1995-2005
Total	134,440	146,198	8.7%
Alabama	2,212	2,402	8.6
Alaska	286	339	18.5
Arizona	2,132	2,652	24.4
Arkansas	1,285	1,422	10.7
California	15,797	17,306	9.6
Colorado	1,889	2,254	19.3
Connecticut	1,687	1,702	0.9
Delaware	368	409	11.1
District of Columbia	295	279	-5.4
Florida	7,301	8,412	15.2
Georgia	3,700	4,320	16.8
Hawaii	587	669	14.0
Idaho	583	743	27.4
Illinois	6,067	6,277	3.5
Indiana	2,982	3,182	6.7
Iowa	1,459	1,505	3.2
Kansas	1,304	1,399	7.3
Kentucky	1,988	2,106	5.9
Louisiana	2,252	2,351	4.4
Maine	637	657	3.1
Maryland	2,593	2,812	8.4
Massachusetts	3,148	3,243	3.0
Michigan	4,904	5,004	2.0
Minnesota	2,341	2,540	8.5
Mississippi	1,404	1,513	7.8
Missouri	2,750	2,941	6.9
Montana	438	508	16.0
Nebraska	837	897	7.2
Nevada	751	1,035	37.8
New Hampshire	584	651	11.5
New Jersey	4,098	4,324	5.5
New Mexico	855	1,021	19.4
New York	9,417	9,448	0.3
North Carolina	3,704	4,230	14.2

(continued)

(continued from previous page)

	1995	2005	percent change 1995-2005
North Dakota	322	341	5.9%
Ohio	5,764	5,885	2.1
Oklahoma	1,678	1,784	6.3
Oregon	1,591	1,833	15.2
Pennsylvania	6,270	6,348	1.2
Rhode Island	514	521	1.4
South Carolina	1,902	2,084	9.6
South Dakota	370	411	11.1
Tennessee	2,720	3,080	13.2
Texas	9,489	10,919	15.1
Utah	981	1,210	23.3
Vermont	297	324	9.1
Virginia	3,380	3,724	10.2
Washington	2,732	3,152	15.4
West Virginia	948	959	1.2
Wisconsin	2,608	2,786	6.8
Wyoming	239	284	18.8

Source: Bureau of the Census, Internet web site, http://www.census.gov; *calculations by New Strategist*

Baby Boomlet to Be Felt in Most States

Nationally, there will be 1.8 million more girls aged 5 to 17 by 2005.

Beginning in the late 1970s, the number of births in the U.S. began to rise, reaching levels by the late 1980s equaling the original baby boom. The children of what is sometimes called the "baby boomlet" will boost the population of school-aged children by 2005.

The number of girls aged 5 to 17 will increase in most states between 1995 and 2005. The fastest increases will be in Nevada (22 percent) and California (20 percent). Only a few states will see a decline in school-aged girls—such as Maine, where the number of girls aged 5 to 17 will decline by 10 percent.

Nationally, the number of preschool girls (under age 5) will decline by 2 percent between 1995 and 2005, although some states will see increases. Growth in the toddler market will be greatest in Wyoming, Idaho, and Alaska. The largest declines in the number of girls under age 5 will be in New York, Connecticut, and Massachusetts.

❖ The rising number of school girls in most states is an opportunity for many businesses. There will be more girls buying make-up, going to proms, learning to drive, and applying to college.

Projections of Females under Age 18 by State, 1995 and 2005

(number of females under age 18 by state and age, 1995 and 2005; percent change 1995-2005; numbers in thousands)

	total under age 18			aged 0 to 4			aged 5 to 17		
	1995	2005	% change 1995-2005	1995	2005	% change 1995-2005	1995	2005	% change 1995-2005
Total	33,522	35,102	4.7%	9,568	9,338	-2.4%	23,954	25,764	7.6%
Alabama	528	546	3.4	146	139	-4.8	382	407	6.5
Alaska	91	104	14.3	26	30	15.4	65	74	13.8
Arizona	583	672	15.3	174	182	4.6	409	490	19.8
Arkansas	316	318	0.6	84	82	-2.4	232	236	1.7
California	4,280	4,853	13.4	1,371	1,360	-0.8	2,909	3,493	20.1
Colorado	478	525	9.8	132	141	6.8	346	384	11.0
Connecticut	390	378	-3.1	111	100	-9.9	279	278	-0.4
Delaware	87	93	6.9	25	24	-4.0	62	69	11.3
Dist. of Columbia	57	64	12.3	20	18	-10.0	37	46	24.3
Florida	1,644	1,739	5.8	472	451	-4.4	1,172	1,288	9.9
Georgia	940	1,052	11.9	269	273	1.5	671	779	16.1
Hawaii	150	173	15.3	47	50	6.4	103	123	19.4
Idaho	169	195	15.4	44	52	18.2	125	143	14.4
Illinois	1,524	1,536	0.8	450	419	-6.9	1,074	1,117	4.0
Indiana	724	742	2.5	199	193	-3.0	525	549	4.6
Iowa	353	337	-4.5	90	89	-1.1	263	248	-5.7
Kansas	337	341	1.2	89	91	2.2	248	250	0.8
Kentucky	473	463	-2.1	127	119	-6.3	346	344	-0.6
Louisiana	607	589	-3.0	165	156	-5.5	442	433	-2.0
Maine	149	138	-7.4	36	36	0.0	113	102	-9.7
Maryland	623	651	4.5	180	173	-3.9	443	478	7.9
Massachusetts	698	725	3.9	202	186	-7.9	496	539	8.7
Michigan	1,230	1,198	-2.6	334	316	-5.4	896	882	-1.6
Minnesota	607	594	-2.1	157	159	1.3	450	435	-3.3
Mississippi	372	376	1.1	102	96	-5.9	270	280	3.7
Missouri	673	677	0.6	180	179	-0.6	493	498	1.0
Montana	115	118	2.6	28	32	14.3	87	86	-1.1
Nebraska	216	216	0.0	55	58	5.5	161	158	-1.9
Nevada	194	228	17.5	58	62	6.9	136	166	22.1
New Hampshire	144	148	2.8	38	38	0.0	106	110	3.8
New Jersey	958	988	3.1	282	261	-7.4	676	727	7.5
New Mexico	245	278	13.5	68	76	11.8	177	202	14.1

(continued)

(continued from previous page)

	total under age 18			aged 0 to 4			aged 5 to 17		
	1995	2005	% change 1995-2005	1995	2005	% change 1995-2005	1995	2005	% change 1995-2005
New York	2,216	2,248	1.4%	664	591	-11.0%	1,552	1,657	6.8%
North Carolina	880	945	7.4	252	235	-6.7	628	710	13.1
North Dakota	83	80	-3.6	20	21	5.0	63	59	-6.3
Ohio	1,394	1,348	-3.3	377	356	-5.6	1,017	992	-2.5
Oklahoma	427	415	-2.8	113	109	-3.5	314	306	-2.5
Oregon	388	400	3.1	102	107	4.9	286	293	2.4
Pennsylvania	1,417	1,385	-2.3	382	356	-6.8	1,035	1,029	-0.6
Rhode Island	115	119	3.5	33	31	-6.1	82	88	7.3
South Carolina	463	479	3.5	129	121	-6.2	334	358	7.2
South Dakota	101	103	2.0	26	28	7.7	75	75	0.0
Tennessee	638	686	7.5	178	177	-0.6	460	509	10.7
Texas	2,636	2,918	10.7	772	796	3.1	1,864	2,122	13.8
Utah	329	369	12.2	90	102	13.3	239	267	11.7
Vermont	71	73	2.8	18	18	0.0	53	55	3.8
Virginia	788	844	7.1	227	217	-4.4	561	627	11.8
Washington	690	728	5.5	188	196	4.3	502	532	6.0
West Virginia	205	192	-6.3	52	48	-7.7	153	144	-5.9
Wisconsin	659	644	-2.3	168	169	0.6	491	475	-3.3
Wyoming	67	71	6.0	16	19	18.8	51	52	2.0

Source: Bureau of the Census, Internet web site, http://www.census.gov; *calculations by New Strategist*

Women Aged 25 to 64 Will Grow in All 50 States

But the number of women aged 18 to 24 will decline in some states.

Nationally, the number of women aged 18 to 24 will increase by nearly 14 percent between 1995 and 2005. The number of women aged 25 to 64 will grow by 11 percent during the same period. Growth in the number of women aged 18 to 64 will vary sharply by state, however.

The largest increase in the number of women aged 18 to 64 will occur in Nevada (up 44 percent). Other states in which this age group will grow rapidly include Idaho, Utah, and Arizona. In some southern states (Alabama, Kentucky, Mississippi, South Carolina, and West Virginia), the number of college-aged women will decline between 1995 and 2005. The number of women aged 25 to 64 is projected to grow in every state except the District of Columbia.

❖ Businesses targeting college-aged women should carefully examine growth rates by state, since some areas will see hefty increases in this age group while others see declines.

Projections of Women Aged 18 to 64 by State, 1995 and 2005

(number of women aged 18 to 64 by state and age, 1995 and 2005; percent change 1995-2005; numbers in thousands)

	total aged 18 to 64			aged 18 to 24			aged 25 to 64		
	1995	2005	% change 1995-2005	1995	2005	% change 1995-2005	1995	2005	% change 1995-2005
Total	81,069	90,119	11.2%	12,230	13,915	13.8%	68,839	76,204	10.7%
Alabama	1,349	1,490	10.5	221	218	-1.4	1,128	1,272	12.8
Alaska	180	212	17.8	30	39	30.0	150	173	15.3
Arizona	1,234	1,583	28.3	193	262	35.8	1,041	1,321	26.9
Arkansas	757	869	14.8	125	125	0.0	632	744	17.7
California	9,507	10,485	10.3	1,397	1,779	27.3	8,110	8,706	7.3
Colorado	1,192	1,435	20.4	170	226	32.9	1,022	1,209	18.3
Connecticut	1,018	1,058	3.9	133	148	11.3	885	910	2.8
Delaware	228	259	13.6	34	40	17.6	194	219	12.9
Dist. Columbia	189	176	-6.9	27	34	25.9	162	142	-12.3
Florida	4,157	5,006	20.4	572	695	21.5	3,585	4,311	20.3
Georgia	2,321	2,764	19.1	360	426	18.3	1,961	2,338	19.2
Hawaii	356	403	13.2	53	61	15.1	303	342	12.9
Idaho	339	448	32.2	62	74	19.4	277	374	35.0
Illinois	3,651	3,865	5.9	543	596	9.8	3,108	3,269	5.2
Indiana	1,818	1,976	8.7	289	301	4.2	1,529	1,675	9.5
Iowa	849	904	6.5	135	141	4.4	714	763	6.9
Kansas	758	846	11.6	119	140	17.6	639	706	10.5
Kentucky	1,223	1,326	8.4	197	189	-4.1	1,026	1,137	10.8
Louisiana	1,348	1,434	6.4	232	241	3.9	1,116	1,193	6.9
Maine	386	419	8.5	55	55	0.0	331	364	10.0
Maryland	1,629	1,808	11.0	214	257	20.1	1,415	1,551	9.6
Massachusetts	1,926	2,030	5.4	269	313	16.4	1,657	1,717	3.6
Michigan	2,975	3,106	4.4	458	463	1.1	2,517	2,643	5.0
Minnesota	1,395	1,586	13.7	205	253	23.4	1,190	1,333	12.0
Mississippi	831	920	10.7	153	144	-5.9	678	776	14.5
Missouri	1,634	1,811	10.8	250	278	11.2	1,384	1,533	10.8
Montana	259	309	19.3	41	45	9.8	218	264	21.1
Nebraska	486	538	10.7	79	89	12.7	407	449	10.3
Nevada	463	668	44.3	62	94	51.6	401	574	43.1
New Hampshire	360	418	16.1	49	61	24.5	311	357	14.8
New Jersey	2,488	2,698	8.4	329	362	10.0	2,159	2,336	8.2
New Mexico	506	615	21.5	82	98	19.5	424	517	21.9

(continued)

(*continued from previous page*)

	total aged 18 to 64			aged 18 to 24			aged 25 to 64		
	1995	2005	% change 1995-2005	1995	2005	% change 1995-2005	1995	2005	% change 1995-2005
New York	5,735	5,835	1.7%	810	871	7.5%	4,925	4,964	0.8%
North Carolina	2,281	2,647	16.0	345	392	13.6	1,936	2,255	16.5
North Dakota	185	201	8.6	30	37	23.3	155	164	5.8
Ohio	3,478	3,627	4.3	534	544	1.9	2,944	3,083	4.7
Oklahoma	989	1,076	8.8	161	175	8.7	828	901	8.8
Oregon	958	1,138	18.8	137	163	19.0	821	975	18.8
Pennsylvania	3,700	3,859	4.3	534	551	3.2	3,166	3,308	4.5
Rhode Island	303	317	4.6	44	48	9.1	259	269	3.9
South Carolina	1,174	1,300	10.7	192	190	-1.0	982	1,110	13.0
South Dakota	209	243	16.3	37	42	13.5	172	201	16.9
Tennessee	1,684	1,944	15.4	255	283	11.0	1,429	1,661	16.2
Texas	5,725	6,674	16.6	947	1,160	22.5	4,778	5,514	15.4
Utah	555	712	28.3	125	155	24.0	430	557	29.5
Vermont	185	207	11.9	27	31	14.8	158	176	11.4
Virginia	2,151	2,387	11.0	318	352	10.7	1,833	2,035	11.0
Washington	1,680	1,999	19.0	241	296	22.8	1,439	1,703	18.3
West Virginia	575	591	2.8	94	77	-18.1	481	514	6.9
Wisconsin	1,548	1,723	11.3	238	273	14.7	1,310	1,450	10.7
Wyoming	142	174	22.5	23	28	21.7	119	146	22.7

Source: Bureau of the Census, Internet web site, http://www.census.gov; *calculations by New Strategist*

Slowing Growth for Women Aged 65+

The number of women aged 65 or older will decline in some states between 1995 and 2005.

Nationally, the number of women aged 65 or older has been growing rapidly. This growth should slow between 1995 and 2005. As the small generation born during the Depression fills the older age groups, the number of women aged 65 or older will be only 6 percent greater in 2005 than in 1995.

A few states will see dramatic increases in the number of elderly women between 1995 and 2005. In Alaska, for example, there will be 53 percent more women aged 65 or older in 2005 than in 1995. Nevada will experience a 48 percent increase and Colorado a 34 percent gain.

But the number of elderly women will decline in many states, including California, Connecticut, and New York. This decline is only temporary, however. When the baby-boom generation ages into its late 60s beginning in 2011, the number of elderly Americans will rise in every state.

❖ Businesses targeting older women should pay close attention to their distribution by state. One in four women aged 65 or older lives in California, Florida, or Texas.

Projections of Women Aged 65 or Older by State, 1995 to 2005

(number of women aged 65 or older by state, 1995 and 2005; percent change 1995-2005; numbers in thousands)

	1995	2005	percent change 1995-2005
Total	19,849	20,977	5.7%
Alabama	335	366	9.3
Alaska	15	23	53.3
Arizona	315	397	26.0
Arkansas	212	235	10.8
California	2,010	1,968	-2.1
Colorado	219	294	34.2
Connecticut	279	266	-4.7
Delaware	53	57	7.5
District of Columbia	49	39	-20.4
Florida	1,500	1,667	11.1
Georgia	439	504	14.8
Hawaii	81	93	14.8
Idaho	75	100	33.3
Illinois	892	876	-1.8
Indiana	440	464	5.5
Iowa	257	264	2.7
Kansas	209	212	1.4
Kentucky	292	317	8.6
Louisiana	297	328	10.4
Maine	102	100	-2.0
Maryland	341	353	3.5
Massachusetts	524	488	-6.9
Michigan	699	700	0.1
Minnesota	339	360	6.2
Mississippi	201	217	8.0
Missouri	443	453	2.3
Montana	64	81	26.6
Nebraska	135	143	5.9
Nevada	94	139	47.9
New Hampshire	80	85	6.3
New Jersey	652	638	-2.1
New Mexico	104	128	23.1
New York	1,466	1,365	-6.9

(continued)

(continued from previous page)

	1995	2005	percent change 1995-2005
North Carolina	543	638	17.5%
North Dakota	54	60	11.1
Ohio	892	910	2.0
Oklahoma	262	293	11.8
Oregon	245	295	20.4
Pennsylvania	1,153	1,104	-4.2
Rhode Island	96	85	-11.5
South Carolina	265	305	15.1
South Dakota	60	65	8.3
Tennessee	398	450	13.1
Texas	1,128	1,327	17.6
Utah	97	129	33.0
Vermont	41	44	7.3
Virginia	441	493	11.8
Washington	362	425	17.4
West Virginia	168	176	4.8
Wisconsin	401	419	4.5
Wyoming	30	39	30.0

Source: Bureau of the Census, Internet web site, http://www.census.gov; *calculations by New Strategist*

Hispanics and Asians Will Grow Rapidly in Every State

The number of Asian females will grow by 43 percent nationally between 1995 and 2005, while Hispanics will increase by 35 percent.

Although the number of Asian females will increase in every state between 1995 and 2005, California will continue to be home to the largest share—39 percent in 1995. Hispanic females are also likely to be found in California, with one-third living there.

Black females are distributed more evenly around the country. Five states had more than 1 million black females in 1995: California, Florida, Georgia, New York, and Texas.

The largest numbers of Native American females can be found in Arizona, California, and Oklahoma. Overall, there are only 1.1 million Native-Americans females in the U.S.

While the numbers of Asian, black, Hispanic, and Native American women are projected to grow in nearly every state between 1995 and 2005, the number of non-Hispanic white females will decline in many areas. The largest declines are projected for California and New York.

❖ Marketers can reach a majority of Asian and Hispanic women by targeting just a few states. Over half of Asian-American women live in just three states—California, Hawaii, or New York. Most Hispanic women live in California or Texas.

Projections of Asian Females by State, 1995 and 2005

(number of Asian females by state, 1995 and 2005; percent change 1995-2005; numbers in thousands)

	1995	2005	percent change 1995-2005
Total	4,831	6,920	43.2%
Alabama	15	21	40.0
Alaska	15	36	140.0
Arizona	42	68	61.9
Arkansas	8	12	50.0
California	1,873	2,651	41.5
Colorado	44	68	54.5
Connecticut	34	50	47.1
Delaware	6	9	50.0
District of Columbia	9	10	11.1
Florida	117	170	45.3
Georgia	58	88	51.7
Hawaii	388	445	14.7
Idaho	7	10	42.9
Illinois	184	252	37.0
Indiana	25	37	48.0
Iowa	17	27	58.8
Kansas	21	31	47.6
Kentucky	13	17	30.8
Louisiana	27	37	37.0
Maine	4	6	50.0
Maryland	96	137	42.7
Massachusetts	97	157	61.9
Michigan	68	99	45.6
Minnesota	55	88	60.0
Mississippi	8	12	50.0
Missouri	28	38	35.7
Montana	3	5	66.7
Nebraska	9	15	66.7
Nevada	33	55	66.7
New Hampshire	6	9	50.0
New Jersey	192	302	57.3
New Mexico	11	18	63.6

(continued)

(continued from previous page)

	1995	2005	percent change 1995-2005
New York	440	620	40.9%
North Carolina	39	59	51.3
North Dakota	2	3	50.0
Ohio	59	86	45.8
Oklahoma	22	30	36.4
Oregon	48	71	47.9
Pennsylvania	91	134	47.3
Rhode Island	11	18	63.6
South Carolina	16	20	25.0
South Dakota	2	3	50.0
Tennessee	23	35	52.2
Texas	231	347	50.2
Utah	24	39	62.5
Vermont	2	4	100.0
Virginia	111	168	51.4
Washington	153	228	49.0
West Virginia	5	7	40.0
Wisconsin	37	65	75.7
Wyoming	2	3	50.0

Source: Bureau of the Census, Internet web site, http://www.census.gov; *calculations by New Strategist*

Projections of Black Females by State, 1995 and 2005

(number of black females by state, 1995 and 2005; percent change 1995-2005; numbers in thousands)

	1995	2005	percent change 1995-2005
Total	17,416	19,863	14.1%
Alabama	585	634	8.4
Alaska	12	14	16.7
Arizona	70	101	44.3
Arkansas	211	226	7.1
California	1,216	1,275	4.9
Colorado	80	112	40.0
Connecticut	157	183	16.6
Delaware	69	83	20.3
District of Columbia	192	172	-10.4
Florida	1,083	1,349	24.6
Georgia	1,073	1,332	24.1
Hawaii	11	13	18.2
Idaho	3	5	66.7
Illinois	961	1,017	5.8
Indiana	248	279	12.5
Iowa	28	35	25.0
Kansas	79	95	20.3
Kentucky	144	156	8.3
Louisiana	737	809	9.8
Maine	2	2	0.0
Maryland	711	852	19.8
Massachusetts	193	239	23.8
Michigan	733	790	7.8
Minnesota	62	92	48.4
Mississippi	519	561	8.1
Missouri	314	352	12.1
Montana	1	3	200.0
Nebraska	33	42	27.3
Nevada	53	80	50.9
New Hampshire	3	5	66.7
New Jersey	605	703	16.2
New Mexico	20	27	35.0

(continued)

(continued from previous page)

	1995	2005	percent change 1995-2005
New York	1,706	1,825	7.0%
North Carolina	849	988	16.4
North Dakota	1	2	100.0
Ohio	664	735	10.7
Oklahoma	132	160	21.2
Oregon	27	37	37.0
Pennsylvania	622	680	9.3
Rhode Island	24	30	25.0
South Carolina	590	644	9.2
South Dakota	1	2	100.0
Tennessee	456	532	16.7
Texas	1,185	1,450	22.4
Utah	8	13	62.5
Vermont	1	2	100.0
Virginia	679	799	17.7
Washington	84	100	19.0
West Virginia	30	32	6.7
Wisconsin	148	191	29.1
Wyoming	1	3	200.0

Source: Bureau of the Census, Internet web site, http://www.census.gov; *calculations by New Strategist*

Projections of Hispanic Females by State, 1995 and 2005

(number of Hispanic females by state, 1995 and 2005; percent change 1995-2005; numbers in thousands)

	1995	2005	percent change 1995-2005
Total	13,283	17,976	35.3%
Alabama	16	21	31.3
Alaska	12	17	41.7
Arizona	430	635	47.7
Arkansas	13	20	53.8
California	4,453	6,024	35.3
Colorado	253	341	34.8
Connecticut	126	169	34.1
Delaware	9	14	55.6
District of Columbia	18	23	27.8
Florida	996	1,459	46.5
Georgia	68	108	58.8
Hawaii	49	58	18.4
Idaho	34	58	70.6
Illinois	520	704	35.4
Indiana	59	81	37.3
Iowa	22	30	36.4
Kansas	54	81	50.0
Kentucky	13	18	38.5
Louisiana	53	70	32.1
Maine	3	5	66.7
Maryland	86	130	51.2
Massachusetts	179	265	48.0
Michigan	116	144	24.1
Minnesota	35	55	57.1
Mississippi	10	12	20.0
Missouri	37	53	43.2
Montana	8	13	62.5
Nebraska	24	35	45.8
Nevada	90	169	87.8
New Hampshire	6	10	66.7
New Jersey	449	604	34.5
New Mexico	332	415	25.0

(continued)

(continued from previous page)

	1995	2005	percent change 1995-2005
New York	1,306	1,585	21.4%
North Carolina	45	66	46.7
North Dakota	2	4	100.0
Ohio	81	104	28.4
Oklahoma	50	70	40.0
Oregon	69	113	63.8
Pennsylvania	140	196	40.0
Rhode Island	30	46	53.3
South Carolina	17	23	35.3
South Dakota	3	4	33.3
Tennessee	22	33	50.0
Texas	2,580	3,332	29.1
Utah	54	81	50.0
Vermont	2	3	50.0
Virginia	101	158	56.4
Washington	134	211	57.5
West Virginia	5	8	60.0
Wisconsin	55	77	40.0
Wyoming	14	21	50.0

Source: Bureau of the Census, Internet web site, http://www.census.gov; *calculations by New Strategist*

Projections of Native American Females by State, 1995 and 2005

(number of Native American females by state, 1995 and 2005; percent change 1995-2005; numbers in thousands)

	1995	*2005*	*percent change 1995-2005*
Total	1,128	1,301	15.3%
Alabama	8	9	12.5
Alaska	46	46	0.0
Arizona	125	143	14.4
Arkansas	7	8	14.3
California	150	148	-1.3
Colorado	18	23	27.8
Connecticut	4	4	0.0
Delaware	1	1	0.0
District of Columbia	1	-	-
Florida	22	29	31.8
Georgia	8	9	12.5
Hawaii	3	3	0.0
Idaho	8	13	62.5
Illinois	12	14	16.7
Indiana	7	8	14.3
Iowa	4	6	50.0
Kansas	11	15	36.4
Kentucky	3	3	0.0
Louisiana	10	10	0.0
Maine	3	3	0.0
Maryland	7	8	14.3
Massachusetts	7	7	0.0
Michigan	30	32	6.7
Minnesota	28	36	28.6
Mississippi	4	4	0.0
Missouri	11	13	18.2
Montana	27	34	25.9
Nebraska	7	9	28.6
Nevada	13	16	23.1
New Hampshire	1	1	0.0
New Jersey	10	12	20.0
New Mexico	78	96	23.1

(continued)

(continued from previous page)

	1995	2005	percent change 1995-2005
New York	36	40	11.1%
North Carolina	45	50	11.1
North Dakota	14	19	35.7
Ohio	11	12	9.1
Oklahoma	136	151	11.0
Oregon	22	28	27.3
Pennsylvania	8	11	37.5
Rhode Island	2	4	100.0
South Carolina	4	4	0.0
South Dakota	27	34	25.9
Tennessee	5	7	40.0
Texas	41	53	29.3
Utah	15	22	46.7
Vermont	1	1	0.0
Virginia	8	9	12.5
Washington	50	58	16.0
West Virginia	1	1	0.0
Wisconsin	22	26	18.2
Wyoming	6	8	33.3

Note: (-) means leass than 500.
Source: Bureau of the Census, Internet web site, http://www.census.gov; *calculations by New Strategist*

Projections of Non-Hispanic White Females by State, 1995 and 2005

(number of non-Hispanic white females by state, 1995 and 2005; percent change 1995-2005; numbers in thousands)

	1995	2005	percent change 1995-2005
Total	98,975	101,855	2.9%
Alabama	1,591	1,721	8.2
Alaska	206	227	10.2
Arizona	1,491	1,749	17.3
Arkansas	1,047	1,156	10.4
California	8,393	7,612	-9.3
Colorado	1,510	1,733	14.8
Connecticut	1,383	1,318	-4.7
Delaware	283	303	7.1
District of Columbia	79	78	-1.3
Florida	5,154	5,546	7.6
Georgia	2,503	2,798	11.8
Hawaii	164	170	3.7
Idaho	535	662	23.7
Illinois	4,424	4,340	-1.9
Indiana	2,648	2,787	5.2
Iowa	1,391	1,411	1.4
Kansas	1,143	1,186	3.8
Kentucky	1,817	1,913	5.3
Louisiana	1,434	1,434	0.0
Maine	624	640	2.6
Maryland	1,710	1,708	-0.1
Massachusetts	2,713	2,635	-2.9
Michigan	3,971	3,954	-0.4
Minnesota	2,164	2,274	5.1
Mississippi	864	924	6.9
Missouri	2,364	2,491	5.4
Montana	400	456	14.0
Nebraska	766	802	4.7
Nevada	569	729	28.1
New Hampshire	568	626	10.2
New Jersey	2,908	2,802	-3.6
New Mexico	426	484	13.6
New York	6,244	5,779	-7.4

(continued)

(continued from previous page)

	1995	2005	percent change 1995-2005
North Carolina	2,732	3,077	12.6%
North Dakota	301	313	4.0
Ohio	4,959	4,961	0.0
Oklahoma	1,345	1,381	2.7
Oregon	1,431	1,595	11.5
Pennsylvania	5,431	5,361	-1.3
Rhode Island	453	433	-4.4
South Carolina	1,278	1,395	9.2
South Dakota	336	366	8.9
Tennessee	2,216	2,478	11.8
Texas	5,534	5,883	6.3
Utah	885	1,063	20.1
Vermont	291	314	7.9
Virginia	2,493	2,609	4.7
Washington	2,329	2,577	10.6
West Virginia	907	912	0.6
Wisconsin	2,350	2,438	3.7
Wyoming	217	251	15.7

Source: Bureau of the Census, Internet web site, http://www.census.gov; *calculations by New Strategist*

Projections of White Females by State, 1995 and 2005

(number of white females by state, 1995 and 2005; percent change 1995-2005; numbers in thousands)

	1995	2005	percent change 1995-2005
Total	111,058	118,112	6.4%
Alabama	1,604	1,739	8.4
Alaska	215	242	12.6
Arizona	1,894	2,341	23.6
Arkansas	1,059	1,174	10.9
California	12,558	13,232	5.4
Colorado	1,747	2,050	17.3
Connecticut	1,493	1,464	-1.9
Delaware	291	315	8.2
District of Columbia	92	97	5.4
Florida	6,078	6,863	12.9
Georgia	2,561	2,892	12.9
Hawaii	185	207	11.9
Idaho	566	715	26.3
Illinois	4,910	4,994	1.7
Indiana	2,702	2,860	5.8
Iowa	1,411	1,438	1.9
Kansas	1,192	1,259	5.6
Kentucky	1,828	1,929	5.5
Louisiana	1,479	1,495	1.1
Maine	627	645	2.9
Maryland	1,779	1,814	2.0
Massachusetts	2,852	2,841	-0.4
Michigan	4,074	4,082	0.2
Minnesota	2,195	2,323	5.8
Mississippi	872	935	7.2
Missouri	2,397	2,538	5.9
Montana	407	467	14.7
Nebraska	788	833	5.7
Nevada	651	884	35.8
New Hampshire	574	635	10.6
New Jersey	3,292	3,308	0.5
New Mexico	746	878	17.7

(continued)

(continued from previous page)

	1995	***2005***	***percent change 1995-2005***
New York	7,233	6,963	-3.7%
North Carolina	2,770	3,134	13.1
North Dakota	303	317	4.6
Ohio	5,031	5,053	0.4
Oklahoma	1,387	1,442	4.0
Oregon	1,494	1,698	13.7
Pennsylvania	5,549	5,525	-0.4
Rhode Island	477	469	-1.7
South Carolina	1,292	1,415	9.5
South Dakota	339	370	9.1
Tennessee	2,235	2,507	12.2
Texas	8,032	9,069	12.9
Utah	935	1,137	21.6
Vermont	293	317	8.2
Virginia	2,581	2,747	6.4
Washington	2,446	2,765	13.0
West Virginia	912	919	0.8
Wisconsin	2,400	2,506	4.4
Wyoming	230	270	17.4

Source: Bureau of the Census, Internet web site, http://www.census.gov; *calculations by New Strategist*

Young Women Are Most Likely to Move

Mobility is highest among women aged 18 to 34.

Only 16 percent of females moved between March 1993 and March 1994. Those most likely to move are young adults, aged 20 to 24. Thirty-six percent of women in this age group moved between 1993 and 1994, according to the Census Bureau. Most of the moves in this age group occur as women leave their parents' home and establish their own household. Mobility rates fall with age as people buy homes and establish roots in a community. The lowest mobility rate is found among women aged 75 to 79—only 4 percent of women in this age group moved between 1993 and 1994.

Most women who move don't move very far. Only 35 percent of women who moved between 1993 and 1994 left the county. Just 16 percent moved out of state. Women in their 20s are most likely to move out of county or out of state.

❖ Americans are less likely to move today than they were in the 1950s and 1960s, when about 20 percent moved each year. Behind this decline are two-income couples. When both husband and wife have jobs, moving to a new city or state is much more difficult.

Geographical Mobility of Females by Age, 1993-1994

(number of females aged 1 or older, and number and percent who moved between March 1993 and March 1994, by age and type of move; numbers in thousands)

					different house in the U.S.					
							different county			
								different state		
	total	same house (non-movers)	total movers	same county	total	same state	total	same region	different region	movers from abroad
Total, aged 1 or older	130,896	109,435	20,887	13,499	7,388	4,111	3,277	1,796	1,481	573
Aged 1 to 4	8,063	6,315	1,722	1,161	561	304	257	136	121	27
Aged 5 to 9	9,434	7,714	1,683	1,132	551	308	243	150	93	38
Aged 10 to 14	9,372	8,081	1,262	858	404	235	169	94	75	29
Aged 15 to 19	8,723	7,030	1,629	1,050	579	333	246	132	114	63
Aged 15 to 17	5,268	4,487	759	483	277	154	123	81	42	22
Aged 18 and 19	3,454	2,543	870	568	302	179	123	52	71	42
Aged 20 to 24	9,338	5,831	3,392	2,222	1,170	740	430	238	192	114
Aged 25 to 29	9,857	6,990	2,785	1,832	953	509	444	248	195	82
Aged 30 to 34	11,211	8,748	2,399	1,569	830	468	362	174	188	64
Aged 35 to 39	11,077	9,393	1,660	1,072	588	296	292	147	145	24
Aged 40 to 44	9,906	8,673	1,191	708	483	292	192	113	79	42
Aged 45 to 49	8,420	7,496	890	553	337	152	186	101	85	35
Aged 50 to 54	6,647	6,073	560	350	210	109	100	57	43	14
Aged 55 to 59	5,593	5,206	370	207	163	85	78	36	43	17
Aged 60 to 64	5,212	4,887	318	206	112	67	45	27	19	7
Aged 60 and 61	2,083	1,950	132	89	43	30	13	7	5	1
Aged 62 to 64	3,129	2,937	186	117	69	37	33	19	13	6

(continued)

(continued from previous page)

			different house in the U.S.							
					different county					
							different state			
	total	same house (non-movers)	total movers	same county	total	same state	total	same region	different region	movers from abroad
Aged 65 to 69	5,365	4,996	360	186	174	84	89	57	32	9
Aged 70 to 74	4,798	4,538	258	160	98	44	54	34	20	2
Aged 75 to 79	3,514	3,354	156	93	63	29	34	25	8	4
Aged 80 to 84	2,455	2,312	141	75	66	35	31	19	12	2
Aged 85 or older	1,911	1,798	111	65	46	21	25	8	17	1
Median age	34.8	37.1	26.4	25.9	27.3	26.3	28.3	28.0	28.7	26.0
Percent										
Total, aged 1 or older	100.0%	83.6%	16.0%	10.3%	5.6%	3.1%	2.5%	1.4%	1.1%	0.4%
Aged 1 to 4	100.0	78.3	21.4	14.4	7.0	3.8	3.2	1.7	1.5	0.3
Aged 5 to 9	100.0	81.8	17.8	12.0	5.8	3.3	2.6	1.6	1.0	0.4
Aged 10 to 14	100.0	86.2	13.5	9.2	4.3	2.5	1.8	1.0	0.8	0.3
Aged 15 to 19	100.0	80.6	18.7	12.0	6.6	3.8	2.8	1.5	1.3	0.7
Aged 15 to 17	100.0	85.2	14.4	9.2	5.3	2.9	2.3	1.5	0.8	0.4
Aged 18 and 19	100.0	73.6	25.2	16.4	8.7	5.2	3.6	1.5	2.1	1.2
Aged 20 to 24	100.0	62.4	36.3	23.8	12.5	7.9	4.6	2.5	2.1	1.2
Aged 25 to 29	100.0	70.9	28.3	18.6	9.7	5.2	4.5	2.5	2.0	0.8
Aged 30 to 34	100.0	78.0	21.4	14.0	7.4	4.2	3.2	1.6	1.7	0.6
Aged 35 to 39	100.0	84.8	15.0	9.7	5.3	2.7	2.6	1.3	1.3	0.2
Aged 40 to 44	100.0	87.6	12.0	7.1	4.9	2.9	1.9	1.1	0.8	0.4

(continued)

(continued from previous page)

			different house in the U.S.							
					different county					
							different state			
	total	same house (non-movers)	total movers	same county	total	same state	total	same region	different region	movers from abroad
Aged 45 to 49	100.0%	89.0%	10.6%	6.6%	4.0%	1.8%	2.2%	1.2%	1.0%	0.4%
Aged 50 to 54	100.0	91.4	8.4	5.3	3.2	1.6	1.5	0.9	0.6	0.2
Aged 55 to 59	100.0	93.1	6.6	3.7	2.9	1.5	1.4	0.6	0.8	0.3
Aged 60 to 64	100.0	93.8	6.1	4.0	2.1	1.3	0.9	0.5	0.4	0.1
Aged 60 and 61	100.0	93.6	6.3	4.3	2.1	1.4	0.6	0.3	0.2	0.0
Aged 62 to 64	100.0	93.9	5.9	3.7	2.2	1.2	1.1	0.6	0.4	0.2
Aged 65 to 69	100.0	93.1	6.7	3.5	3.2	1.6	1.7	1.1	0.6	0.2
Aged 70 to 74	100.0	94.6	5.4	3.3	2.0	0.9	1.1	0.7	0.4	0.0
Aged 75 to 79	100.0	95.4	4.4	2.6	1.8	0.8	1.0	0.7	0.2	0.1
Aged 80 to 84	100.0	94.2	5.7	3.1	2.7	1.4	1.3	0.8	0.5	0.1
Aged 85 or older	100.0	94.1	5.8	3.4	2.4	1.1	1.3	0.4	0.9	0.1

Source: Bureau of the Census, Geographical Mobility: March 1993 to March 1994, *Current Population Reports, P20-485, 1995; calculations by New Strategist*

Nine Percent of Females Are Foreign-Born

Women account for 51 percent of the nation's foreign-born population.

Over 11 million women and girls in the U.S. are immigrants. The largest number are from Mexico (2.9 million), accounting for 37 percent of the female foreign-born population in 1994. Slightly fewer than half (45 percent) of the Mexican foreign born are females. The proportion of females among the foreign born varies by country. Fully 71 percent of the German foreign born are female, versus only 42 percent of the foreign born from India.

With more immigrants arriving in the U.S. every day, the foreign-born population is growing. In 1994, 804,000 immigrants entered the country. Slightly more than half (54 percent) were women. In 1994, female immigrants were most likely to be from Mexico (14 percent), followed by the former Soviet Union (8 percent), the Philippines (8 percent), and China (6 percent).

❖ The sizable and growing immigrant population of the U.S. makes the female population increasingly multicultural. Understanding the interests and needs of women from different cultures is of great importance to many consumer businesses.

Foreign-Born Population by Country of Birth, 1994

(number of total and female foreign-born persons by country of birth and percent female, for the 14 largest foreign-born populations in the United States ranked by size, 1994; numbers in thousands)

		female	
	number	*number*	*percent*
Total persons	259,752	132,838	51.1%
Total native born	237,184	121,402	51.2
Total foreign born	22,568	11,436	50.7
Mexico	6,264	2,860	45.7
Philippines	1,033	565	54.7
Cuba	805	423	52.5
El Salvador	718	345	48.1
Canada	679	399	58.8
Germany	625	446	71.4
China	565	282	49.9
Dominican Republic	556	314	56.5
Korea	533	303	56.8
Vietnam	496	259	52.2
India	493	209	42.4
Italy	483	259	53.6
England	454	265	58.4
Russia	454	256	56.4

Source: Bureau of the Census, The Foreign-Born Population: 1994, *Current Population Reports, P20-486, 1995; and Internet web site,* http://www.census.gov; *calculations by New Strategist*

Immigrants by Country of Birth, 1994

(number of total and female immigrants to the U.S. and percent female, for countries sending at least 6,000 immigrants to the U.S., 1994)

		female	
	total	number	percent
Total immigrants	804,416	431,684	53.7%
Mexico	111,398	62,198	55.8
Soviet Union (former)	63,420	34,093	53.8
China, mainland	53,985	27,792	51.5
Philippines	53,535	32,377	60.5
Dominican Republic	51,189	26,321	51.4
Vietnam	41,345	21,264	51.4
India	34,921	18,846	54.0
Poland	28,048	14,567	51.9
El Salvador	17,644	9,586	54.3
Ireland	17,256	7,639	44.3
United Kingdom	16,326	7,742	47.4
Canada	16,068	8,258	51.4
Korea	16,011	9,244	57.7
Cuba	14,727	6,977	47.4
Jamaica	14,349	7,665	53.4
Haiti	13,333	7,506	56.3
Iran	11,422	6,272	54.9
Colombia	10,847	6,422	59.2
Taiwan	10,032	5,613	56.0
Peru	9,177	5,161	56.2
Pakistan	8,698	4,430	50.9
Hong Kong	7,731	4,017	52.0
Guyana	7,662	4,060	53.0
Guatemala	7,389	4,018	54.4
Germany	6,992	4,812	68.8
Trinidad & Tobago	6,292	3,458	55.0
Japan	6,093	4,197	68.9

Source: U.S. Immigration and Naturalization Service, Statistical Yearbook of the Immigration and Naturalization Service, 1994

CHAPTER

8

Spending

❖ **Married couples with children spend the most.**

They spent an average of $44,989 in 1995—or 39 percent more than average. In contrast, single parents spent an average of only $22,626.

❖ **Married couples without children also spend a lot on some items.**

These couples, many of whom are empty-nesters, spend much more than average on cruises and airline fares, health insurance and drugs, household furnishings and equipment.

❖ **Women who live alone spent an average of $17,677 in 1994-95.**

Those aged 35 to 44 spent the most, an average of $24,646, while those under age 25 spent the least—just $11,925.

❖ **Although they spend the least overall, women under age 25 spend more than average on some items.**

They spend more than four times the average on education, 21 percent more on food away from home, and 35 percent more on alcoholic beverages.

Married Couples with Children Are the Biggest Spenders

Single parents spend only about half as much.

Married couples spent $41,139 in 1995, 27 percent more than the $32,277 spent by the average household. But married couples with children spent even more, an average of $44,989—or 39 percent more than average. Spending by households headed by single parents was only 70 percent of the average ($22,626), primarily because they have less money to spend.

The Bureau of Labor Statistics does not collect spending data by sex—except for single-person households. See the tables beginning on page 367 for the spending of women who live alone. To get an idea of how women spend in households with more than one person, spending data by household type are the best approximation.

The Indexed Spending table beginning on page 362 shows spending by type of household in comparison to what the average household spends. An index of 100 means the household type spends an average amount on an item. An index above 100 means the household type spends more than average on an item, while an index below 100 signifies below-average spending. A look at the table reveals spending well below average for single-parent households, although they spend close to the average on most foods.

Married couples with children at home spend much more than average on most items. They are big spenders on personal services (day care). They also spend well above average on children's clothes, entertainment, and education. Married couples without children at home (many of them empty nesters) spend much more than average on such items as public transportation (cruises and airline fares), health insurance and drugs, household furnishings and equipment.

❖ Because women handle the checkbook and make the bulk of day-to-day spending decisions in most families, knowing how to reach women with a compelling message is vital to consumer businesses.

Spending by Household Type, 1995

(selected characteristics of consumer units and average annual spending by category and type of consumer unit, 1995)

		married couples			
	total consumer units	total	couples only	couples with children of any age at home	single parents with children under age 18 at home
Number of consumer units (in thousands)	103,024	53,999	22,034	27,928	6,702
Average income before taxes	$36,948	$49,526	$44,765	$53,715	$19,595
Average number of persons in cu	2.5	3.2	2.0	3.9	2.9
Average number of earners in cu	1.3	1.7	1.2	2.1	0.9
Aver. no. of vehicles owned by cu	1.9	2.5	2.3	2.7	1.1
Percent homeowners	64%	80%	85%	78%	33%
With mortgage	38	53	41	61	23
Without mortgage	26	28	45	16	10
Percent renters	36	20	15	22	67
Percent black	11	7	5	7	32
Average spending	**$32,277**	**$41,139**	**$36,052**	**$44,989**	**$22,626**
FOOD	**$4,505**	**$5,725**	**$4,722**	**$6,368**	**$3,586**
Food at home	**2,803**	**3,558**	**2,772**	**4,041**	**2,529**
Cereals and bakery products	441	562	430	649	406
Cereals and cereal products	165	209	151	249	172
Bakery products	276	352	279	400	234
Meats, poultry, fish, and eggs	752	947	717	1,078	752
Beef	228	287	214	322	241
Pork	156	192	148	218	164
Other meats	104	131	93	159	105
Poultry	138	173	126	201	134
Fish and seafood	97	126	109	135	79
Eggs	30	37	28	42	29
Dairy products	297	377	285	437	273
Fresh milk and cream	123	154	107	185	128
Other dairy products	174	222	179	252	146
Fruits and vegetables	457	577	490	621	372
Fresh fruits	144	182	161	189	115
Fresh vegetables	137	173	153	179	90

(continued)

(continued from previous page)

	total consumer units	married couples: total	couples only	couples with children of any age at home	single parents with children under age 18 at home
Processed fruits	$96	$122	$93	$142	$90
Processed vegetables	80	101	82	112	77
Other food at home	856	1,096	849	1,256	726
Sugar and other sweets	112	145	118	163	95
Fats and oils	82	104	85	114	72
Miscellaneous foods	377	482	348	574	338
Nonalcoholic beverages	240	300	230	343	202
Food prep by cu, out-of-town trips	45	64	68	62	20
Food away from home	**1,702**	**2,166**	**1,950**	**2,327**	**1,057**
ALCOHOLIC BEVERAGES	**277**	**318**	**338**	**303**	**95**
HOUSING	**10,465**	**12,940**	**11,512**	**13,997**	**8,171**
Shelter	**5,932**	**7,145**	**6,176**	**7,863**	**4,710**
Owned dwellings*	3,754	5,356	4,637	5,963	1,788
Mortgage interest and charges	2,107	3,137	2,190	3,857	1,176
Property taxes	932	1,307	1,419	1,263	404
Maintenance/repair/insurance/other	716	913	1,029	843	208
Rented dwellings	1,786	1,224	909	1,376	2,808
Other lodging	392	565	630	524	114
Utilities, fuels, and public services	**2,193**	**2,629**	**2,396**	**2,751**	**1,880**
Natural gas	268	319	304	328	238
Electricity	870	1,065	956	1,128	761
Fuel oil and other fuels	87	105	112	99	42
Telephone	708	805	723	845	658
Water and other public services	260	334	301	351	180
Household operations	**508**	**680**	**451**	**888**	**589**
Personal services	258	360	93	586	468
Other household expenses	250	320	358	302	121
Housekeeping supplies	**430**	**569**	**548**	**584**	**270**
Laundry and cleaning supplies	110	143	115	160	93
Other household products	194	264	262	263	110
Postage and stationery	125	162	171	160	67
Household furnishings & equip.	**1,403**	**1,916**	**1,941**	**1,911**	**722**
Household textiles	100	129	144	115	54
Furniture	327	452	367	520	236
Floor coverings	177	259	437	145	24

(continued)

(continued from previous page)

	total consumer units	married couples: total	married couples: couples only	married couples: couples with children of any age at home	single parents with children under age 18 at home
Major appliances	$155	$206	$194	$207	$92
Small appliances, misc. housewares	85	106	109	106	51
Miscellaneous household equipment	557	763	689	818	265
APPAREL AND SERVICES	**1,704**	**2,100**	**1,588**	**2,477**	**1,655**
Men and boys	**425**	**532**	**380**	**647**	**441**
Men, 16 and over	329	419	360	462	121
Boys, 2 to 15	96	113	20	184	321
Women and girls	**660**	**807**	**666**	**914**	**624**
Women, 16 and over	559	671	635	697	376
Girls, 2 to 15	101	136	31	217	248
Children under 2	**81**	**112**	**41**	**159**	**120**
Footwear	**278**	**334**	**199**	**431**	**286**
Other apparel products and services	**259**	**315**	**301**	**326**	**184**
TRANSPORTATION	**6,016**	**7,941**	**6,535**	**8,936**	**3,919**
Vehicle purchases	**2,639**	**3,516**	**2,584**	**4,169**	**1,913**
Cars and trucks, new	1,194	1,620	1,417	1,776	617
Cars and trucks, used	1,411	1,855	1,128	2,343	1,274
Other vehicles	34	42	40	50	22
Gasoline and motor oil	**1,006**	**1,315**	**1,096**	**1,463**	**642**
Other vehicle expenses	**2,016**	**2,652**	**2,337**	**2,899**	**1,151**
Vehicle finance charges	261	361	286	408	167
Maintenance and repairs	653	831	759	888	406
Vehicle insurance	713	915	797	1,002	450
Vehicle rent, leasing, licenses, other charges	390	546	494	601	128
Public transportation	**355**	**458**	**518**	**404**	**213**
HEALTH CARE	**1,732**	**2,244**	**2,438**	**2,102**	**803**
Health insurance	860	1,117	1,314	959	385
Medical services	511	675	567	777	237
Drugs	280	349	460	257	129
Medical supplies	80	103	96	109	53
ENTERTAINMENT	**1,612**	**2,077**	**1,830**	**2,319**	**1,082**
Fees and admissions	433	593	543	658	195
Television, radios, sound equipment	542	640	517	728	457

(continued)

(continued from previous page)

	total consumer units	married couples total	married couples: couples only	married couples: couples with children of any age at home	single parents with children under age 18 at home
Pets, toys, and playground equipment	$322	$421	$348	$485	$286
Other supplies, equip., and services	315	422	422	447	144
PERSONAL CARE PRODUCTS AND SERVICES	**403**	**498**	**451**	**530**	**305**
READING	**163**	**205**	**211**	**206**	**77**
EDUCATION	**471**	**631**	**391**	**847**	**264**
TOBACCO PRODUCTS AND SMOKING SUPPLIES	**269**	**296**	**242**	**312**	**234**
MISCELLANEOUS	**766**	**817**	**798**	**822**	**514**
CASH CONTRIBUTIONS	**925**	**1,191**	**1,457**	**1,033**	**550**
PERSONAL INSURANCE AND PENSIONS	**2,967**	**4,159**	**3,541**	**4,738**	**1,372**
Life and other personal insurance	374	551	505	598	194
Pensions and Social Security	2,593	3,607	3,035	4,140	1,177
GIFTS**	**987**	**1,202**	**1,359**	**1,120**	**462**
Food	**88**	**121**	**132**	**114**	**27**
Housing	**250**	**315**	**325**	**313**	**159**
Housekeeping supplies	38	50	56	48	25
Household textiles	10	13	14	10	12
Appliances and misc. housewares	27	35	42	31	11
Major appliances	5	6	8	4	3
Small appl. and misc. housewares	23	29	35	28	8
Miscellaneous household equipment	66	79	90	72	15
Other housing	109	139	123	151	95
Apparel and services	**258**	**282**	**320**	**261**	**161**
Males 2 and over	70	70	81	68	52
Females 2 and over	94	108	151	79	49
Children under 2	39	54	41	62	42
Other apparel products and services	55	49	47	52	17
Jewelry and watches	27	19	27	13	8
All other apparel products and serv.	29	30	21	39	10
Transportation	**48**	**61**	**71**	**48**	**14**
Health care	**22**	**21**	**28**	**16**	**12**

(continued)

(continued from previous page)

	total consumer units	married couples: total	married couples: couples only	married couples: couples with children of any age at home	single parents with children under age 18 at home
Entertainment	**$86**	**$103**	**$122**	**$92**	**$31**
Toys, games, hobbies, and tricycles	29	36	46	28	13
Other entertainment	57	67	75	64	18
Education	**120**	**181**	**214**	**175**	**21**
All other gifts	**114**	**118**	**146**	**103**	**38**

** This figure does not include the amount paid for mortgage principle, which is considered an asset.*
*** Expenditures on gifts are also included in the preceding product and service categories.*
Note: The Bureau of Labor Statistics uses consumer units rather than households as the sampling unit in the Consumer Expenditure survey. For the definition of consumer unit, see the Glossary. Expenditures listed for items in a given category may not add to the total for that category because the listing is incomplete.
Source: Bureau of Labor Statistics, Internet web site, http://www.bls.gov

Indexed Spending by Household Type, 1995

(indexed spending of consumer units by category and type of consumer unit, 1995)

	total consumer units	married couples: total	married couples: couples only	married couples: couples with children of any age at home	single parents with children under age 18 at home
Average spending	**100**	**127**	**112**	**139**	**70**
FOOD	**100**	**127**	**105**	**141**	**80**
Food at home	**100**	**127**	**99**	**144**	**90**
Cereals and bakery products	100	127	98	147	92
Cereals and cereal products	100	127	92	151	104
Bakery products	100	128	101	145	85
Meats, poultry, fish, and eggs	100	126	95	143	100
Beef	100	126	94	141	106
Pork	100	123	95	140	105
Other meats	100	126	89	153	101
Poultry	100	125	91	146	97
Fish and seafood	100	130	112	139	81
Eggs	100	123	93	140	97
Dairy products	100	127	96	147	92
Fresh milk and cream	100	125	87	150	104
Other dairy products	100	128	103	145	84
Fruits and vegetables	100	126	107	136	81
Fresh fruits	100	126	112	131	80
Fresh vegetables	100	126	112	131	66
Processed fruits	100	127	97	148	94
Processed vegetables	100	126	103	140	96
Other food at home	100	128	99	147	85
Sugar and other sweets	100	129	105	146	85
Fats and oils	100	127	104	139	88
Miscellaneous foods	100	128	92	152	90
Nonalcoholic beverages	100	125	96	143	84
Food prep by cu, out-of-town trips	100	142	151	138	44
Food away from home	**100**	**127**	**115**	**137**	**62**
ALCOHOLIC BEVERAGES	**100**	**115**	**122**	**109**	**34**
HOUSING	**100**	**124**	**110**	**134**	**78**
Shelter	**100**	**120**	**104**	**133**	**79**

(continued)

(continued from previous page)

	total consumer units	married couples: total	married couples: couples only	married couples: couples with children of any age at home	single parents with children under age 18 at home
Owned dwellings	100	143	124	159	48
Mortgage interest and charges	100	149	104	183	56
Property taxes	100	140	152	136	43
Maintenance/repair/insurance/other	100	128	144	118	29
Rented dwellings	100	69	51	77	157
Other lodging	100	144	161	134	29
Utilities, fuels, and public services	**100**	**120**	**109**	**125**	**86**
Natural gas	100	119	113	122	89
Electricity	100	122	110	130	87
Fuel oil and other fuels	100	121	129	114	48
Telephone	100	114	102	119	93
Water and other public services	100	128	116	135	69
Household operations	**100**	**134**	**89**	**175**	**116**
Personal services	100	140	36	227	181
Other household expenses	100	128	143	121	48
Housekeeping supplies	**100**	**132**	**127**	**136**	**63**
Laundry and cleaning supplies	100	130	105	145	85
Other household products	100	136	135	136	57
Postage and stationery	100	130	137	128	54
Household furnishings & equip.	**100**	**137**	**138**	**136**	**51**
Household textiles	100	129	144	115	54
Furniture	100	138	112	159	72
Floor coverings	100	146	247	82	14
Major appliances	100	133	125	134	59
Small appliances, misc. housewares	100	125	128	125	60
Miscellaneous household equipment	100	137	124	147	48
APPAREL AND SERVICES	**100**	**123**	**93**	**145**	**97**
Men and boys	**100**	**125**	**89**	**152**	**104**
Men, 16 and over	100	127	109	140	37
Boys, 2 to 15	100	118	21	192	334
Women and girls	**100**	**122**	**101**	**138**	**95**
Women, 16 and over	100	120	114	125	67
Girls, 2 to 15	100	135	31	215	246
Children under 2	**100**	**138**	**51**	**196**	**148**
Footwear	**100**	**120**	**72**	**155**	**103**
Other apparel products and services	**100**	**122**	**116**	**126**	**71**

(continued)

(continued from previous page)

	total consumer units	married couples: total	married couples: couples only	married couples: couples with children of any age at home	single parents with children under age 18 at home
TRANSPORTATION	**100**	**132**	**109**	**149**	**65**
Vehicle purchases	**100**	**133**	**98**	**158**	**72**
Cars and trucks, new	100	136	119	149	52
Cars and trucks, used	100	131	80	166	90
Other vehicles	100	124	118	147	65
Gasoline and motor oil	**100**	**131**	**109**	**145**	**64**
Other vehicle expenses	**100**	**132**	**116**	**144**	**57**
Vehicle finance charges	100	138	110	156	64
Maintenance and repairs	100	127	116	136	62
Vehicle insurance	100	128	112	141	63
Vehicle rent, leasing, licenses, other charges	100	140	127	154	33
Public transportation	**100**	**129**	**146**	**114**	**60**
HEALTH CARE	**100**	**130**	**141**	**121**	**46**
Health insurance	100	130	153	112	45
Medical services	100	132	111	152	46
Drugs	100	125	164	92	46
Medical supplies	100	129	120	136	66
ENTERTAINMENT	**100**	**129**	**114**	**144**	**67**
Fees and admissions	100	137	125	152	45
Television, radios, sound equipment	100	118	95	134	84
Pets, toys, and playground equipment	100	131	108	151	89
Other supplies, equip., and services	100	134	134	142	46
PERSONAL CARE PRODUCTS AND SERVICES	**100**	**124**	**112**	**132**	**76**
READING	**100**	**126**	**129**	**126**	**47**
EDUCATION	**100**	**134**	**83**	**180**	**56**
TOBACCO PRODUCTS AND SMOKING SUPPLIES	**100**	**110**	**90**	**116**	**87**
MISCELLANEOUS	**100**	**107**	**104**	**107**	**67**
CASH CONTRIBUTIONS	**100**	**129**	**158**	**112**	**59**
PERSONAL INSURANCE AND PENSIONS	**100**	**140**	**119**	**160**	**46**
Life and other personal insurance	100	147	135	160	52
Pensions and Social Security	100	139	117	160	45

(continued)

(continued from previous page)

	total consumer units	married couples: total	married couples: couples only	married couples: couples with children of any age at home	single parents with children under age 18 at home
GIFTS	**100**	**122**	**138**	**113**	**47**
Food	**100**	**138**	**150**	**130**	**31**
Housing	**100**	**126**	**130**	**125**	**64**
Housekeeping supplies	100	132	147	126	66
Household textiles	100	130	140	100	120
Appliances and misc housewares	100	130	156	115	41
Major appliances	100	120	160	80	60
Small appl and misc housewares	100	126	152	122	35
Miscellaneous household equipment	100	120	136	109	23
Other housing	100	128	113	139	87
Apparel and services	**100**	**109**	**124**	**101**	**62**
Males 2 and over	100	100	116	97	74
Females 2 and over	100	115	161	84	52
Children under 2	100	138	105	159	108
Other apparel products and services	100	89	85	95	31
Jewelry and watches	100	70	100	48	30
All other apparel products and serv	100	103	72	134	34
Transportation	**100**	**127**	**148**	**100**	**29**
Health care	**100**	**95**	**127**	**73**	**55**
Entertainment	**100**	**120**	**142**	**107**	**36**
Toys, games, hobbies, and tricycles	100	124	159	97	45
Other entertainment	100	118	132	112	32
Education	**100**	**151**	**178**	**146**	**18**
All other gifts	**100**	**104**	**128**	**90**	**33**

Note: The index compares the spending of each type of consumer unit with the spending of the average consumer unit. 100 is the average. An index of 132 means the spending of the consumer unit type is 32 percent above average, while an index of 75 means the spending of the consumer unit type is 25 percent below average. The Bureau of Labor Statistics uses consumer units rather than households as the sampling unit in the Consumer Expenditure Survey. For the definition of consumer unit, see the Glossary.
Source: Bureau of Labor Statistics, Internet web site, http://www.bls.gov; *calculations by New Strategist*

Among Women Who Live Alone, Spending Patterns Vary

Older women have different priorities than their younger counterparts.

Women who live alone spent an average of $17,677 a year in 1994-95. Those aged 35 to 44 spent the most, an average of $24,646, while those under age 25 spent the least—just $11,925.

The Indexed Spending table beginning on page 371 shows spending by age in comparison to what the average women who lives alone spends. An index of 100 means women in the age group spend an average amount on an item. An index above 100 means women in the age group spend more than average on an item, while an index below 100 signifies below-average spending.

Women under age 25 spend much more on education than the average woman who lives alone, with an index of 538. Many of these young women are in college. This age group also spent 21 percent more than average on food away from home (with an index of 121), 35 percent more on alcoholic beverages, and 45 percent more on used cars and trucks.

Women aged 25 to 54 have higher incomes and consequently spend more than the average woman who lives alone. They spend more on food away from home, entertainment, reading, and apparel, for example. One of the few categories in which their spending is less than average is health care.

Women aged 65 or older who live alone have relatively low incomes. Their spending in most categories is well below average. This group spends considerably more than average on health care, however.

❖ As baby-boom women become widowed and live alone, their tastes will change the spending patterns of older women. Businesses should prepare for these sophisticated and demanding older consumers.

Spending of Women Who Live Alone by Age, 1994-95

(selected characteristics of single-person consumer units headed by women and average annual spending by category and age, 1994-95)

	total	< 25	25 to 34	35 to 44	45 to 54	55 to 64	65+
Number of consumer units (in thousands)	16,063	1,531	1,907	1,506	1,643	1,988	7,487
Aver. income before taxes	$18,087	$9,646	$24,951	$28,073	$28,640	$19,645	$13,359
Aver. no. of earners in cu	0.5	0.9	0.9	0.9	0.9	0.6	0.1
Average number of vehicles owned by cu	0.8	0.7	0.9	1.0	0.9	1.0	0.7
Percent homeowners	51%	1%	18%	43%	57%	63%	67%
With mortgage	16	0	16	37	36	29	7
Without mortgage	35	1	2	7	22	33	60
Percent renters	49	99	82	57	43	37	33
Percent black	10	9	11	12	11	11	9
Average spending	**$17,677**	**$11,925**	**$23,395**	**$24,646**	**$24,094**	**$19,822**	**$14,003**
FOOD	**$2,237**	**$1,684**	**$2,743**	**$2,388**	**$2,837**	**$2,463**	**$2,012**
Food at home	**1,459**	**743**	**1,478**	**1,309**	**1,686**	**1,596**	**1,577**
Cereals and bakery products	236	147	231	205	267	252	255
Cereals and cereal products	80	60	91	75	87	70	84
Bakery products	156	88	139	130	179	182	171
Meats, poultry, fish, and eggs	356	129	326	290	460	451	385
Beef	98	35	86	80	128	141	102
Pork	74	14	62	53	96	106	82
Other meats	45	18	34	43	58	40	54
Poultry	77	36	78	62	95	92	82
Fish and seafood	46	19	54	40	60	53	47
Eggs	16	6	12	13	24	19	18
Dairy products	163	107	143	155	155	157	189
Fresh milk and cream	65	37	49	52	62	63	81
Other dairy products	98	70	95	103	93	93	107
Fruits and vegetables	274	118	289	208	285	292	316
Fresh fruits	90	39	99	60	85	88	109
Fresh vegetables	90	33	110	76	81	105	99
Processed fruits	54	25	42	44	60	57	64
Processed vegetables	41	22	37	28	58	43	45

(continued)

(continued from previous page)

	total	< 25	25 to 34	35 to 44	45 to 54	55 to 64	65+
Other food at home	$430	$241	$489	$451	$519	$445	$432
Sugar and other sweets	61	32	78	47	74	65	62
Fats and oils	47	17	38	40	48	47	59
Miscellaneous foods	183	105	208	213	213	178	183
Nonalcoholic beverages	120	72	133	124	158	129	116
Food prepared by cu, out-of-town trips	20	15	32	27	27	27	12
Food away from home	**777**	**941**	**1,265**	**1,079**	**1,151**	**866**	**435**
ALCOHOLIC BEVERAGES	**119**	**161**	**229**	**249**	**122**	**132**	**46**
HOUSING	**6,734**	**3,802**	**8,372**	**9,100**	**8,781**	**7,994**	**5,664**
Shelter	**3,954**	**2,590**	**5,466**	**6,093**	**5,456**	**4,270**	**3,005**
Owned dwellings*	1,765	54	1,021	3,168	2,990	2,513	1,556
Mortgage interest and charges	637	12	695	2,006	1,495	1,058	175
Property taxes	561	19	183	612	743	763	664
Maintenance/repair/ insurance/other expenses	567	23	143	549	752	692	717
Rented dwellings	2,017	2,354	4,287	2,748	2,188	1,490	1,326
Other lodging	172	182	158	178	277	267	123
Utilities, fuels, public services	**1,509**	**724**	**1,413**	**1,625**	**1,723**	**1,756**	**1,557**
Natural gas	201	39	124	180	194	213	257
Electricity	554	212	428	607	656	686	587
Fuel oil and other fuels	79	2	14	45	71	91	116
Telephone	510	448	762	645	611	560	396
Water and other public services	165	24	85	149	192	206	201
Household operations	**303**	**34**	**199**	**230**	**286**	**413**	**374**
Personal services	71	6	99	1	57	147	74
Other household expenses	232	28	100	229	229	266	300
Housekeeping supplies	**259**	**88**	**279**	**229**	**284**	**289**	**289**
Laundry and cleaning supplies	56	15	65	59	68	75	55
Other household products	112	29	104	81	99	116	143
Postage and stationery	91	44	110	88	116	98	91
Household furnishings and equipment	**709**	**367**	**1,015**	**922**	**1,032**	**1,266**	**439**
Household textiles	74	13	69	121	126	72	69
Furniture	170	121	329	224	219	282	87
Floor coverings	55	4	30	83	88	134	38
Major appliances	80	37	49	70	94	143	80
Small appl., misc. housewares	67	34	113	117	74	124	34
Misc. household equipment	263	159	426	307	430	510	131

(continued)

(continued from previous page)

	total	< 25	25 to 34	35 to 44	45 to 54	55 to 64	65+
APPAREL AND SERVICES	**$1,008**	**$959**	**$1,900**	**$1,676**	**$1,260**	**$1,181**	**$535**
Men and boys	**58**	**73**	**71**	**53**	**105**	**78**	**36**
Men, 16 and over	46	72	69	47	90	43	25
Boys, 2 to 15	12	1	1	6	15	35	12
Women and girls	**625**	**596**	**1,249**	**1,077**	**784**	**649**	**326**
Women, 16 and over	608	595	1,239	1,068	768	621	304
Girls, 2 to 15	17	1	11	8	16	27	22
Children under 2	**19**	**14**	**26**	**12**	**39**	**30**	**13**
Footwear	**158**	**144**	**279**	**302**	**98**	**195**	**101**
Other apparel products, svcs.	**147**	**132**	**275**	**231**	**233**	**229**	**59**
TRANSPORTATION	**2,397**	**1,929**	**4,381**	**4,158**	**3,211**	**2,422**	**1,448**
Vehicle purchases	**824**	**643**	**2,105**	**1,702**	**906**	**481**	**431**
Cars and trucks, new	523	208	1,494	1,272	459	269	271
Cars and trucks, used	301	435	611	431	447	213	160
Other vehicles	0.0	0.0	0.0	0.0	0.0	0.0	0.0
Gasoline and motor oil	**414**	**442**	**610**	**641**	**598**	**464**	**259**
Other vehicle expenses	**912**	**616**	**1,323**	**1,528**	**1,397**	**1,189**	**564**
Vehicle finance charges	71	57	213	130	128	62	16
Maintenance and repairs	326	248	365	588	515	414	214
Vehicle insurance	359	228	496	497	517	429	270
Vehicle rent, leasing, licenses, other charges	156	83	248	313	238	284	64
Public transportation	**247**	**228**	**343**	**287**	**310**	**287**	**194**
HEALTH CARE	**1,353**	**230**	**642**	**1,154**	**1,119**	**1,376**	**1,849**
Health insurance	667	77	234	341	374	554	1,059
Medical services	350	73	240	488	473	497	342
Drugs	283	51	116	274	193	258	403
Medical supplies	51	29	52	51	79	67	46
ENTERTAINMENT	**775**	**795**	**1,172**	**1,234**	**999**	**1,026**	**455**
Fees and admissions	210	225	318	293	270	313	123
Television, radios, sound equip.	315	373	435	525	342	329	215
Pets, toys, playground equip.	174	96	286	311	308	210	95
Other supplies, equip., services	76	100	133	105	79	175	23
PERSONAL CARE PRODUCTS & SERVICES	**249**	**200**	**397**	**262**	**335**	**242**	**202**
READING	**124**	**64**	**140**	**171**	**157**	**154**	**107**
EDUCATION	**226**	**1,217**	**401**	**166**	**242**	**57**	**30**

(continued)

(continued from previous page)

	total	< 25	25 to 34	35 to 44	45 to 54	55 to 64	65+
TOBACCO PRODUCTS & SMOKING SUPPLIES	**$120**	**$87**	**$124**	**$216**	**$235**	**$201**	**$60**
MISCELLANEOUS	**552**	**236**	**436**	**887**	**1,394**	**599**	**379**
CASH CONTRIBUTIONS	**645**	**55**	**229**	**430**	**805**	**565**	**902**
PERSONAL INSURANCE, PENSIONS	**1,139**	**508**	**2,230**	**2,555**	**2,597**	**1,411**	**312**
Life and other personal insurance	143	18	69	139	201	161	170
Pensions and Social Security	996	490	2,161	2,416	2,396	1,250	143
GIFTS**	**692**	**644**	**746**	**687**	**1,100**	**1,075**	**491**
Food	**56**	**21**	**69**	**39**	**104**	**139**	**30**
Housing	**200**	**186**	**218**	**156**	**282**	**309**	**161**
Housekeeping supplies	33	27	48	40	39	43	26
Household textiles	20	0.0	11	3	35	20	27
Appliances, misc. housewares	25	10	28	24	36	70	13
Major appliances	5	0.0	1	0.0	11	15	4
Small appl., misc. housewares	20	10	27	24	25	55	9
Misc. household equipment	48	43	59	57	40	59	42
Other housing	74	107	71	32	132	116	53
Apparel and services	**187**	**147**	**251**	**180**	**297**	**287**	**128**
Males 2 and over	58	73	71	53	105	74	36
Females 2 and over	70	33	96	80	107	130	45
Children under 2	19	14	26	12	39	30	13
Other apparel products, services	40	28	59	35	47	53	34
Jewelry and watches	13	8	20	24	11	24	7
All other apparel pdts., svcs.	27	19	40	11	35	29	28
Transportation	**33**	**12**	**14**	**61**	**77**	**59**	**20**
Health care	**12**	**1**	**8**	**17**	**26**	**9**	**12**
Entertainment	**78**	**165**	**76**	**78**	**98**	**110**	**43**
Toys, games, hobbies, tricycles	23	10	27	29	33	47	16
Other entertainment	55	155	49	49	65	63	28
Education	**32**	**73**	**15**	**33**	**69**	**18**	**24**
All other gifts	**94**	**38**	**94**	**122**	**147**	**144**	**73**

** This figure does not include the amount paid for mortgage principle, which is considered an asset.*
*** Expenditures on gifts are also included in the preceding product and service categories.*
Note: The Bureau of Labor Statistics uses consumer units rather than households as the sampling unit in the Consumer Expenditure survey. For the definition of consumer unit, see the Glossary. Expenditures listed for items in a given category may not add to the total for that category because the listing is incomplete.
Source: Bureau of Labor Statistics, Internet web site, http://www.bls.gov

Indexed Spending of Women Who Live Alone by Age, 1994-95

(indexed spending of single-person consumer units headed by women by category and age, 1994-95)

	total	*< 25*	*25 to 34*	*35 to 44*	*45 to 54*	*55 to 64*	*65+*
Average spending	**100**	**67**	**132**	**139**	**136**	**112**	**79**
FOOD	**100**	**75**	**123**	**107**	**127**	**110**	**90**
Food at home	**100**	**51**	**101**	**90**	**116**	**109**	**108**
Cereals and bakery products	100	62	98	87	113	107	108
Cereals and cereal products	100	75	114	94	109	88	105
Bakery products	100	56	89	83	115	117	110
Meats, poultry, fish, and eggs	100	36	92	81	129	127	108
Beef	100	36	88	82	131	144	104
Pork	100	19	84	72	130	143	111
Other meats	100	40	76	96	129	89	120
Poultry	100	47	101	81	123	119	106
Fish and seafood	100	41	117	87	130	115	102
Eggs	100	38	75	81	150	119	113
Dairy products	100	66	88	95	95	96	116
Fresh milk and cream	100	57	75	80	95	97	125
Other dairy products	100	71	97	105	95	95	109
Fruits and vegetables	100	43	105	76	104	107	115
Fresh fruits	100	43	110	67	94	98	121
Fresh vegetables	100	37	122	84	90	117	110
Processed fruits	100	46	78	81	111	106	119
Processed vegetables	100	54	90	68	141	105	110
Other food at home	100	56	114	105	121	103	100
Sugar and other sweets	100	52	128	77	121	107	102
Fats and oils	100	36	81	85	102	100	126
Miscellaneous foods	100	57	114	116	116	97	100
Nonalcoholic beverages	100	60	111	103	132	108	97
Food prep by cu, out-of-town trips	100	75	160	135	135	135	60
Food away from home	**100**	**121**	**163**	**139**	**148**	**111**	**56**
ALCOHOLIC BEVERAGES	**100**	**135**	**192**	**209**	**103**	**111**	**39**
HOUSING	**100**	**56**	**124**	**135**	**130**	**119**	**84**
Shelter	**100**	**66**	**138**	**154**	**138**	**108**	**76**

(continued)

(continued from previous page)

	total	< 25	25 to 34	35 to 44	45 to 54	55 to 64	65+
Owned dwellings*	100	3	58	179	169	142	88
Mortgage interest and charges	100	2	109	315	235	166	27
Property taxes	100	3	33	109	132	136	118
Maintenance/repair/ insurance/other expenses	100	4	25	97	133	122	126
Rented dwellings	100	117	213	136	108	74	66
Other lodging	100	106	92	103	161	155	72
Utilities, fuels, public services	**100**	**48**	**94**	**108**	**114**	**116**	**103**
Natural gas	100	19	62	90	97	106	128
Electricity	100	38	77	110	118	124	106
Fuel oil and other fuels	100	3	18	57	90	115	147
Telephone	100	88	149	126	120	110	78
Water and other public services	100	15	52	90	116	125	122
Household operations	**100**	**11**	**66**	**76**	**94**	**136**	**123**
Personal services	100	8	139	1	80	207	104
Other household expenses	100	12	43	99	99	115	129
Housekeeping supplies	**100**	**34**	**108**	**88**	**110**	**112**	**112**
Laundry and cleaning supplies	100	27	116	105	121	134	98
Other household products	100	26	93	72	88	104	128
Postage and stationery	100	48	121	97	127	108	100
Household furnishings and equipment	**100**	**52**	**143**	**130**	**146**	**179**	**62**
Household textiles	100	18	93	164	170	97	93
Furniture	100	71	194	132	129	166	51
Floor coverings	100	7	55	151	160	244	69
Major appliances	100	46	61	88	118	179	100
Small appl., misc. housewares	100	51	169	175	110	185	51
Misc. household equipment	100	60	162	117	163	194	50
APPAREL AND SERVICES	**100**	**95**	**188**	**166**	**125**	**117**	**53**
Men and boys	**100**	**126**	**122**	**91**	**181**	**134**	**62**
Men, 16 and over	100	157	150	102	196	93	54
Boys, 2 to 15	100	8	8	50	125	292	100
Women and girls	**100**	**95**	**200**	**172**	**125**	**104**	**52**
Women, 16 and over	100	98	204	176	126	102	50
Girls, 2 to 15	100	6	65	47	94	159	129
Children under 2	**100**	**74**	**137**	**63**	**205**	**158**	**68**
Footwear	**100**	**91**	**177**	**191**	**62**	**123**	**64**
Other apparel products, svcs.	**100**	**90**	**187**	**157**	**159**	**156**	**40**

(continued)

(continued from previous page)

	total	< 25	25 to 34	35 to 44	45 to 54	55 to 64	65+
TRANSPORTATION	**100**	**80**	**183**	**173**	**134**	**101**	**60**
Vehicle purchases	**100**	**78**	**255**	**207**	**110**	**58**	**52**
Cars and trucks, new	100	40	286	243	88	51	52
Cars and trucks, used	100	145	203	143	149	71	53
Other vehicles	0	0	0	0	0	0	0
Gasoline and motor oil	**100**	**107**	**147**	**155**	**144**	**112**	**63**
Other vehicle expenses	**100**	**68**	**145**	**168**	**153**	**130**	**62**
Vehicle finance charges	100	80	300	183	180	87	23
Maintenance and repairs	100	76	112	180	158	127	66
Vehicle insurance	100	64	138	138	144	119	75
Vehicle rent, leasing, licenses, other charges	100	53	159	201	153	182	41
Public transportation	**100**	**92**	**139**	**116**	**126**	**116**	**79**
HEALTH CARE	**100**	**17**	**47**	**85**	**83**	**102**	**137**
Health insurance	100	12	35	51	56	83	159
Medical services	100	21	69	139	135	142	98
Drugs	100	18	41	97	68	91	142
Medical supplies	100	57	102	100	155	131	90
ENTERTAINMENT	**100**	**103**	**151**	**159**	**129**	**132**	**59**
Fees and admissions	100	107	151	140	129	149	59
Television, radios, sound equip.	100	118	138	167	109	104	68
Pets, toys, playground equip.	100	55	164	179	177	121	55
Other supplies, equip., services	100	132	175	138	104	230	30
PERSONAL CARE PRODUCTS & SERVICES	**100**	**80**	**159**	**105**	**135**	**97**	**81**
READING	**100**	**52**	**113**	**138**	**127**	**124**	**86**
EDUCATION	**100**	**538**	**177**	**73**	**107**	**25**	**13**
TOBACCO PRODUCTS & SMOKING SUPPLIES	**100**	**73**	**103**	**180**	**196**	**168**	**50**
MISCELLANEOUS	**100**	**43**	**79**	**161**	**253**	**109**	**69**
CASH CONTRIBUTIONS	**100**	**9**	**36**	**67**	**125**	**88**	**140**
PERSONAL INSURANCE, PENSIONS	**100**	**45**	**196**	**224**	**228**	**124**	**27**
Life and other personal insurance	100	13	48	97	141	113	119
Pensions and Social Security	100	49	217	243	241	126	14
GIFTS	**100**	**93**	**108**	**99**	**159**	**155**	**71**
Food	**100**	**38**	**123**	**70**	**186**	**248**	**54**

(continued)

(continued from previous page)

	total	< 25	25 to 34	35 to 44	45 to 54	55 to 64	65+
Housing	**100**	**93**	**109**	**78**	**141**	**155**	**81**
Housekeeping supplies	100	82	145	121	118	130	79
Household textiles	100	0	55	15	175	100	135
Appliances, misc. housewares	100	40	112	96	144	280	52
Major appliances	100	0	20	0	220	300	80
Small appl., misc. housewares	100	50	135	120	125	275	45
Misc. household equipment	100	90	123	119	83	123	88
Other housing	100	145	96	43	178	157	72
Apparel and services	**100**	**79**	**134**	**96**	**159**	**153**	**68**
Males 2 and over	100	126	122	91	181	128	62
Females 2 and over	100	47	137	114	153	186	64
Children under 2	100	74	137	63	205	158	68
Other apparel products, services	100	70	148	88	118	133	85
Jewelry and watches	100	62	154	185	85	185	54
All other apparel pdts., svcs.	100	70	148	41	130	107	104
Transportation	**100**	**36**	**42**	**185**	**233**	**179**	**61**
Health care	**100**	**8**	**67**	**142**	**217**	**75**	**100**
Entertainment	**100**	**212**	**97**	**100**	**126**	**141**	**55**
Toys, games, hobbies, tricycles	100	43	117	126	143	204	70
Other entertainment	100	282	89	89	118	115	51
Education	**100**	**228**	**47**	**103**	**216**	**56**	**75**
All other gifts	**100**	**40**	**100**	**130**	**156**	**153**	**78**

Note: The index compares the spending of women in each age group with the spending of the average woman who lives alone. 100 is the average. An index of 132 means the spending of women in the age group is 32 percent above the average for all women who live alone, while an index of 75 means the spending of women in the age group is 25 percent below the average for all women who live alone. The Bureau of Labor Statistics uses consumer units rather than households as the sampling unit in the Consumer Expenditure Survey. For the definition of consumer unit, see the Glossary.
Source: Bureau of Labor Statistics, Internet web site, http://www.bls.gov; *calculations by New Strategist*

CHAPTER

9

Wealth

❖ **Since most older Americans are women, women control most wealth.**

The net worth of householders aged 75 or older—at $95,000—was far greater than the net worth of householders up to age 55.

❖ **The average household owned a median of $13,000 in financial assets in 1995.**

Stocks have grown as a share of total financial assets, from 26 percent in 1989 to 40 percent in 1995.

❖ **American homes were worth a median of $90,000 in 1995.**

For homeowners, the value of their house is greater than the value of any other single asset they own.

❖ **Seventy-five percent of households were in debt in 1995, owing a median of $22,500.**

Although the percentage of households with debt rises with income, debt levels decline with age after peaking in the 35-to-54 age group.

❖ **Wives and women who live alone are increasingly likely to own a home.**

Between 1982 and 1996, the homeownership rate increased for married couples, women who live alone, and women who head households that include nonrelatives.

❖ **Although most working women are offered pension coverage, many don't participate.**

Men and women are equally likely to work for an employer who offers pension coverage, although men are more likely to participate—80 versus 71 percent.

Net Worth Rises with Age

Since most older Americans are women, women control most wealth.

The median net worth (assets minus liabilities) of American households stood at $56,400 in 1995, according to the Federal Reserve Board's 1995 Survey of Consumer Finances. This was 7 percent greater than the median net worth of households in 1992, after adjusting for inflation.

Net worth rises to a peak in middle age as people accumulate assets and pay off debts. In 1995, net worth peaked in the 55-to-64 age group at $111,000. After that age, net worth declines as older Americans spend down their wealth in retirement. Nevertheless, the net worth of householders aged 75 or older—at $95,000—was far greater than the net worth of householders up to age of 55.

❖ Wives and widows are the majority of customers for businesses targeting households with relatively high net worth.

Net Worth of Households, 1992 and 1995

(median net worth of households by household income and age of householder, 1992 and 1995, and percent change, 1992-95; in 1995 dollars; numbers in thousands)

	1995	*1992*	*percent change 1992-95*
Total households	$56.4	$52.8	6.8%
Income			
Under $10,000	4.8	3.3	45.5
$10,000 to $24,999	30.0	28.2	6.4
$25,000 to $49,999	54.9	54.8	0.2
$50,000 to $99,999	121.1	121.2	-0.1
$100,000 or more	485.9	506.1	-4.0
Age of householder			
Under age 35	11.4	10.1	12.9
Aged 35 to 44	48.5	46.0	5.4
Aged 45 to 54	90.5	83.4	8.5
Aged 55 to 64	110.8	122.5	-9.6
Aged 65 to 74	104.1	105.8	-1.6
Aged 75 or older	95.0	92.8	2.4

Source: Federal Reserve Board, Family Finances in the U.S.: Recent Evidence from the Survey of Consumer Finances, *Federal Reserve Bulletin, January 1997*

Women's Financial Assets Are Growing

The median value of the financial assets owned by the average household stood at $13,000 in 1995.

The financial assets of Americans are growing as people pour money into the stock market. Financial assets accounted for 34 percent of total household assets in 1995, up from 28 percent in 1989. During those years, direct and indirect stock ownership grew sharply as a share of total financial assets, rising from 26 percent in 1989 to 40 percent in 1995.

Nine out of ten households own financial assets, with the proportion showing little variation by age. The value of financial assets does vary by age, however, peaking at $32,000 among householders aged 55 to 64. The value then declines as people spend their wealth in retirement.

The proportion of households with financial assets does not vary much by income, but their value is greater the higher the income. Households with incomes of $100,000 or more have a median of $214,500 in financial assets, with the largest share in retirement accounts.

❖ With millions of American women concerned with saving for retirement, the financial assets of households should expand substantially in the years ahead.

Financial Assets of Households, 1995

(percentage of households owning financial assets and median value of assets for owners, by household income, age of householder, and type of asset, 1995)

	any financial asset	transaction accounts	CDs	savings bonds	bonds	stocks	mutual funds	retirement accounts	life insurance	other managed	other financial
Percent owning, total households	90.8%	87.1%	14.1%	22.9%	3.0%	15.3%	12.0%	43.0%	31.4%	3.8%	11.0%
Income											
Under $10,000	68.1	61.1	7.2	5.9	-	2.5	1.8	5.9	15.8	-	8.9
$10,000 to $24,999	87.6	82.3	16.0	11.8	-	9.2	4.9	24.2	25.2	3.2	8.6
$25,000 to $49,999	97.8	94.7	13.7	27.4	3.2	14.3	12.4	52.6	33.1	4.2	13.2
$50,000 to $99,999	99.5	98.6	15.6	39.9	4.8	26.0	20.9	69.8	42.5	5.3	11.3
$100,000 or more	100.0	100.0	21.1	36.3	14.5	45.2	38.0	84.6	54.1	8.0	15.2
Age of householder											
Under age 35	87.0	80.8	7.1	21.1	0.5	11.1	8.8	39.2	22.3	1.6	13.5
Aged 35 to 44	92.0	87.4	8.2	31.0	1.6	14.5	10.5	51.5	28.9	3.4	10.5
Aged 45 to 54	92.4	88.9	12.5	25.1	4.6	17.5	16.0	54.3	37.5	2.9	13.0
Aged 55 to 64	90.5	88.2	16.2	19.6	2.9	14.9	15.2	47.2	37.5	7.1	9.0
Aged 65 to 74	92.0	91.1	23.9	17.0	5.1	18.0	13.7	35.0	37.0	5.6	10.4
Aged 75 or older	93.8	93.0	34.1	15.3	7.0	21.3	10.4	16.5	35.1	5.7	5.3

(continued)

(continued from previous page)

	any financial asset	transaction accounts	CDs	savings bonds	bonds	stocks	mutual funds	retirement accounts	life insurance	other managed	other financial
Median value, total households	$13.0	$2.1	$10.0	$1.0	$26.2	$8.0	$19.0	$15.6	$5.0	$30.0	$3.0
Income											
Under $10,000	1.2	0.7	7.0	0.4	-	2.0	25.0	3.5	1.5	-	2.0
$10,000 to $24,999	5.4	1.4	10.0	0.8	-	5.7	8.0	6.0	3.0	19.7	2.0
$25,000 to $49,999	12.1	2.0	10.0	0.7	29.0	6.9	12.5	10.0	5.0	25.0	2.5
$50,000 to $99,999	40.7	4.5	13.0	1.2	9.4	5.7	15.0	23.0	7.0	35.0	3.0
$100,000 or more	214.5	15.8	15.6	1.5	58.0	30.0	48.0	85.0	12.0	62.5	23.0
Age of householder											
Under age 35	5.3	1.2	6.0	0.5	2.0	3.7	5.0	5.2	3.4	3.8	1.0
Aged 35 to 44	11.6	2.0	6.0	1.0	11.0	4.0	10.0	12.0	5.0	10.8	2.0
Aged 45 to 54	24.8	2.7	12.0	1.0	17.0	10.0	17.5	25.0	6.5	43.0	5.0
Aged 55 to 64	32.3	3.0	14.0	1.1	10.0	17.0	55.0	32.8	6.0	42.0	9.0
Aged 65 to 74	19.1	3.0	17.0	1.5	58.0	15.0	50.0	28.5	5.0	26.0	9.0
Aged 75 or older	20.9	5.0	11.0	4.0	40.0	25.0	50.0	17.5	5.0	100.0	35.0

Note: (-) means sample is too small to make a reliable estimate.
Source: Federal Reserve Board, Family Finances in the U.S.: Recent Evidence from the Survey of Consumer Finances, *Federal Reserve Bulletin, January 1997*

For Women, a House Is Most Important Asset

American homes were worth a median of $90,000 in 1995.

Although a larger percentage of households own a vehicle (84 percent) than own a home (65 percent), the median value of vehicles was just $10,000 in 1995. For homeowners, the value of their house is greater than the value of any other single asset they own.

Not surprisingly, the ownership of nonfinancial assets rises with income, as does the median value of those assets. The ownership of non-financial assets also rises with age, peaking at 94 percent in the 45-to-64 age group. The median value of non-financial assets peaks at over $112,000 in the 45-to-54 age group.

❖ The rising homeownership rate for married couples and for women who live alone means greater wealth for American women.

Households with Nonfinancial Assets, 1995

(percentage of households owning nonfinancial assets and median value of assets for owners, by household income, age of householder, and type of asset, 1995; numbers in thousands)

	any nonfinancial asset	vehicles	primary residence	investment real estate	business	other non-financial
Percent owning,						
total households	91.1%	84.2%	64.7%	17.5%	11.0%	9.0%
Income						
Under $10,000	69.8	57.7	37.6	6.9	4.8	3.8
$10,000 to $24,999	89.4	82.7	55.4	11.5	6.2	6.2
$25,000 to $49,999	96.6	92.2	68.4	16.5	9.8	9.6
$50,000 to $99,999	99.1	93.3	84.4	24.9	17.5	11.5
$100,000 or more	99.4	90.2	91.1	52.3	32.1	22.6
Age of householder						
Under age 35	87.6	83.9	37.9	7.2	9.3	7.6
Aged 35 to 44	90.9	85.1	64.6	14.4	13.9	10.2
Aged 45 to 54	93.7	88.2	75.4	23.9	14.8	10.7
Aged 55 to 64	94.0	88.7	82.1	26.9	11.7	9.8
Aged 65 to 74	92.5	82.0	79.0	26.5	7.9	8.9
Aged 75 or older	90.2	72.8	73.0	16.6	3.8	5.4
Median value, total households	$83.0	$10.0	$90.0	$50.0	$41.0	$10.0
Income						
Under $10,000	13.1	3.6	40.0	16.2	50.6	2.5
$10,000 to $24,999	44.5	6.1	65.0	30.0	30.0	8.0
$25,000 to $49,999	81.5	11.1	80.0	40.0	26.3	6.0
$50,000 to $99,999	145.2	16.2	120.0	57.3	30.0	14.0
$100,000 or more	319.3	22.8	200.0	130.0	300.0	20.0
Age of householder						
Under age 35	21.5	9.0	80.0	33.5	20.0	5.0
Aged 35 to 44	95.6	10.7	95.0	45.0	35.0	9.0
Aged 45 to 54	111.7	12.4	100.0	55.0	60.0	12.0
Aged 55 to 64	107.0	11.9	85.0	82.5	75.0	10.0
Aged 65 to 74	93.5	8.0	80.0	55.0	100.0	16.0
Aged 75 or older	79.0	5.3	80.0	20.0	30.0	15.0

Source: Federal Reserve Board, Family Finances in the U.S.: Recent Evidence from the Survey of Consumer Finances,*Federal Reserve Bulletin, January 1997*

Most Women Have Debts

Seventy-five percent of households were in debt in 1995, owing a median of $22,500.

Although three out of four households have debts, no single type of debt is held by a majority of households. Credit card debt is most common, with 48 percent of households owing a median of $1,500 on their credit cards in 1995. Forty-seven percent of households have installment debt (primarily car loans), owing a median of $6,100. Forty-one percent of households have mortgage or home equity debt, with a median balance of $51,000.

The percentage of households with debt rises with income. But debt levels decline with age after peaking in the 35-to-54 age group. The expenses of buying a home and raising children explain why 87 percent of 35-to-54-year-olds are in debt. The proportion is a smaller 75 percent among 55-to-64 year olds, then falls to 54 percent among 65-to-74-year-olds. Only among householders aged 75 or older are a minority of householders in debt.

❖ With baby-boom women now in the most debt-prone age group, 35 to 54, debt is a fact of life for millions of women. As boomers get older and pay off their loans, they will have more money to spend on themselves.

Households with Debt, 1995

(percentage of households with debt, and median value of debt for debtors, by household income, age of householder, and type of debt, 1995; numbers in thousands)

	any debt	mortgage & home equity	installment	other lines of credit	credit card	investment real estate	other debt
Percent with debt,							
total households	75.2%	41.1%	46.5%	1.9%	47.8%	6.3%	9.0%
Income							
Under $10,000	48.5	8.9	25.9	-	25.4	1.6	6.6
$10,000 to $24,999	67.3	24.8	41.3	1.4	41.9	2.5	8.7
$25,000 to $49,999	83.9	47.3	54.3	2.0	56.7	5.8	8.5
$50,000 to $99,999	89.9	68.7	60.7	3.2	62.8	9.5	10.0
$100,000 or more	86.4	73.6	37.0	4.0	37.0	27.9	15.8
Age of householder							
Under age 35	83.8	32.9	62.2	2.6	55.4	2.6	7.8
Aged 35 to 44	87.2	54.1	60.7	2.2	55.8	6.5	11.1
Aged 45 to 54	86.5	61.9	54.0	2.3	57.3	10.4	14.1
Aged 55 to 64	75.2	45.8	36.0	1.4	43.4	12.5	7.5
Aged 65 to 74	54.2	24.8	16.7	1.3	31.3	5.0	5.5
Aged 75 or older	30.1	7.1	9.6	-	18.3	1.5	3.6
Median value of debt,							
total households	$22.5	$51.0	$6.1	$3.5	$1.5	$28.0	$2.0
Income							
Under $10,000	2.6	14.0	2.9	-	0.6	15.0	2.0
$10,000 to $24,999	9.2	26.0	3.9	3.0	1.2	18.3	1.2
$25,000 to $49,999	23.4	46.0	6.6	3.0	1.4	25.0	1.5
$50,000 to $99,999	65.0	68.0	9.0	2.2	2.2	34.0	2.5
$100,000 or more	112.2	103.4	8.5	19.5	3.0	36.8	7.0
Age of householder							
Under age 35	15.2	63.0	7.0	1.4	1.4	22.8	1.5
Aged 35 to 44	37.6	60.0	5.6	2.0	1.8	30.0	1.7
Aged 45 to 54	41.0	48.0	7.0	5.7	2.0	28.1	2.5
Aged 55 to 64	25.8	36.0	5.9	3.5	1.3	26.0	4.0
Aged 65 to 74	7.7	19.0	4.9	3.8	0.8	36.0	2.0
Aged 75 or older	2.0	15.9	3.9	-	0.4	8.0	3.0

Note: (-) means sample is too small to make a reliable estimate.
Source: Federal Reserve Board, Family Finances in the U.S.: Recent Evidence from the Survey of Consumer Finances, *Federal Reserve Bulletin, January 1997*

Gains in Homeownership for Women

Wives and women who live alone are increasingly likely to own a home.

Americans were more likely to be homeowners in 1996 than in 1982, with the homeownership rate rising by 0.6 percentage points—to 65.4 percent—during those years. The homeownership rate increased for married couples, women who live alone, and women who head households that include nonrelatives.

Regardless of household type, homeownership rates rise with age. Married couples are most likely to own their home, with a homeownership rate of 80.2 percent in 1996. Among couples, the rate ranges from 29.8 percent for householders under age 25 to 91.3 percent for those aged 65 or older. Over half of women who live alone own their home, including 67 percent of those aged 65 or older. Among female-headed families, the homeownership rate fell by 1 percentage point between 1982 and 1996, to 46.1 percent.

❖ With most older women owning a home, businesses have an opportunity to provide a range of services to customers who lack the technical skills or physical ability to maintain and repair their homes themselves.

Homeownership by Type of Household, 1982 and 1996

(percent of householders who own their home by household type and age of householder, 1982 and 1996; percentage point change 1982-96)

	1996	1982	percentage point change, 1982-96
Total households	65.4%	64.8%	0.6
Under age 25	18.0	19.3	-1.3
Aged 25 to 29	34.7	38.6	-3.9
Aged 30 to 34	53.0	57.1	-4.1
Aged 35 to 44	66.3	70.0	-3.7
Aged 45 to 54	75.2	77.4	-2.2
Aged 55 to 64	79.3	80.0	-0.7
Aged 65 or older	76.3	74.4	1.9
Married-couple families	80.2	78.5	1.7
Under age 25	29.8	32.6	-2.8
Aged 25 to 29	53.0	53.9	-0.9
Aged 30 to 34	68.2	71.9	-3.7
Aged 35 to 44	79.6	82.0	-2.4
Aged 45 to 54	87.5	87.4	0.1
Aged 55 to 64	90.3	89.5	0.8
Aged 65 or older	91.3	86.6	4.7
Female-headed family, no spouse present	46.1	47.1	-1.0
Under age 25	15.4	8.9	6.5
Aged 25 to 29	16.3	17.3	-1.0
Aged 30 to 34	28.9	31.3	-2.4
Aged 35 to 44	42.8	48.3	-5.5
Aged 45 to 54	60.2	61.7	-1.5
Aged 55 to 64	69.2	68.7	0.5
Aged 65 or older	81.1	75.1	6.0

(continued)

(continued from previous page)

	1996	*1982*	*percentage point change, 1982-96*
NONFAMILY HOUSEHOLDS			
Female-headed single-person households	56.0%	51.2%	4.8
Under age 25	8.3	7.5	0.8
Aged 25 to 29	15.0	14.3	0.7
Aged 30 to 34	29.9	24.7	5.2
Aged 35 to 44	40.4	37.0	3.4
Aged 45 to 54	55.5	49.1	6.4
Aged 55 to 64	63.8	62.4	1.4
Aged 65 or older	67.2	62.2	5.0
Female-headed household with two or more persons	35.9	30.1	5.8
Under age 35	15.4	12.7	2.7
Aged 35 to 44	52.9	37.9	15.0
Aged 45 to 54	62.1	60.2	1.9
Aged 55 to 64	68.0	72.6	-4.6
Aged 65 or older	70.8	77.2	-6.4

Source: Bureau of the Census, Internet web site, http://www.census.gov*; calculations by New Strategist*

Most Working Women Are Offered Pension Coverage

But many do not participate in their company's pension plan.

Men and women are equally likely to work for an employer who offers pension coverage (62 percent). But men are more likely than women to participate in their employer's plan—80 versus 71 percent. Consequently, men are more likely than women to have pension coverage—50 percent of working men versus 44 percent of working women.

Pension-plan participation peaks among people in their 50s—when retirement planning becomes a serious pursuit. Eighty-nine percent of workers aged 51 to 60 whose employer offers a pension participate in the plan. Among workers in this age group, over half are vested in a pension plan—meaning they will receive some pension income in retirement.

❖ As career-oriented, baby-boom women retire, a growing share of women will have pension coverage. This should boost their economic well-being in retirement and narrow the income gap between elderly men and women.

Pension Plan Participation by Sex and Age, 1993

(total number of civilian, nonagricultural workers aged 16 or older; percent with employers who sponsor a pension plan, participation rates of total workers and those with plans, and vesting rates of total workers and those with plans, by sex and age, 1993; numbers in thousands)

	total workers	sponsorship rate	participation rate (total workers)	sponsored participation rate	vesting rate (total workers)	participant vesting rate
Total	105,815	62.1%	47.1%	75.9%	40.3%	85.8%
Women	50,233	61.8	44.0	71.2	37.6	85.3
Men	55,582	62.3	50.0	80.2	42.8	85.6
Aged 16 to 20	6,634	32.2	3.5	11.0	1.6	45.6
Aged 21 to 30	26,359	56.6	33.8	59.8	25.8	76.2
Aged 31 to 40	31,047	65.8	52.7	80.1	45.0	85.3
Aged 41 to 50	23,459	70.6	61.5	87.1	54.5	88.7
Aged 51 to 60	13,164	66.8	59.3	88.8	53.3	89.9
Aged 61 to 64	2,781	62.4	51.3	82.3	47.7	92.9
Aged 65 or older	2,371	46.1	29.0	63.0	26.6	91.6

Note: Sponsorship rate is the percent of total workers who work for an employer where a plan was sponsored for any of the employees. Participation rate is the percent of total workers who participate in a pension plan. Sponsored participation rate is the percent of employees working for an employer where a retirement plan was sponsored who participated in the plan. Vesting rate is the percent of all workers who are vested in a pension plan. Participant vesting rate is the percent of workers who participate in an employer-sponsored plan and are vested in a plan.
Source: Employee Benefit Research Institute, Baby Boomers in Retirement: What Are Their Prospects? *Special Report and Issue Brief Number 151, July 1994*

Glossary

adjusted for inflation Income or a change in income that has been adjusted for the rise in the cost of living, or the consumer price index (CPI-U-XI).

Asian In this book, the term "Asian" includes both Asians and Pacific Islanders.

baby boom Americans born between 1946 and 1964. Baby boomers are aged 33 to 51 in 1997.

baby bust Americans born between 1965 and 1976, also known as Generation X. In 1997, Generation Xers are aged 21 to 32.

central cities The largest city in a metropolitan area is called the central city. The balance of the metropolitan area outside the central city is regarded as the "suburbs."

consumer unit (on spending tables only) For convenience, the term consumer unit and households are used interchangeably in the spending section of this book, although consumer units are somewhat different from the Census Bureau's households. Consumer units are all related members of a household, or financially independent members of a household. A household may include more than one consumer unit.

dual-earner couple A married couple in which both the householder and the householder's spouse are in the labor force.

employed All civilians who did any work as a paid employee or farmer/self-employed worker, or who worked 15 hours or more as an unpaid farm worker or in a family-owned business, during the reference period. All those who have jobs but who are temporarily absent from their jobs due to illness, bad weather, vacation, labor management dispute, or personal reasons are considered employed.

expenditure The transaction cost including excise and sales taxes of goods and services acquired during the survey period. The full cost of each purchase is recorded even though full payment may not have been made at the date of purchase. Average expenditure figures may be artifically low for infrequently purchased items such as cars because figures are calculated using all consumer units within a demographic segment rather than just purchasers. Expenditure estimates include money spent on gifts for others.

family A group of two or more people (one of whom is the householder) related by birth, marriage, or adoption and living in the same household.

family household A household maintained by a householder who lives with one or more people related to him or her by blood, marriage, or adoption.

female/male householder A woman or man who maintains a household without a spouse present. May head family or nonfamily households.

full-time employment Full-time is 35 or more hours of work per week during a majority of the weeks worked during the preceding calendar year.

full-time, year-round Indicates 50 or more weeks of full-time employment during the preceding calendar year.

geographic regions The four major regions and nine census divisions of the United States are the state groupings as shown below:

Northeast:

—New England: Connecticut, Maine, Massachusetts, New Hampshire, Rhode Island, and Vermont

—Middle Atlantic: New Jersey, New York, and Pennsylvania

Midwest:

—East North Central: Illinois, Indiana, Michigan, Ohio, and Wisconsin

—West North Central: Iowa, Kansas, Minnesota, Missouri, Nebraska, North Dakota, and South Dakota

South:

—South Atlantic: Delaware, District of Columbia, Florida, Georgia, Maryland, North Carolina, South Carolina, Virginia, and West Virginia

—East South Central: Alabama, Kentucky, Mississippi, and Tennessee

—West South Central: Arkansas, Louisiana, Oklahoma, and Texas

West:

—Mountain: Arizona, Colorado, Idaho, Montana, Nevada, New Mexico, Utah, and Wyoming

—Pacific: Alaska, California, Hawaii, Oregon, and Washington

Generation X *See* baby bust.

Hispanic Persons or householders who identify their origin as Mexican, Puerto Rican, Central or South American, or some other Hispanic origin. Persons of Hispanic origin may be of any race. In other words, there are black Hispanics, white Hispanics, and Asian Hispanics.

household All the persons who occupy a housing unit. A household includes the related family members and all the unrelated persons, if any, such as lodgers, foster children, wards, or employees who share the housing unit. A person living alone is counted as a household. A group of unrelated people who share a housing unit as roommates or unmarried partners is also counted as a household. Households do not include group quarters such as college dormitories, prisons, or nursing homes.

household, race/ethnicity of Households are categorized according to the race or ethnicity of the householder only.

householder The householder is the person (or one of the persons) in whose name the housing unit is owned or rented or, if there is no such person, any adult member. With married couples, the householder may be either the husband or wife. The householder is the reference person for the household.

householder, age of The age of the householder is used to categorize households into age groups such as those used in this book. Married couples, for example, are classified according to the age of either the husband or wife, depending on which one identified him or herself as the householder.

income Money received in the preceding calendar year by each person aged 15 or older from each of the following sources: (1) earnings from longest job (or self-employment); (2) earnings from jobs other than longest job; (3) unemployment compensation; (4) workers' compensation; (5) Social Security; (6) Supplemental Security income; (7) public assistance; (8) veterans' payments; (9) survivor benefits; (10) disability benefits; (11) retirement pensions; (12) interest; (13) dividends; (14) rents and royalties or estates and trusts; (15) educational assistance; (16) alimony; (17) child support; (18) financial assistance from outside the household, and other periodic income. Income is reported in several ways in this book. Household income is the combined income of all household members. Income of persons is all income accruing to a person from all sources. Earnings is the amount of money a person receives from his or her job.

industry Refers to the industry in which a person worked longest in the preceding calendar year.

labor force The labor force tables in this book are for the civilian labor force, which includes both the employed and the unemployed—people who are looking for work. Persons are counted as in the labor force if they were working or looking for work during the reference week in which the Census Bureau fields the Current Population Survey.

labor force participation rate The percent of the civilian noninstitutional population that is in the civilian labor force, which includes both the employed and the unemployed.

married couples with or without children under age 18 Refers to married couples with or without own children under age 18 living in the same household. Couples without children under age 18 may be parents of grown children who live elsewhere, or they could be childless couples.

median The median is the amount that divides the population or households into two equal portions: one below and one above the median. Medians can be calculated for income, age, and many other characteristics.

median income The amount that divides the income distribution into two equal groups, half having incomes above the median, half having incomes below the median. The medians for households or families are based on all households or families. The median for persons are based on all persons aged 15 or older with income.

metropolitan area An area qualifies for recognition as a metropolitan area if: (1) it includes a city of at least 50,000 population, or (2) it includes a Census Bureau-defined urbanized area of at least 50,000 with a total metropolitan population of at least 100,000 (75,000 in New England). In addition to the county containing the main city or urbanized area, a metropolitan area may include other counties having strong commuting ties to the central county.

nonfamily household A household maintained by a householder who lives alone or who lives with people to whom he or she is not related.

nonfamily householder A householder who lives alone or with nonrelatives.

non-Hispanic People who do not identify themselves as Hispanic are classified as non-Hispanic. Non-Hispanics may be of any race.

nonmetropolitan area Counties that are not classified as metropolitan areas.

occupation Occupational classification is based on the kind of work a person did at his or her job during the previous calendar year. If a person changed jobs during the year, the data refer to the occupation of the job held the longest during that year.

outside central city The portion of a metropolitan county or counties that falls outside of the central city or cities; generally regarded as the suburbs.

part-time employment Part-time is less than 35 hours of work per week in a majority of the weeks worked during the year.

percent change The change (either positive or negative) in a measure that is expressed as a proportion of the starting measure. When median income changes from $20,000 to $25,000, for example, this is a 25 percent increase.

percentage point change The change (either positive or negative) in a value which is already expressed as a percentage. When a labor force participation rate changes from 70 percent of 75 percent, for example, this is a 5 percentage point increase.

poverty level The official income threshold below which families and persons are classified as living in poverty. The threshold rises each year with inflation and varies depending on family size and age of householder. In 1995, the poverty threshold for a family of four was $15,569.

proportion or share The value of a part expressed as a percentage of the whole. If there are 4 million people aged 25 and 3 million of them are white, then the white proportion is 75 percent.

race Race is self-reported and appears in four categories in this book: white, black, Native American, and Asian. A household is assigned the race of the householder.

rounding Percentages are rounded to the nearest tenth of a percent; therefore, the percentages in a distribution do not always add exactly to 100.0 percent. The totals, however, are always shown as 100.0. Moreover, individual figures are rounded to the nearest thousand without being adjusted to group totals, which are independently rounded; percentages are based on the unrounded numbers.

suburbs *See* Outside central city.

tenure, housing A housing unit is "owner occupied" if the owner lives in the unit, even if it is mortgaged or not fully paid for. A cooperative or condominium unit is "owner occupied" only if the owner lives in it. All other occupied units are classified as "renter occupied."

tenure, job The length of time a worker has been with his current employer, usually expressed in years.

Index